THE ART OF
D. H. LAWRENCE

KEITH SAGAR

Senior Staff Tutor in Literature
Extra-Mural Department, University of Manchester

D0001362

CAMBRIDGE UNIVERSITY PRESS

CAMBRIDGE

LONDON   NEW YORK   NEW ROCHELLE

MELBOURNE   SYDNEY

SOUTHGATE VETERANS
MEMORIAL LIBRARY
14680 DIX-TOLEDO ROAD
SOUTHGATE, MI 48195

Published by the Press Syndicate of the University of Cambridge
The Pitt Building, Trumpington Street, Cambridge CB2 IRP
32 East 57th Street, New York, NY 10022, USA
296 Beaconsfield Parade, Middle Park, Melbourne 3206, Australia

© Cambridge University Press 1966

Library of Congress catalogue card number: 66-10086

ISBN 0 521 06181 4 hard covers
ISBN 0 521 09387 2 paperback

First published 1966
Reprinted 1975, 1978, 1981

Printed in Great Britain at the
University Press, Cambridge

CONTENTS

SOUTHGATE VETERANS
MEMORIAL LIBRARY
14680 DIX-TOLEDO ROAD
SOUTHGATE, MI 48195

CONTENTS

ACKNOWLEDGEMENTS

I welcome this opportunity to acknowledge my debt to the editorial staff of the Cambridge University Press for reading the work in preparation and making valuable suggestions, to Mrs O. Hopkin, Mrs F. N. Miller, Mrs E. Needham, Miss J. King and Mr G. L. Lazarus for their hospitality and for allowing me to rummage through their Lawrence material, to Mr Walter Stein and Mr Philip Hobsbaum for many stimulating conversations, and to the many correspondents who have so promptly and fully answered my inquiries.

I am aware of a great debt to the Lawrence scholarship of Edward Nehls and Harry T. Moore. One's debt to other critics is much more difficult to pin down. I am deeply indebted, as all subsequent Lawrence critics must be, to the work of F. R. Leavis, particularly in relation to my chapters on *The Rainbow*, *Women in Love*, and *St Mawr*. Other major debts of which I am aware are to Julian Moynahan on *The White Peacock*; Seymour Betsky on *Sons and Lovers*; Mark Spilka on *Sons and Lovers* and *The Man Who Died*; Marvin Modrick on *The Rainbow*; Mark Schorer on *Women in Love* and *Lady Chatterley's Lover*; Neil Myers on *Aaron's Rod*; Ian Gregor on *The Fox*; Gamini Salgado, Vivian de Sola Pinto, A. Alvarez and Harold Bloom on the poems; L. D. Clark, John B. Vickery and Jascha Kessler on *The Plumed Serpent*.

My thanks are also due to Messrs William Heinemann Ltd, Laurence Pollinger Ltd and the Estate of the late Mrs Frieda Lawrence for permission to quote freely from Lawrence's published works, and to the Trustees of the John Galsworthy Estate for permission to print a previously unpublished letter.

Manchester   K. M. S.
November 1965

ABBREVIATIONS

AH   *The Letters of D. H. Lawrence*, ed. Aldous Huxley, Heinemann, 1932.

Brewster *D. H. Lawrence, Reminiscences and Correspondence*, by Earl and Achsah Brewster, Secker, 1934.

CL   *The Collected Letters of D. H. Lawrence*, ed. H. T. Moore, Heinemann, 1962.

ET   *D. H. Lawrence, A Personal Record*, by E(unice) T(emple), Cape, 1935.

Frieda   *Frieda Lawrence, The Memoirs and Correspondence*, ed. E. W. Tedlock, Heinemann, 1961.

Nehls   *D. H. Lawrence, A Composite Biography* (3 vols.), by Edward Nehls, Madison, 1959.

Phoenix   *Phoenix, The Posthumous Papers of D. H. Lawrence*, ed. E. D. McDonald, Heinemann, 1936.

SLC   *Sex, Literature and Censorship*, ed. H. T. Moore, Heinemann, 1955.

Tedlock   *The Frieda Lawrence Collection of D. H. Lawrence Manuscripts, A Descriptive Bibliography*, by E. W. Tedlock, Albuquerque, 1948.

All quotations from Lawrence not otherwise specified are from the Heinemann Phoenix Edition.

INTRODUCTION

Any new thing must find a new shape, then afterwards one can call it 'art' (Frieda Lawrence).

LAWRENCE said that his books would not be understood for three hundred years. When we read the early critics we can understand his pessimism. J. M. Murry wrote of the characters in *Women in Love*:

> Their creator believes that he can distinguish the writhing of one from the writhing of another; he spends pages and pages in describing the contortions of the first, the second, the third, and the fourth. To him they are all utterly and profoundly different; to us they are all the same (*Athenaeum*, 13 August 1921).

Edwin Muir complained that we should not recognise these characters if we met them in the street, to which Lawrence replied:

> Alas, that I should recognize people in the street, by their noses, bonnets or beauty. I don't care about their noses, bonnets or beauty. Does nothing exist beyond that which is recognizable in the street?—How does my cat recognize me in the dark?—Ugh, thank God there are more and other sorts of vision than the kodak sort which Mr Muir esteems above all others (*Phoenix* 802).

Lawrence's vision strips away appearances, even personalities, and penetrates to being.

Even those who admired (like Murry) could not formulate their approval in coherent critical terms. The old terminology was useless, for they were confronted with something quite new: 'Lawrence was that, and so rare a thing, genius, and Murry, as he says himself, did not have the least idea what Lawrence "was after"' (*Frieda* 273). Murry wrote to Frieda in 1953: 'Why, half *The Rainbow* was completely beyond my ken when it was published' (*ibid.* 330). Murry saw quicker than most the immense superiority of Lawrence to the other writers of the time. Yet, by all the accepted canons, his work was flawed. Murry was forced into a false choice between Lawrence and art. He chose Lawrence:

I

Much better 'art' has been produced by Lawrence's contemporaries; books better shaped, novels more objectively conceived, poems more concentrated. Beside Lawrence's work they seem frigid and futile. It is simply that they are not commensurate with our deep needs today. Our modern art is all obviously, irremediably minor. And it must necessarily be minor, so long as its aim is to be art (*Son of Woman* 173).

Lawrence's greatness is attributed to the fact that 'at bottom he was not concerned with art':

He gave up, deliberately, the pretence of being an artist. The novel became for him simply a means by which he could make explicit his own 'thought-adventures'...His aim was to discover authority, not to create art...To charge him with a lack of form, or of any other of the qualities which are supposed to be necessary to art, is to be guilty of irrelevance. Art was not Lawrence's aim (*ibid.* 173).

Murry here comes to the very brink of understanding, but turns aside into chaos: 'But he was not a great artist. He was a prophet, a psychologist, a philosopher, what you will—but more than any other single thing, the great life-adventurer of modern times' (*ibid.* 174). If Lawrence is 'what you will', he is vulnerable to all the subjective criticism anyone cares to level at him. 'Destructive hagiography' is Aldous Huxley's phrase for Murry's criticism. He constructs an apparatus of psychology-cum-gossip to 'account for' Lawrence's work and to evaluate it in inverse ratio to its merit as art. The ideas Murry found most accessible and seminal were contained in *Fantasia of the Unconscious* and *Aaron's Rod*, so these were acclaimed as the twin pinnacles of Lawrence's achievement. Neither Murry, nor Eliot, nor even Leavis, could see what Lawrence 'was after' during his lifetime.

F. R. Leavis notes the 'Flaubertian' use of the word 'aesthetic' by Eliot in relation to Pound's art—he was not so much interested in what the Cantos said, as in the way they said it. If there is no separation between the man who lives and the man who creates, if he creates directly out of his living, making art the servant of life, then he has no possible use for the word 'aesthetic'. Eliot's use of it indicates, according to Leavis, a lack of wholeness, a denial of the need of the artist to be a person and to have a deep responsibility towards experience. In a letter of 1915 Lawrence wrote of Van Gogh:

But best of all, if he could have known a great humanity, where to live one's animal would be to create oneself, *in fact, be the artist creating a man in living*

2

fact (not like Christ, as he wrongly said)—and where the art was the final expression of the created animal or man—not the be-all and being of man—but the end, the climax. And some men would end in artistic utterance, and some wouldn't. But each one would create the work of art, the living man, achieve that piece of supreme art, a man's life (*CL* 327).

Lawrence believed that a complete imaginative experience, which goes through the whole soul and body, can renew our strength and our vitality. He saw the novel as the utterance of the consciousness of the whole man, drawing the consciousness of the reader towards health, sanity and wholeness: 'it can inform and lead into new places the flow of our sympathetic consciousness, and it can lead our sympathy away in recoil from things gone dead'. The morality is not injected, but discovered. The artist must keep his thumb out of the balance. The control must be imposed at source. The form corresponds to a pattern in consciousness—a vision—which is itself a product of the interaction between the reality within the writer, the naked self, and the reality outside him, the circumambient universe. As Hart Crane has it:

No work of true genius dares want its appropriate form, neither indeed is there any danger of this. As it must not, so genius cannot, be lawless: for it is even this that constitutes its genius—the power of acting creatively under laws of its own origination (quoted by James E. Miller, Jr. in *Start with the Son*).

My aim in this study is to try to discover the 'appropriate form' which Lawrence's genius takes in all his major imaginative works. This will involve a kind of spiritual-artistic biography—an examination of the relationship between Lawrence's vision of life, at every stage of his career, and the form in which that vision finds utterance in art. How can the same man, within six years, produce the superbly constructed *Women in Love* and the rambling, almost formless *Kangaroo*? Why is the form of the late works so different from that of the middle and early ones? Why is the main creative force channelled, at one stage, into full-length novels, and at another, diffused through tales, poems, essays and even paintings? This inquiry will involve, in turn, a study of Lawrence's development, and the accurate dating of the works, according to composition, so as to see them in the right order.

I hope to demonstrate that the works fall into a well-defined pattern:

(1) 1906–11: a period of gradual discovery and growth;

(2) 1912–16: the first phase of mature achievement;

(3) 1917–24: a period of moral and artistic uncertainty or even perversity;

(4) 1925–30: regeneration to a new art and vision.

The fine and distinctive work of the fourth phase is seldom recognised and is not widely read. Almost all coherent critical hostility towards Lawrence is directed against works of the third phase, but in the belief that the conclusions are valid for the whole corpus. By recognising these phases, a more balanced and just estimate of Lawrence's achievement should be possible.

For reasons of space and continuity I have chosen to restrict myself to imaginative work—fiction, poems, paintings—and the other works which relate most closely to them. Some of Lawrence's best work, for example his literary criticism, is therefore given little attention. I have assumed that the novels and long stories carry more of Lawrence's creative effort than the short stories, fine as they are. I have devoted space to a work more or less in proportion to my evaluation of it. The accounts are not intended to be exhaustive, for I have tried to avoid merely reformulating existing commentaries. It is, of course, impossible to avoid covering some familiar ground.

My method is, first, to let each text speak for itself, to examine its structure and texture with close attention to key passages, to try to discover its inner coherence (or incoherence) and to judge its achievement against its own apparent intentions, within the given frame of reference. Second, to draw upon other works of the same period for confirmation or elucidation. Third, to look at each work within the context of the total *œuvre* and to judge it by Lawrence's own best standards. By this approach I hope to avoid the formal preconceptions which have vitiated so much Lawrence criticism ever since Arnold Bennett:

Tell Arnold Bennett that all rules of construction hold good only for novels which are copies of other novels. A book which is not a copy of other books has its own construction, and what he calls faults, he being an old imitator, I call characteristics. I shall repeat till I am grey—when they have as good a work to show, they may make their pronouncements *ex cathedra*. Till then, let them learn decent respect (*CL* 399).

4

Any work of art must, by definition, be a new thing. Originality does not, of course, exclude a vital relationship with the tradition. In *The Great Tradition* Dr Leavis examined the way in which the tradition of the English novel through Jane Austen, George Eliot, Dickens, Conrad and Henry James made for continuity, vitality and human centrality, particularly in the handling of moral and social themes. In *D. H. Lawrence Novelist* we see Lawrence using this tradition as a place to start from: he is at the growing tip of a living tradition, extending and transforming it. Dr Leavis's approach yields countless valuable insights, and the most definitive account yet of Lawrence's art. This study will be largely a matter of confirming Dr Leavis's findings, though from a somewhat different approach.

In such contexts as 'the Scott tradition that imposed on the novelist a romantic resolution of his themes', or even 'the tradition coming down from the eighteenth century that demanded a plane-mirror reflection of the surface of "real" life', Dr Leavis seems to me to be using the word 'tradition' in a sense which comes perilously close to the word 'convention'. I want to approach Lawrence as uncompromisingly unconventional, and taking his place in a much larger, two-thousand- rather than two-hundred-year-old tradition. Eliot defines tradition as all the art of the past which has remained alive. The tradition in which Lawrence virtually places himself in the *Study of Thomas Hardy* is much nearer to this than to Leavis's great tradition: he shares with Sophocles, Shakespeare, Tolstoy and Hardy the quality of 'setting behind the small action of the protagonists the terrific action of unfathomed nature'. *Studies in Classic American Literature* adds more names to this list, including Melville and Whitman. We can add other names from other sources; but the list is not likely to include any of the names in Leavis's more parochial tradition. Lawrence himself spoke of Jane Austen as 'this old maid'; after the very early days, George Eliot is not mentioned, except for her inadequacy in handling sex; Conrad is 'so good', but 'gives in before he starts', and *Lord Jim* is 'snivel in a wet hanky'; while Henry James 'was always on a different line—subtle conventional design was his aim'. Lawrence knew that James would hate *The Rainbow*; 'I have trifled with the exordia', James later confessed.

By concentrating more on Lawrence's reaction *against* the

English realist tradition (it is significant that Dr Leavis should have felt it to be necessary to apologise for the word 'real' in this context), and on his search for access to a deeper and more permanent reality, I hope to contribute some insights complementary to those of Dr Leavis, and to bring us a little nearer to understanding the nature and magnitude of Lawrence's achievement.

CHAPTER I

CHRONOLOGY

Lawrence was born in Eastwood, Nottinghamshire, in 1885. He attended Nottingham High School from 1898 to 1901 and worked as a student-teacher from 1902 to 1906. He entered Nottingham University College in September 1906 for a two-year course. Lawrence met Jessie Chambers in 1901 and became unofficially engaged to her in 1904.

EARLY POEMS (*Complete Poems*, Heinemann, 1964, Vol. 2).

Guelder Roses and *Campions* were written in the spring of 1905; *The Piano*, *The Death of the Baron* and *Married in June* between September 1906 and October 1908; *Baby Songs: Ten Months Old* and *After School* in January 1909.

THE WHITE PEACOCK (Heinemann, 1911).

Begun, as *Laetitia*, Easter 1906, then set aside until the autumn (*CL* 8). First version completed by June 1907 (*CL* 9). Second version completed by April 1908 (*CL* 4). Third version begun January 1909 (*CL* 47), sent to Hueffer at the end of October (*CL* 57), and to Heinemann on 15 December (*CL* 58); now called *Nethermere*. There was some further revision in the spring of 1910.

A COLLIER'S FRIDAY NIGHT (Secker, 1934; *Complete Plays*, Heinemann, 1965).

'Written when I was twenty-one, almost before I'd done anything, it is most horribly green' (Nottingham Exhibition Catalogue—*D. H. Lawrence after Thirty Years*, 14). Lawrence did not show this play to Jessie Chambers until November 1909 (ET 166).

RHYMING POEMS (*Love Poems and Others*, Duckworth, 1913; *Amores*, Duckworth, 1916; *New Poems*, Secker, 1918).

The first nineteen poems with the possible addition of *Lightning* and *A Tarantella* were written between September 1906 and October 1908.

A PRELUDE (*Nottinghamshire Guardian*, 7 December 1907; Merle Press, 1949).
LEGEND (later *A Fragment of Stained Glass*; *English Review*, September 1911; *The Prussian Officer*, Duckworth, 1914).
THE WHITE STOCKING (*The Smart Set*, October 1914; *The Prussian Officer*).

These were entered for a competition in the *Nottinghamshire Guardian* at Christmas 1907.

THE SHADOW IN THE ROSE GARDEN (*The Smart Set*, March 1914; *The Prussian Officer*).

Probably written about the same time, as *The Vicar's Garden*.

7

THE ART OF D. H. LAWRENCE

LOVE AMONG THE HAYSTACKS (Nonesuch Press, 1930).
GOOSE FAIR (*English Review*, February 1910; *The Prussian Officer*).
A SICK COLLIER (*New Statesman*, 13 September 1913; *The Prussian Officer*).
THE CHRISTENING (*The Prussian Officer*).
ODOUR OF CHRYSANTHEMUMS (*English Review*, June 1911; *The Prussian Officer*).
All these may have been written as early as the summer of 1908.

ART AND THE INDIVIDUAL (*The Early Life of D.H.L.*, 1930).
Begun before May 1908 (*CL* 12) and finished by mid-July (*CL* 20).

In October 1908 Lawrence took up a teaching post at Davidson Road School, Croydon.

A FLY IN THE OINTMENT (*New Statesman*, 13 August 1913; *The Early Life of D.H.L.*).
Written in the winter of 1908–9.

A MODERN LOVER (*Life and Letters*, Autumn 1933; Secker, 1934).
Written before June 1909 (*CL* 102).

RHYMING POEMS
Flat Suburbs, S.W., in the Morning is the first of the Croydon poems. *Dreams Old and Nascent: Nascent* also belongs to this period.

THE TRESPASSER (Duckworth, 1912).
Begun as *The Saga of Siegmund* in March 1910 and finished within three months (*CL* 66). Heinemann accepted it, but Lawrence, on Hueffer's advice, withdrew it (*CL* 88). Encouraged by Garnett, he rewrote the book in January and February 1912 (*CL* 91–7).

RACHEL ANNAND TAYLOR (*The Early Life of D.H.L.*).
Lecture delivered to the Croydon English Association in mid-November 1910 (*CL* 68).

A SORT OF BALANCE
1906–1910

The White Peacock
Odour of Chrysanthemums

§1

The White Peacock is hardly worth attention as a novel in its own right. Ford Maddox Hueffer, Lawrence's first literary adviser, said: 'It's got every fault that the English novel can have.' But he added: 'You've got GENIUS.' For Hueffer recognised the authentic eye, the fine sensibility, the original handling of distinctive themes, most of all the life that runs through even the most cloying prose—qualities not altogether cancelled out by immaturity and formlessness. The very evasions and desperate measures are significant; we can trace the problems Lawrence had to face, and the solutions he came through to, before he could render his own deepest experiences into art with the poise and assurance of *Sons and Lovers*.

Our main concern in looking more closely at the novel here, will be to relate its faults of tone, style and form to the coherence, or lack of it, of Lawrence's vision of life, and to show how the struggle with formal difficulties itself leads to a clarifying of moral insight. This relationship is hinted at by Lawrence himself in his retrospective account many years later:

I had been tussling away for four years, getting out *The White Peacock* in inchoate bits, from the underground of my consciousness. I must have written most of it five or six times, but only in intervals, never as a task or a divine labour, or in the groans of parturition (*Assorted Articles* 149).

Even while writing it Lawrence called *The White Peacock* 'a florid prose poem':

All about love—and rhapsodies on Spring scattered here and there— heroines galore—no plot—nine-tenths adjectives—every colour in the spectrum descanted upon—a poem or two—scraps of Latin and French— altogether a sloppy, spicy mess (*CL* 5).

9

What form there is is second-hand:

> The usual plan is to take two couples and develop their relationships...Most of George Eliot's are on that plan. Anyhow, I don't want a plot, I should be bored with it (ET 103).

Lawrence is, as always, concerned to evaluate these relationships; but the Cyril–Emily story, which adumbrates the Paul–Miriam relationship of *Sons and Lovers*, is dropped when it comes too close. Lawrence is not yet sufficiently in control of his own experience to handle it directly in art: the mining background and the home situation are similarly evaded, kept in the margins of the novel.

The Lettie–Leslie–George triangle is at the heart of the book. Yet how many essential questions about it remain unanswered at the end. We can vaguely perceive, from our knowledge of Lawrence's other writings or from the traditional treatment of similar material in George Eliot, Hardy or Emily Brontë, what we are supposed to think about Lettie. Like Catherine Earnshaw, she chooses wealth, security, adoration, a life of elegance and frivolity, thus betraying her 'true' lover and her own heart.

> Having reached that point in a woman's career when most, perhaps all, of the things in life seem worthless and insipid, she had determined to put up with it, to ignore her own self, to empty her own potentialities into the vessel of another or others, and to live her life at second-hand. This peculiar abnegation of self is the resource of a woman for the escaping of the responsibilities of her own development. Like a nun, she puts over her living face a veil, as a sign that the woman no longer exists for herself: she is the servant of God, of some man, of her children, or maybe of some cause. As a servant, she is no longer responsible for her self, which would make her terrified and lonely...Like so many women, she seemed to live, for the most part contentedly, a small indoor existence with artificial light and padded upholstery. Only occasionally, hearing the winds of life outside, she clamoured to be out in the black, keen storm (280–7).

The wayward Lettie is perhaps the most convincing characterisation in the novel (with the obvious exception of Annable, whose looming presence reduces all the other characters to shadows).

George is less successful. Something of his physical aura comes across, and a sense of suspended animation, awaiting Lettie's quickening touch. We can see Lawrence painfully struggling to draw on the farm setting, George's work in the fields, to charge him with some more than personal, some 'elemental' significance. To judge the extent of his failure, we need only look at the opening pages of *The Rainbow*.

Leslie won't do at all. We are simply asked to assume that because he is wealthy and not a manual worker he must be deficient as a human being. As in all Lawrence's subsequent negative males, Leslie's failings manifest themselves sexually; but here, uniquely, the key sexual scenes are as muffled and evasive as in any Victorian novel. What on earth is supposed to have happened on the night Leslie stays at Lettie's home? We are given the breakfast scene. Leslie comes down nervous and agitated. Lettie comes down late, severely dressed, her face averted, biting her underlip. She refuses to eat or to speak to Leslie as he departs. He makes an excuse to return:

'Why didn't you go away?' she said impulsively. He hung his head and was silent.
'I don't see why—why it should make trouble between us, Lettie,' he faltered. She made a swift gesture of repulsion, whereupon, catching sight of her hand, she hid it swiftly against her skirt again.
'You make my hands—my very hands disclaim me,' she struggled to say. He looked at her clenched fist pressed against the folds of her dress.
'But—,' he began, much troubled.
'I tell you, I can't bear the sight of my own hands,' she said in low passionate tones.
'But surely, Lettie, there's no need—if you love me—'
She seemed to wince (175–6).

This is all we are given. The relationship continues much as before. At last Lettie asks to be freed from the engagement:

'Love—love—I don't know anything about it. But I can't—we can't be—don't you see—oh, what do they say—flesh of one flesh' (195).

Yet they marry. The sexual theme is never raised again except to say that Lettie seeks all her satisfaction in motherhood. Lawrence seems to have no means of bypassing the squeamishness of the characters, for the narrator, Cyril, is the most squeamish of all.

The women of the novel undermine the men's hold on life, rejecting manhood for refinement: the men either capitulate or burn themselves up. All the analysis offers is the suggestion that some essential knowledge has been lost without which sex is nothing but strife, fear and futility. The author/narrator cannot supply any norms or sanctions because he has not yet discovered any means of breaking the sexual stalemate. In the absence of a plot, Cyril cannot hold the novel together. The first-person narrative means that Lawrence cannot place Cyril's priggishness or communicate any insights beyond Cyril's. He has to abandon, half-way through the novel, the attempt to restrict the narrative to those scenes which Cyril might have witnessed. The language is always either would-be naturalistic dialogue or Cyril's narration; it can only be heightened for those rhapsodies of natural description which so impressed the early reviewers. In *Sons and Lovers* such passages are integral—nature offers a touchstone for the evaluation of human response. In *The White Peacock* they are, for the most part, mere indulgence, as Lawrence himself admitted. When the language is occasionally heightened in other ways—'If we move the blood rises in our heel-prints'—the context will not carry the access of weight.

George tries to be serious about life. He speaks passionately of 'her and them frittering away themselves and money in that idiocy—'; but Lawrence dare not let him become too articulate. Cyril interrupts him flippantly: 'You are quoting Longfellow, "Life is real, life is earnest—".' This, of course, is to be Lawrence's perpetual message. He must discover how to embody it in story and character, myth and symbol, in the poetic resonances of his prose, and in the architecture of a 'dramatic' novel.

Despite the word 'architecture', the required discipline is not aesthetic. It is a matter of vision. In 1914 Lawrence wrote to Gordon Campbell:

I think there is the dual way of looking at things: our way, which is to say '*I* am all. All other things are but radiation out from me.'—The other way is to try to conceive the whole, to build up a whole by means of symbolism, because symbolism avoids the I and puts aside the egotist; and, in the whole, to take our decent place. That was how man built the cathedrals. He didn't say 'out of my breast springs this cathedral!' But 'in this vast whole I am a small part, I move and live and have my being' (*CL* 302).

We shall trace, in subsequent pages, the development of this vision.

The immediate problem in *The White Peacock* is to achieve a certain objectivity, impersonality, a clearer focus, a fulcrum. First the restricted personal focus must go:

I will write the thing again, and stop up the mouth of Cyril—I will kick him out—I hate the fellow (*CL* 25).

Cyril, unfortunately, remained. But his centrality is, in the last version, usurped by Annable. Annable is able to respond to life altogether more directly than the other characters who are 'social beings'. He is the natural man, freed, by his extra-social status as a gamekeeper, from all their inhibitions of action and language. Jessie Chambers commented acutely: 'Annable seemed to be a focus for all Lawrence's despair over the materialistic view of life he felt compelled to accept for lack of an alternative' (ET 117). But Annable, who appears 'like some malicious Pan', is more than a focus of despair. The pagan or demonic outcast is to serve Lawrence well as embodying both the destructive element in his vision—his hatred of materialism and society—and also the whole range of Lawrentian positives, here baldly expressed in Annable's motto 'Be a good animal', but undergoing many subsequent metamorphoses and refinements, returning at last to that more notorious gamekeeper whose motto might have been 'Be a good lover'.

Annable is too much of a desperate last-minute interpolation to save *The White Peacock* structurally; but the principle behind his inclusion is sound enough:

He *has* to be there. Don't you see why? He makes a sort of balance. Otherwise it's too much one thing, too much me (ET 117).

§2

In *The White Peacock*, Lawrence uses the mining scene, marginally, for a variety of 'effects':

As you walk home past Selsby, the pit stands up against the west, with beautiful tapering chimneys marked in black against the swim of sunset, and the headstocks etched with tall significance on the brightness (179).

The slow red fires and smoke of the pit-hill are described in the same tone as the bonfires of scarlet lilies in the cottage gardens and the smoke of the tall larkspur (240). For the most part, the scene is avoided, particularly in its human implications:

Pity to hunt out the ugly side of the picture when nature has given you an eye for the pretty, and a soul for flowers, and for lounging in the lozenge-lighted shade of a lilac tree (*CL* 15).

When, rarely, he tries to convey the negative aspect, the prose is undistinguished:

13

We came near to the ugly rows of houses that back up against the pit-hill. Everywhere is black and sooty: the houses are back-to-back, having only one entrance, which is from a square garden where black speckled weeds grow sulkily, and which looks onto a row of evil little ash-pit huts. The road everywhere is trodden over with a crust of soot and coal-dust and cinders (180).

We need only compare this with the masterly analysis and evocation of the same scene in the first two pages of *Sons and Lovers* to recognise a simultaneous maturing of prose and vision.

The first sign of the mature style, apparently sparse and restrained, yet able to draw on real poetic resources, and applied to the human predicament within the domestic and mining scene, is *Odour of Chrysanthemums*. Hueffer has recorded his reaction when this story was submitted to him as editor of the *English Review*:

At once you read:

'The small locomotive engine, Number 4, came clanking, stumbling down from Selston', and at once you know that this fellow with the power of observation is going to write of whatever he writes about from the inside. [. . .] 'It appeared round the corner with loud threats of speed.'. . . Good writing; slightly, but not *too* arresting. . . 'But the colt that it startled from among the gorse. . . outdistanced it at a canter.' Good again. This fellow does not 'state'. He doesn't say: 'It was coming slowly', or—what would have been a little better—'at seven miles an hour' [. . .]. But anyone knows that an engine that makes a great deal of noise and yet cannot overtake a colt at a canter must be a ludicrously ineffective machine. We know then that this fellow knows his job. 'The gorse still flickered indistinctly in the raw afternoon.'. . . Good too, distinctly good. This is the just-sufficient observation of Nature that gives you, in a single phrase, landscape, time of day, weather, season. It is a raw afternoon in autumn in a rather accented countryside [. . .]. You are, then, for as long as the story lasts, to be in one of those untidy, unfinished landscapes where locomotives wander innocuously amongst women with baskets. That is to say, you are going to learn how what we used to call 'the other half'—though we might as well have said the other ninety-nine hundredths— lives. And if you are an editor and that is what you are after, you know that you have got what you want and you can pitch the story straight away into your wicker tray with a few accepted manuscripts and go on to some other occupation. . .Because this man knows. He knows how to open a story with a sentence of the right cadence for holding the attention. He knows how to construct a paragraph. He knows the life he is writing about in a landscape just sufficiently constructed with a casual word here and there. You can trust him for the rest (Nehls 1, 108-9).

The passage indeed represents Lawrence's prose of this period at its best and gives us a foretaste of the prose of *Sons and Lovers*.

The locomotive, 'clanking' and 'stumbling', only threatening speed, so that the colt can outdistance it at a canter, is a paltry, rather ridiculous example of man's mechanical inventiveness. Nevertheless, both nature and human life are subjected to it. The woman stands 'insignificantly trapped' by its jolting waggons which pass with 'slow, inevitable movement'. The colt canters away, the birds make off into the dusk. The woman would make off if she could. Nature seems unable to compete, has given up the struggle. Withered oak leaves drop from the trees; the fowls 'had already abandoned their run among the alders'; the fields are 'dreary and forsaken', the grass filmed with soot from the engine-smoke which sank and cleaved to it. The air is raw and the light stagnant. Nature has gone dead, sterile, here, trapped between the railway and the pit-bank—'flames, like red sores licking its ashy sides'. From the pit-bank the sterility spreads outwards, to the pit-pond, over the dusky fields, up the railway line, to the houses where the colliers live. They, too, are subjects and victims; for the pit, with its clumsy headstocks, is only a larger version of the small engine. The little spasms of the winding-engine signify that the miners are being turned up. Occasionally they are turned up dead or maimed. Men and women, at the mercy of the machine, breathe an atmosphere of death, heightened by the odour of chrysanthemums.

CHAPTER 2

CHRONOLOGY

In November 1910 Lawrence broke his 'betrothal of six years' standing' to Jessie Chambers, and on 3 December became engaged to Louie Burrows. Mrs Lawrence died on 9 December.

RHYMING POEMS.

Suspense is the first poem about the dying mother. *Submergence* marks the end of the period of intensive mourning. The poems from *The Enkindled Spring* to *Two Wives* were all probably written in 1911, as were the last five poems in *Rhyming Poems*.

SONS AND LOVERS (Duckworth, 1913).

Begun, as *Paul Morel*, in October 1910 (*CL* 66). Begun again early in 1911 (*CL* 74). Half-written by October (*CL* 83). Set aside for *The Trespasser* until February 1912. Finished early in April (*CL* 106). Revised throughout May (*CL* 121–6). Begun again in August 1912 (*CL* 137) and finished by November (*CL* 160). Foreword added in January 1913.

SECOND BEST (*English Review*, February 1912; *The Prussian Officer*).

Probably one of the stories 'in the hands of the editor of the *English Review*' in June 1911 (*CL* 78).

WITCH A LA MODE (*Lovat Dickson's Magazine*, June 1934; *A Modern Lover*).

By July 1911 (*CL* 78–81)—earlier titles *Intimacy* and *The White Woman*.

THE OLD ADAM (*A Modern Lover*).

Also 1911.

DAUGHTERS OF THE VICAR.

By September 1911. (*Time and Tide*, 24 March 1934, as *Two Marriages*; *The Prussian Officer*). Revised in October (*CL* 80–1).

THE SHADES OF SPRING (*Forum*, March 1913, as *The Soiled Rose*; *The Prussian Officer*).

December 1911 (*CL* 206). Revised by March 1912 (*CL* 102).

TWO ANONYMOUS REVIEWS—H. G. Fiedler's *Oxford Book of German Verse*, and Jethro Bithell's *The Minnesingers* (*English Review*, January 1912).

December 1911 (*CL* 87).

Lawrence left Croydon in January 1912, having been forced by his tuberculosis to abandon teaching as a profession.

THE BASES OF THE NORMAL

LOOK! WE HAVE COME THROUGH! (Chatto and Windus, 1917).
From *Moonrise* to *Hymn to Priapus*, late 1911 to January 1912.

THE MINER AT HOME (*Nation*, 16 March 1912; *Phoenix*).
February 1912. The strike situation of this month also gave rise to another article,
THE COLLIER'S WIFE SCORES (*CL* 105), and two stories,
HER TURN and STRIKE PAY (*Saturday Westminster Gazette*, 6 and 13 September 1913; *A Modern Lover*), both written by 12 February (*CL* 100).

Lawrence met Frieda Weekley in March 1912 and eloped to Germany with her on 3 May.

THE MERRY-GO-ROUND (*Virginia Quarterly*, Winter 1941; *Complete Plays*, 1965).

THE DAUGHTER-IN-LAW (*Complete Plays*, 1965).

THE MARRIED MAN (*Virginia Quarterly*, Autumn 1940; *Complete Plays*, 1965).
Probably the 'middling good comedy' referred to on 23 April (*CL* 109).

GERMAN IMPRESSIONS (*Saturday Westminster Gazette*, 3 and 10 August 1912; *Phoenix*).
May 1912 (*CL* 115).

LOOK! WE HAVE COME THROUGH!
From *Ballad of a Wilful Woman* to *She Looks Back*, May 1912. From *On the Balcony* to *A Doe at Evening*, June–July 1912.

NEW EVE AND OLD ADAM (*A Modern Lover*)—earlier titles *Renegade Eve* and *The New Eve*.

DELILAH AND MR BIRCUMSHAW (*Virginia Quarterly*, Spring 1940).

ONCE (*Love Among the Haystacks*, 1930).
Probably August 1912.

A CHAPEL AMONG THE MOUNTAINS (*Love Among the Haystacks*).
A HAY HUT AMONG THE MOUNTAINS (*Love Among the Haystacks*).
THE CRUCIFIX ACROSS THE MOUNTAINS (*Saturday Westminster Gazette*, 22 March 1913 as *Christs in the Tirol*; *Twilight in Italy*, Duckworth, 1916).
August–September 1912.

LOOK! WE HAVE COME THROUGH!
From *Song of a Man Who is Not Loved* to *Why Does She Weep?* August–October 1912.

THE FIGHT FOR BARBARA (*Argosy*, December 1933 as *Keeping Barbara*; *Complete Plays*, 1965).
27–29 October 1912.

LOOK! WE HAVE COME THROUGH!
From *Giorno dei Morti* to *December Night*. November–December 1912.

MY MOTHER MADE A FAILURE OF HER LIFE
1912–1913 (Tedlock 44).

A BURNS NOVEL (Nehls 1, 184).
Possibly the novel 'of the common people' conceived in August 1912 (*CL* 137) to be called *Scargill Street* (*CL* 152). Burns was to be treated as a Derbyshire man (*CL* 167). Begun by 29 December (*CL* 174). Abandoned by mid-January 1913 (*CL* 176).

THE WIDOWING OF MRS HOLROYD (Mitchell Kennerley, 1914; *Plays*, Secker, 1932; *Complete Plays*, 1965).
Probably the new play sent to Garnett on 16 January 1913 (*CL* 175). Revised August 1913 (*CL* 218).

LOOK! WE HAVE COME THROUGH!
From *New Year's Eve* to *Coming Awake*, January–March 1913.

REVIEW OF 'GEORGIAN POETRY' (*Rhythm*, March 1913; *Phoenix*).
Probably February 1913 (*CL* 181).

THE LOST GIRL (Secker, 1920).
Begun, as *The Insurrection of Miss Houghton*, in mid-January 1913 (*CL* 176). Set aside half-written (200 pages) in March (*CL* 183, 186, 193, 197), not to be taken up again until 1920.

THE BASES OF THE NORMAL

1910–1913

Sons and Lovers
The Insurrection of Miss Houghton

I mean that always, at first, for a second or two, he seemed like the reckless robber of hen-roosts with gleaming eyes and a mouth watering for adventure and then, with the suddenness of a switched-off light, he became the investigator into the bases of the normal that he essentially was (Ford Maddox Hueffer: Nehls I, 115).

§1

IN *Sons and Lovers* there is much more immediacy, realisation, than in the callow and conventional earlier novels. Lawrence himself describes the treatment as 'visualised'—'in that hard, violent style full of sensation and presentation'. '*Paul Morel* will be a novel—not a florid prose-poem, or a decorated idyll running to seed in realism' (*CL* 66). The autobiographical and intensely personal subject-matter contributes much in these terms. But *Paul Morel* will be a 'somewhat impersonal novel'—not an autobiography, however well done. There is ample evidence in *Sons and Lovers* that Lawrence is now mature enough to create the real, without being slavishly naturalistic; that form is more important to him than autobiographical accuracy; and that his distinctive use of imagery carries a great deal of the novel's significance. Too close a concentration on the autobiographical, the personal problem, has persistently led critics away from the novel's value as a work of art towards its interest as a case-history.

In *A Personal Record* Jessie Chambers epitomises this non-literary criticism:

...I felt that the theme, if treated adequately, had in it the stuff of a magnificent story. It only wanted setting down, and Lawrence possessed the miraculous power of translating the raw material of life into significant form...Since he had elected to deal with the big and difficult subject of his family, and the interactions of the various relationships, I felt he ought to do it faithfully—'with both hands earnestly', as he was fond of quoting. It seemed to me that if he was able to treat the theme with strict integrity he would thereby walk into freedom, and cast off the trammelling past like an old skin (192).

It seems that 'significant form' was not perceived by Jessie Chambers in any of Lawrence's deviations from 'truth':

The Clara of the second half of the story was a clever adaptation of elements from three people, and her creation arose as a complement to Lawrence's mood of failure and defeat. The events related had no foundation in fact, whatever their psychological significance. Having utterly failed to come to grips with his problem in real life, he created the imaginary Clara as a compensation. Even in the novel the compensation is unreal and illusory, for at the end Paul Morel calmly hands her back to her husband, and remains suspended over the abyss of his despair...I realised that I had naively credited Lawrence with superhuman powers of detachment (202).

The issue seemed simple enough to Jessie Chambers:

'I've loved her like a lover. That's why I could never love you.'...The situation was simply that his mother had claimed his love, all the spontaneous tenderness without which 'love' is a mockery. And having given it to her fully and unreservedly Lawrence had in truth no love to give anyone else... (184–5).

There is some truth in this account, as the novel itself establishes. Indeed, Lawrence himself shortly afterwards came round to a similar position, under the influence of Frieda and Freud. The well-known letter to Edward Garnett (14 November 1912) will bear requoting:

It follows this idea: a woman of character and refinement goes into the lower class, and has no satisfaction in her own life. She has had a passion for her husband, so the children are born of passion, and have heaps of vitality. But as her sons grow up, she selects them as lovers—first the eldest, then the second. These sons are urged into life by their reciprocal love of their mother—urged on and on. But when they come into manhood, they can't love, because their mother is the strongest power in their lives, and holds them. As soon as the young men come into contact with women, there's a split. William gives his sex to a fribble, and his mother holds his soul. But the split kills him, because he doesn't know where he is. The next son gets a woman who fights for his soul—fights his mother. The son loves the mother—all the sons hate and are jealous of the father. The battle goes on between the mother and the girl, with the son as object. The mother gradually proves the stronger, because of the tie of blood. The son decides to leave his soul in his mother's hands and, like his elder brother, go for passion. He gets passion. Then the split begins to tell again. But, almost unconsciously, the mother realises what is the matter, and begins to die. The son casts off his mistress to attend to his mother dying. He is left in the end naked of everything, with the drift towards death (*CL* 160).

This account has elicited almost unqualified approval. If this were offered as an analysis of Lawrence's own experience as he then saw it, we could not demur. That it should be offered, however, as the 'idea' which *Sons and Lovers* follows, and as evidence that the novel 'has got form—*form*: haven't I made it patiently, out of sweat as well as blood', means that, testing it against the novel we have, we can only find it loaded and misleading. Certainly it bears no resemblance to Jessie Chambers's account of the novel ('a slander—a fearful treachery'):

In *Sons and Lovers* Lawrence handed his mother the laurels of victory...

I realised that the entire structure of the story rested upon the attitude he had adopted. To do any kind of justice to our relationship would involve a change in his attitude towards his mother's influence, and of that I was now convinced he was incapable (ET 212).

Lawrence's 1912 account is of the novel he might then have written—not the novel we have:

I would write a different *Sons and Lovers* now; my mother was wrong, and I thought she was absolutely right (Frieda Lawrence, *Not I But the Wind* 52).

Right or wrong as Lydia Lawrence may have been, Gertrude Morel is right, though the novel qualifies her rightness—it is not absolute, but relative to the alternatives which are offered. And, as Jessie Chambers observes, it is this attitude towards her which determines 'the entire structure of the story'. The novel does not attribute the split in Paul's consciousness to his mother's possessiveness and jealousy; nor does it present the failure of the two love-affairs as a 'neurotic refusal of life' (Hough, *The Dark Sun* 42) engendered in him by his parents' failure.

Morel is held responsible for his own collapse ('he had denied the God in him'). It is true that the father is later, in *The Lost Girl*, for example, to receive his apotheosis. But it does not follow that Mrs Morel must be in the tradition of destructive women. Her role in *Sons and Lovers* is nearer to that of Lydia Lensky (it is no coincidence that Lydia was Mrs Lawrence's name) in *The Rainbow*. There is a destructive element in her relations with both husband and sons; but the overriding impression is of a normality and strength of character which serves as a standard against which the other women in the novel are judged, and found wanting.

§ 2

The talk was lively and Mrs Lawrence seemed to be the pivot on which the liveliness centred. She struck me as a bright, vivacious little woman, full of vitality, and amusingly emphatic in her way of speaking (E.T. 24).

This was Jessie Chambers's impression of Mrs Lawrence, before the 'little woman' became her rival. And it is in just these terms— liveliness, brightness, vivaciousness, vitality—that she dominates *Sons and Lovers* and takes on a pivotal significance in its structure.

It is this same vitality in Morel which draws Gertrude Coppard to him:

He was so full of colour and animation, his voice ran so easily into comic grotesque, he was so ready and so pleasant with everybody. Her own father had a rich fund of humour, but it was satiric. This man's was different: soft, non-intellectual, warm, a kind of gambolling...He danced well, as if it were natural and joyous in him to dance (9).

This, for her, is manhood, contrasting with her own earnestness, with her father's puritanism, with the lack of manliness in her former suitor, John Field, who had allowed his father to browbeat him into business when he wanted to enter the clergy ('"But if you're a MAN?" she had cried. "Being a man isn't everything", he replied, frowning with puzzled helplessness'). She is fascinated:

Therefore the dusky, golden softness of this man's sensuous flame of life, that flowed off his flesh like the flame from a candle, not baffled and gripped into incandescence by thought and spirit as her life was, seemed to her something wonderful, beyond her...A warmth radiated through her as if she had drunk wine (10).

In Walter Morel, she seeks to complete herself, to achieve fulfilment, through marriage:

The next Christmas they were married, and for three months she was perfectly happy: for six months she was very happy (11).

But the happiness continues to dwindle. 'There was nothing at the back of all his show.'

Sometimes, when she herself wearied of love-talk, she tried to open her heart seriously to him. She saw him listen deferentially, but without understanding. This killed her efforts at a finer intimacy, and she had flashes of fear. Sometimes he was restless of an evening: it was not enough for him just to be near her, she realised (11).

He drifts back to his drinking, and begins to ill-treat her.

There began a battle between them the husband and wife—a fearful, bloody battle that ended only with the death of one. She fought to make him undertake his responsibilities, to make him fulfil his obligations. But he was too different from her. His nature was purely sensuous, and she strove to make him moral, religious. She tried to force him to face things. He could not endure it—it drove him out of his mind (14).

Mrs Morel's religion is presented here not as chapel-going, but as a moral obligation to face reality, to be responsible for one's life, to have integrity. She does not merely make impossible demands of Morel. She goes more than half-way to meet him. She accepts the squalor and poverty. She is a model housewife and mother. She sees in Mr Leivers a man who would have let her help him. Even little Barker is 'ten times the man' Morel is. Through irresponsibility he forfeits his health. He loses the energy even to quarrel and bully, and, when Mrs Morel dies, is left a pathetic lifeless figure. Even if we feel that her demands *were* impossible; that Morel *could* not become responsible, he is not to be forgiven in Lawrence's strictly existential morality: 'for the real tragedy went on in Morel in spite of himself.' He is even responsible for his accidents in the pit:

The essence of tragedy, which is creative crisis, is that a man should go through with his fate, and not dodge it and go bumping into an accident (*Touch and Go* 12).

'Everything deep in him he denied.' It is from his own vital core, which is God in him, that fate emanates. In Tom Brangwen we are to see a man with the courage to go through with his fate; his death by water is a resolution, part of a higher ordering. In dying he is one with his tragedy, which is 'the whole business of life'. Morel lingers on at the end of *Sons and Lovers* adrift even from his own tragedy.

Mrs Morel turns to her sons, but not for sterile compensation. She gives always more than she receives. It is not until she is dying that she begins to sap Paul's life. For, despite the tragedy o. her marriage, she has not been broken. Indeed she has salvaged from the early days something of immense and lasting value:

'My Mother, I believe, got real joy and satisfaction out of my father at first. I believe she had a passion for him; that's why she stayed with him... That's what one must have, I think', he continued—'the real, real flame of feeling through another person—once, only once, if it only lasts three months. She, my mother, looks as if she'd had everything that was necessary for her living and developing. There's not a tiny bit of feeling of sterility about her... And with my father at first, I'm sure she had the real thing. She knows: she has been there. You can feel it about her, and about him, and about hundreds of people you meet every day; and, once it has happened to you, you can go on with anything and ripen.'

'What happened, exactly?' asked Miriam.

'It's so hard to say, but the something big and intense that changes you when you really come together with somebody else. It almost seems to fertilize your soul and make it that you can go on and mature.'

'And you think your mother had it with your father?'

'Yes; and at the bottom she feels grateful to him for giving it her, even now, though they are miles apart' (317).

In the early chapters we see Paul being kindled to life by his mother. They have ecstatic excursions to Nottingham and Lincoln. The words 'jolly' and 'gay' figure prominently. In such scenes the brightness and love is realised largely through naturalistic dialogue. Sometimes it is more concentrated, and poetic:

Once roused, he opened his eyes to see his mother standing on the hearth-rug with the hot iron near her cheek, listening, as it were, to the heat. Her still face, with the mouth closed tight from suffering and disillusion and self-denial, and her nose the smallest bit on one side, and her blue eyes so young, quick, and warm, made his heart contract with love. When she was quiet, so, she looked brave and rich with life... She spat on the iron and a little ball of spit bounded, raced off the dark, glossy surface. She was warm in the ruddy firelight. Paul loved the way she crouched and put her head on one side. Her movements were light and quick. It was always a pleasure to watch her. Nothing she ever did, no movement she ever made, could have been found fault with by her children. The room was warm and full of the scent of hot linen (66).

Young, quick, warm, brave, rich, life—these words have their effect. The warmth has its source in Mrs Morel's eyes as much as in the firelight and the hot linen. And the quickness of her eyes and movements (controlled by a central poise and stillness) uses the alternative meaning of the word to convey life itself ('the quick and the dead'). It is significant that the last word of the novel is 'quickly'.

§3

The second third of the novel is concerned largely with Miriam, though Mrs Morel's presence is always felt. Gradually Paul comes to mediate between Miriam and life. Miriam lives through her soul. She finds difficulty in assimilating sensuous experience.

And she was cut off from ordinary life by her religious intensity which made the world for her either a nunnery garden or a paradise, where sin and knowledge were not, or else an ugly, cruel thing (148).

Miriam's intensity, her inability to be ordinary, is taken up again and again:

'Eh, my Hubert!' she sang, in a voice heavy and surcharged with love. 'Eh, my Hubert!' And folding him in her arms, she swayed slightly from side to side with love, her face half lifted, her eyes half closed, her voice drenched with love. 'Don't!' said the child, uneasy—'don't, Miriam!' (153).

This trance-like ecstasy—'her face half lifted, her eyes half closed'—is typical of Miriam. Paul is as uneasy as the child, contrasting her behaviour with his mother's normality:

'What do you make such a fuss for?' cried Paul, all in suffering because of her extreme emotion. 'Why can't you be ordinary with him?'
  She let the child go, and rose, and said nothing. Her intensity, which would leave no emotion on a normal plane, irritated the youth into a frenzy. And this fearful, naked contact of her on small occasions shocked him. He was used to his mother's reserve. And on such occasions he was thankful in his heart and soul that he had his mother, so sane and wholesome (153).

This intense supplication is evident even in her approach to algebra:

'What do you tremble your soul before it for?' he cried. 'You don't learn algebra with your blessed soul. Can't you look at it with your clear simple wits?' (156).

This humility with its attendant spirituality and religious overtones is most evident in the flower scenes:

He watched her crouching, sipping the flowers with fervid kisses.
  'Why must you always be fondling things?' he said irritably.
  'But I love to touch them', she replied, hurt.
  'Can you never like things without clutching them as if you wanted to pull the heart out of them? Why don't you have a bit more restraint, or reserve, or something?'

She looked up at him full of pain, then continued slowly to stroke her lips against a ruffled flower. Their scent, as she smelled it, was so much kinder than he; it almost made her cry.

'You wheedle the soul out of things', he said. 'I would never wheedle—at any rate I'd go straight...You don't want to love—your eternal and abnormal craving is to be loved. You aren't positive, you're negative. You absorb, absorb, as if you must fill yourself up with love, because you've got a shortage somewhere' (218).

This 'restraint, or reserve, or something', the lack of which constitutes an abnormality, a 'shortage' in Miriam, is, of course, Mrs Morel's:

He loved to sit at home, alone with his mother, at night, working and working. She sewed or read. Then, looking up from his task, he would rest his eyes for a moment on her face, that was bright with living warmth, and he returned gladly to his work. 'I can do my best things when you sit there in your rocking-chair, mother', he said. 'I'm sure!' she said, sniffing with mock scepticism. But she felt it was so, and her heart quivered with brightness. For many hours she sat still, slightly conscious of him labouring away, whilst she worked or read her book. And he, with all his soul's intensity directing his pencil, could feel her warmth inside him like strength. They were both very happy so, and both unconscious of it. These times, that meant so much, and which were real living, they almost ignored (158).

And it is Mrs Morel who first notices that Miriam is pulling the heart out of Paul. Gradually it becomes clear that it is this 'absorption' by Miriam which is causing the 'split' in Paul's consciousness, not any demands made by his mother:

With Miriam he was always on the high plane of abstraction, when his natural fire of love was transmitted into the fine stream of thought. She would have it so. If he were jolly, and, as she put it, flippant, she waited till he came back to her, till the change had taken place in him again, and he was wrestling with his own soul, frowning, passionate in his desire for understanding. And in this passion for understanding her soul lay close to his; she had him all to herself. But he must be made abstract first.

Then, if she put her arm in his, it caused him almost torture. His consciousness seemed to split. The place where she was touching him ran hot with friction. He was one internecine battle, and he became cruel to her because of it (173).

And the frustration which this 'split' causes becomes more and more clearly sexual:

The fact that he might want her as a man wants a woman had in him been suppressed into a shame. When she shrank in her convulsed, coiled torture from the thought of such a thing, he had winced to the depths of his soul. And now this 'purity' prevented even their first love-kiss. It was as if she could scarcely stand the shock of physical love, even a passionate kiss, and then he was too shrinking and sensitive to give it...He loved to think of his mother, and other jolly people...And Paul hated her because, somehow, she spoilt his ease and naturalness. And he writhed himself with a feeling of humiliation (179).

At last he breaks with Miriam and writes a valedictory letter to her:

See, you are a nun. I have given you what I would give a holy nun...In all our relations no body enters. I do not talk to you through the senses—rather through the spirit. That is why we cannot love in the common sense... If people marry, they must live together as affectionate humans, who may be commonplace with each other without feeling awkward—not as two souls (251).

Miriam's abnormality is related to her mother, just as Paul's relative normality is to his. Early in the relationship there is evident a serious maladjustment in both mother and daughter, towards the realities of farm life:

Miriam was exceedingly sensitive, as her mother had always been. The slightest grossness made her recoil almost in anguish. Her brothers were brutal, but never coarse in speech. The men did all the discussing of farm matters outside. But, perhaps because of the continual business of birth and begetting which goes on upon every farm, Miriam was the more hyper-sensitive to the matter, and her blood was chastened almost to disgust of the faintest suggestion of such intercourse. Paul took his pitch from her, and their intimacy went on in an utterly blanched and chaste fashion. It could never be mentioned that the mare was in foal (162).

The placing of that last sentence establishes that the failure towards Paul is only one manifestation of a general failure towards life. Miriam idealises love to purify it from 'the faintest suggestion of such intercourse'. Otherwise 'she felt as if her whole soul coiled into knots of shame' (171). She prays 'make me love him— as Christ would, who died for the souls of men'. All this prepares us for the ultimate failure, when Paul goes back to Miriam to try to break down her spirituality through a physical consummation, and achieves, instead, only a ritual slaughter:

Her big brown eyes were watching him, still and resigned and loving; she lay as if she had given herself up to sacrifice: there was her body for him; but the look at the back of her eyes, like a creature awaiting immolation, arrested him, and all his blood fell back. 'You are sure you want me?' he asked, as if a cold shadow had come over him. 'Yes, quite sure.' She was very quiet, very calm. She only realised that she was doing something for him. He could

27

hardly bear it. She lay to be sacrificed for him because she loved him so much. And he had to sacrifice her. For a second, he wished he were sexless or dead (289–90).

It is the dead hand of the mother once more upon Miriam:

'Mother said to me: "There is one thing in marriage that is always dreadful, but you have to bear it." And I believed it.' (290–1.)

§4

The unnatural intensity, the clenched will of Miriam, relates her unmistakably to Hermione Roddice of *Women in Love*, even in its physical manifestation, a heaviness, almost a clumsiness in her movements:

Her body was not flexible and living. She walked with a swing, rather heavily, her head bowed forward, pondering. She was not clumsy, and yet none of her movements seemed quite *the* movement. Often, when wiping the dishes, she would stand in bewilderment and chagrin because she had pulled in two halves a cup or a tumbler. It was as if, in her fear and self-mistrust, she put too much strength into the effort. There was no looseness or abandon about her. Everything was gripped stiff with intensity and her effort, overcharged, closed in on itself (153–4).

We are reminded again of Mrs Morel:

Her movements were light and quick. It was always a pleasure to watch her. Nothing she ever did, no movement she ever made, could have been found fault with by her children (66).

But, even more than it throws us back to Mrs Morel, this throws us forward to Clara:

She stood on top of the stile, and he held both her hands. Laughing, she looked down into his eyes. Then she leaped. Her breast came against his; he held her, and covered her face with kisses (307–8).

The Miriam passage continues:

But she was physically afraid. If she were getting over a stile, she gripped his hands in a little hard anguish, and began to lose her presence of mind. And he could not persuade her to jump from even a small height. Her eyes dilated, became exposed and palpitating. 'No!' she cried, half laughing in terror—'no!'
'You shall!' he once cried, and, jerking her forward, he brought her falling from the fence. But her wild 'Ah!' of pain, as if she were losing consciousness, cut him (154).

The same physical inhibition prevents Miriam from enjoying the swing. This episode is characteristic of the novel—remarkable for its realism and freshness, embodying resources far greater than those needed for mere presentation, resources which serve to relate the episode closely to the overall structure of the novel and to invest it with a deeper moral significance.

Paul swings 'like a bird that swings for joy of movement'; he finds it 'a treat of a swing—a real treat of a swing'. Miriam is amazed that he takes his enjoyment so seriously. But for Paul life is made up of such moments of intensity, an intensity as relaxed and whole as hers is taut and unbalanced, moments when the body is given over to something outside the will, in this case the rhythm of the swing:

She could feel him falling and lifting through the air, as if he were lying on some force... For the moment he was nothing but a piece of swinging stuff: not a particle of him that did not swing (150-1).

Miriam is roused watching him:

It were almost as if he were a flame that had lit a warmth in her whilst he swung in the middle air (151).

Mrs Morel had been able to yield to joy, to Walter's 'flame of life', but Miriam 'cannot lose herself so'. When her turn comes she grips the rope with fear, resisting the forces which seek to carry her. The sexual implication is clear in the hot waves of fear through her bowels which accompany Paul's rhythmic thrusts. The fiasco of their eventual consummation could be predicted from this scene.

Miriam's reluctance to give herself up to life, and, more specifically, to put herself in the hands of the man she loves, contrasts, again, with Clara:

'Will you go down to the river?' he asked.
She looked at him, leaving herself in his hands. He went over the brim of the declivity and began to climb down.
'It is slippery', he said.
'Never mind', she replied.
The red clay went down almost sheer. He slid, went from one tuft of grass to the next, hanging on to the bushes, making for a little platform at the foot of a tree. There he waited for her, laughing with excitement. Her shoes were clogged with red earth. It was hard for her. He frowned. At last he caught her hand, and she stood beside him. The cliff rose above them and fell away

29

below. Her colour was up, her eyes flashed. He looked at the big drop below them.

'It's risky', he said; 'or messy, at any rate. Shall we go back?'

'Not for my sake', she said quickly...

She was coming perilously down.

'Mind!' he warned her. He stood with his back to the tree, waiting.

'Come now', he called, opening his arms.

She let herself run. He caught her, and together they stood watching the dark water scoop at the raw edge of the bank (309).

Clara's natural abandon makes their first intimacy easy for Paul, despite the hazards. Afterwards, glowing with happiness, they go for tea in the village. An old lady presents Clara with 'three tiny dahlias in full blow, neat as bees, and speckled scarlet and white' (312). The offering is made 'because we were jolly', Paul tells Miriam.

Flower themes are woven into the whole novel so skilfully that only cumulatively does one recognise their symbolism. A scene in the first chapter identifies Mrs Morel with the flowers, and, through them, with all the mysterious potentialities of life:

She became aware of something about her. With an effort she roused herself to see what it was that penetrated her consciousness. The tall white lilies were reeling in the moonlight, and the air was charged with their perfume as with a presence. Mrs Morel gasped slightly in fear. She touched the big, pallid flowers on their petals, then shivered. They seemed to be stretching in the moonlight. She put her hand into one white bin: the gold scarcely showed on her fingers by moonlight. She bent down to look at the binful of yellow pollen; but it only appeared dusky. Then she drank a deep draught of the scent. It almost made her dizzy (24).

She is pregnant with Paul, and it is stressed that this communion is shared by the unborn child. The night she looks out on is not only nature, it is all that the infinite distance offers:

The night was very large, and very strange, stretching its hoary distances infinitely. And out of the silver-grey fog of darkness came sounds vague and hoarse: a corncrake not far off, sound of a train like a sigh, and distant shouts of men (24).

The symbolic character of the passage is underlined on the following page, when Mrs Morel, looking in the mirror, smiles to see 'her face all smeared with the yellow dust of lilies'. The night into which Mrs Morel here merges is moonlit, shiny, hoary, silver-grey, rich with scents and sounds and the dusky gold of the pollen. And Paul is here baptised into life.

At the structural centre of the novel, at the critical moment when Paul rejects Miriam finally for Clara, there is a second night-communion which in part repeats, in part subtly qualifies and extends, the symbolism of the first. The lilies are now described as madonna lilies:

Through the open door, stealthily, came the scent of madonna lilies, almost as if it were prowling abroad (293).

We remember from the earlier scene the overpowering perfume, the streaming white light of the full moon, the whiteness of all the flowers. In the later scene there is a half-moon, dusky gold, which makes the sky dull purple, and which disappears below the hill at the very moment when Paul catches 'another perfume, something raw and coarse':

Hunting round, he found the purple iris, touched their fleshy throats and their dark, grasping hands. At any rate he had found something (294).

The next chapter is called 'Passion'. The intense whiteness of the full moon and the lilies, formerly a condition of Paul's growth within an all-encompassing mother-love, is now becoming a weight upon him, a 'barrier' to his further maturing. The blanched white light is the possession of his soul by women who, as mother and virgin, cannot foster the life of the body and the development of a strong, self-sufficient masculinity.

As the first night-communion gave a blessing to the unborn child, so the second blesses the new self which is coming into being within Paul:

Often, as he talked to Clara Dawes, came that thickening and quickening of his blood, that peculiar concentration in the breast, as if something were alive there, a new self, or a new centre of consciousness (252).

The new self responds to Clara impersonally, as a woman rather than a person, almost physiologically. And Mrs Morel approves: 'At any rate that feeling was wholesome.' She even invites Clara to Sunday tea:

Clara felt she completed the circle, and it was a pleasure to her. But she was rather afraid of the self-possession of the Morels, father and all. She took their tone; there was a feeling of balance. It was a cool, clear atmosphere, where everyone was himself, and in harmony...Miriam realised that Clara was accepted as she had never been (322, 324).

Mrs Morel's verdict is confirmed by the novel:

Yes, I liked her. But you'll tire of her my son; you know you will (329).

The consummation with Clara is wonderfully done. The significance of the experience is conveyed largely in the symbolism of the Trent in flood:

The Trent was very full. It swept silent and insidious under the bridge, travelling in a soft body. There had been a great deal of rain. On the river levels were flat gleams of flood water. The sky was grey, with glisten of silver here and there... There was the faintest haze over the silvery-dark water and the green meadow bank, and the elm-trees that were spangled with gold. The river slid by in a body, utterly silent and swift, intertwining among itself like some subtle, complex creature... Sometimes there below they caught glimpses of the full, soft-sliding Trent, and of water-meadows dotted with small cattle... The far-below water-meadows were very green. He and she stood leaning against one-another, silent, afraid, their bodies touching all along. There came a quick gurgle from the river below (306, 308).

There is more here than a mere water-equals-fertility symbol. The splashes of silver and gold remind us of the positives of the night-communions. The Trent is the great surge of uninhibited instinct, emotion, which carries all before it:

As a rule, when he started love-making, the emotion was strong enough to carry with it everything—reason, soul, blood—in a great sweep, like the Trent carries bodily its back-swirls and intertwinings, noiselessly. Gradually the little criticisms, the little sensations, were lost, thought also went, everything borne along in one flood. He became, not a man with a mind, but a great instinct (363).

The abstraction of his relationship with Miriam—'his natural fire of love... transmitted into the fine stream of thought'—had cut him off from life. Clara puts him in touch again:

Just as he was, so it seemed the vigorous wintry stars were strong also with life. He and they struck with the same pulse of fire, and the same joy of strength which held the bracken-frond stiff near his eyes held his own body firm (364).

Throughout the novel, this faculty for being in touch with life has been stressed in Paul, and its absence in Miriam. It is a matter of respect for the unique otherness of phenomena, the mythic faculty of meeting phenomena in an I–thou relationship, meeting but not merging, as Miriam seeks to do, which is a violation of individuality. Sexual union with Clara is not at all a merging of identities. It is through the very strangeness of the woman that Paul gains access to the darkness which is both the unknown forces and purposes of the wheeling universe, and the equally unknown forces and purposes deep within himself:

All the while the peewits were screaming in the field. When he came to, he wondered what was near his eyes, curving and strong with life in the dark, and what voice it was speaking. Then he realised it was the grass, and the peewit was calling. The warmth was Clara's breathing heaving. He lifted his head, and looked into her eyes. They were dark and shining and strange, life wild at the source staring into his life, stranger to him, yet meeting him; and he put his face down on her throat, afraid. What was she? A strong, strange, wild life, that breathed with his in the darkness through this hour. It was all so much bigger than themselves that he was hushed. They had met, and included in their meeting the thrust of the manifold grass stems, the cry of the peewit, the wheel of the stars (353).

From now on in Lawrence's work, life is not to be judged by merely human standards; rather, human values are themselves exposed to standards drawn from experiences and relationships in an animistic universe:

To know their own nothingness, to know the tremendous living flood which carried them always, gave them rest within themselves. If so great a magnificent power could overwhelm them, identify them altogether with itself, so that they knew that they were only grains in the tremendous heave that lifted every grass blade its little height, and every tree, and living thing, then why fret about themselves? They could let themselves be carried by life, and they felt a sort of peace, each in the other. There was a verification which they had had together. Nothing could nullify it, nothing could take it away; it was almost their belief in life (354).

It is this faith which finally saves Paul from the temptation to merge with the dying mother into the other darkness, of death. Clara has now taken over from the mother the initiation of Paul into life.

But the Trent imagery has also suggested the limitations of this passion; like floodwaters, it is something beyond control, accumulated and unresolved, unless it takes its place in a whole human relationship which Paul finds impossible with Clara.

§5

After the failure with Clara, Paul begins to doubt his capacity for loving any woman other than his mother.

'You haven't met the right woman.'
  'And I never shall meet the right woman while you live', he said.
  She was very quiet. Now she began to feel tired, as if she were done (351).

Mrs Morel has up to this point supplied Paul with the standards with which to judge both Miriam and Clara and find them wanting. But he is unable to separate the moral qualities for which his mother stands (and which the novel never calls in question) from her actual physical presence and his close filial relationship with her. But it is in terms of those very standards that the relationship is now seen to be retarding. If Paul continues to lean on his mother and live through her, he will never discover whether he has succeeded in incorporating her strengths into his own character. Unless he can learn to live without daily reference to her and dependence on her, no complete relationship with another woman will be possible for him, nor will he be able to survive his mother's death. Without her the night which she had made him a part of, containing all the un-realised potentialities of life (its sights and sounds had 'roused' and 'invigorated' Mrs Morel), becomes not the womb of day, but its winding sheet:

The town...stretched away over the bay of railway, a level fume of lights. Beyond the town, the country, little smouldering spots for more towns—the sea—the night—on and on! And he had no place in it!...Everywhere the vastness and terror of the immense night which is roused and stirred for a brief while by the day, but which returns, and will remain at last eternal, holding everything in its silence and living gloom (420).

Paul's will fights to voice his mother's values against his own temptation to follow 'in the wake of his beloved':

'You've got to keep alive for her sake', said his will in him...'You've got to carry forward her living, and what she had done, go on with it' (407).

He turns, at the end, to seek for life in new places:

But no, he would not give in. Turning sharply, he walked towards the city's gold phosphorescence. His fists were shut, his mouth set fast. He would not take that direction, to follow her. He walked towards the faintly humming, glowing town, quickly (420).

'The city's gold phosphorescence' beckons, like the 'dusky gold' of Morel's youthful flame of life, like the pollen and the half-moon, towards the unknown—full of richness and the promise of life.

§6

On 26 April 1913 Lawrence wrote to A. W. McLeod:

Pray to your gods for me that *Sons and Lovers* shall succeed. People should begin to take me seriously now. And I do so break my heart over England when I read *The New Machiavelli*. And I am sure that only through a re-adjustment between men and women, and a making free and healthy of this sex, will she get out of her present atrophy. Oh, Lord, and if I don't 'subdue my art to a metaphysic', as somebody very beautifully said of Hardy, I do write because I want folk—English folk—to alter, and have more sense (*CL* 204).

It seems that the writing of *Sons and Lovers* has emancipated Lawrence not only from the now restricting influence of the mother, but also from the preoccupation with autobiographical material. Lawrence continues to explore his personal problems in his fiction, but there is from now on a highly developed awareness of, for example, the social implications of the sexual lives of individuals.

Frieda's influence is incalculable in these first years together. She helped Lawrence to realise the atrophy of England, the lack of real life offered in English society, the extent to which his mother had been circumscribed by that society, whilst his father had, in some sense, refused to toe the social line. Most of all she convinced him of the regenerative potentiality of free and healthy sex. Frieda was also the first of Lawrence's critics to try to push him forward rather than pull him back. She knew that he could do much better work than *Sons and Lovers*:

The novel is a failure but you must feel something at the back of it struggling, trying to come out. You see, I don't really believe in *Sons and Lovers*; it feels as if there were nothing *behind* all those happenings as if there were no 'Hinterland der Seele', only intensely felt fugitive things. I who am a believer though I don't know in what, to me it seems an irreligious book. It does not seem the deepest and last thing said; if for instance a man loves in a book the pretty curl on the neck of 'her', he loves it ever so intensely and beautifully, there is something behind the curl, *more* than that curl; there is *she*, the living, striving *she*. Writers are so beside the point, not *direct* enough (*Frieda* 202).

By this time (February 1914) Lawrence had already made a further attempt to get directly to the point, to create a 'living, striving *she*'. In the early months of the previous year he had written the first 200 pages of *The Insurrection of Miss Houghton* (later called *The Lost Girl*), which he had then set aside to begin *The Sisters* (later *The Rainbow* and *Women in Love*), a pot-boiler, 'a shorter, absolutely impeccable—as far as morals go—novel' for the *jeunes filles*. But it quickly fell from grace and developed into 'an earnest and painful work'. Miss Houghton was abandoned for several years; but she had been, for a while, very much Lawrence's first love—

so new, so really a stratum deeper than I think anybody has ever gone, in a novel...It is all analytical—quite unlike *Sons and Lovers*, not a bit visualised (*CL* 193).

At first glance it is hard to credit this. Indeed it is almost always quoted as though it referred to *The Rainbow*. When we remember the furore which greeted *Tess of the D'Urbervilles* a generation earlier, we can readily appreciate what is new about the book's subject-matter, and why Lawrence thought he would not be able to find a publisher. But the method, in the first half at least, is as traditional as anything in Lawrence, the social setting as meticulously presented as in Arnold Bennett, full of telling observations and local colour, the characterisation richly Dickensian, drawing to the full on Lawrence's comic gifts. Many readers were later to complain that Lawrence's novels contained no 'lifelike', no 'recognisable' characters. *The Lost Girl* provides as much evidence as we need to demonstrate that he could have rivalled the Bennetts and Galsworthys in their own mode had he chosen to do so.

In creating a world of people recognisable by their appearance and outward behaviour, a world full of furniture and houses and shops, Bennett and Galsworthy thought that they were writing about 'the real world', and so did their readers, including the critics. They wrote on the assumption that people are social beings living entirely within a world of property and manners. Such people may, in fact, be the majority; they are none the less, for Lawrence, abnormal, parasitic:

They are parasites upon the thought, the feelings, the whole body of life of really living individuals who have gone before them and who exist alongside with them. All they can do, having no individual life of their own, is out of fear to rake together property, and to feed upon the life that has been given by living men to mankind (*Phoenix* 543).

In *The Insurrection of Miss Houghton* Lawrence set out to do what Galsworthy almost accomplished:

The Man of Property has the elements of a very great novel, a very great satire. It sets out to reveal the social being in all his strength and inferiority. But the author has not the courage to carry it through. The greatness of the book rests in its new and sincere and amazingly profound satire. It is the ultimate satire on modern humanity, and done from the inside, with really consummate skill and sincere creative passion, something quite new. It seems to be a real effort to show up the social being in all his weirdness. And then it fizzles out (*ibid.* 542).

This is surely the sense in which Lawrence intends the words 'deep', 'new' and 'analytical' in relation to *The Insurrection of Miss Houghton*. Alvina's insurrection is against the social being. The title itself strikes exactly the right note of satire:

Satire exists for the very purpose of killing the social being, showing him what an inferior he is and, with all his parade of social honesty, how subtly and corruptly debased. Dishonest to life, dishonest to the living universe on which he is parasitic as a louse. By ridiculing the social being, the satirist helps the true individual, the real human being, to rise to his feet again and go on with the battle. For it is always a battle, and always will be (*ibid.* 543).

What distinguishes Alvina from almost everyone else in Woodhouse (or England) is that she is not, as they are,

unaware even of the thing most precious to any human being, that core of manhood or womanhood, naïve, innocent at-oneness with the living universe-continuum, which alone makes a man individual and, as an individual, *essentially* happy... even in his greatest misery (*ibid.* 543).

The story changes at the end from satire to something very like tragedy. By deliberately losing herself to the world of convenience, Alvina is exposed to great suffering, but comes through to this essential happiness:

And a wild, terrible happiness would take hold of her, beyond despair, but very like despair. No one would ever find her. She had gone beyond the world into the pre-world, she had reopened an old eternity (326).

Lawrence goes 'really a stratum deeper' because he has created his Woodhouse world in all its 'reality' in order to have an absurd troupe of phony Indians make it disappear at the toss of a feathered head. The unreality, absurdity, of the circus troupe is essential to the satire; they must share none of the standards of the society they invade.

They *were* unreal, Madame and Cicio and the rest. Cicio was just a fantasy blown in on the wind, to blow away again. The real, permanent thing was Woodhouse, the *semper idem* Knarborough Road, and the unchangeable grubby gloom of Manchester House, with the stuffy, padding Miss Pinnegar, and her father, whose fingers, whose very soul seemed dirty with pennies. These were the solid, permanent fact. These were life itself. And Cicio, splashing up on his bay horse and green cloth, he was a mountebank and an extraneous nonentity, a coloured old rag blown down the Knarborough Road into Limbo (149).

But it is England itself which finally sinks into Limbo:

She watched, away off, behind all the sunshine and the sea, the grey, snow-streaked substance of England slowly receding and sinking, submerging. She felt she could not believe it. It was like looking at something else. What? It was like a long, ash-grey coffin, winter, slowly submerging into the sea. England? (303).

The ridiculous get-up of the Natcha-Kee-Tawaras masks living individuals; the propriety of Woodhouse masks a void. In Califano the standards of English social life exist only in the letters from home, including this from Dr Mitchell:

I little thought, at the time when I was hoping to make you my wife, that you were carrying on with a dirty Italian organ-grinder. So your fair-seeming face covered the schemes and vice of your true nature. Well, I can only thank Providence which spared me the disgust and shame of marrying you, and I hope that, when I meet you on the streets of Leicester Square, I shall have forgiven you sufficiently to be able to throw you a coin (339).

Dr Mitchell is more deeply absurd here than Cicio ever was.

What is behind all the happenings of *The Lost Girl* is Alvina's 'true nature', 'the living, striving *she*'. In Frieda's terms it is a religious book.

CHAPTER 3

CHRONOLOGY

TWILIGHT IN ITALY (Duckworth, 1916).

The Spinner and the Monks, December 1912 or January 1913. *The Lemon Gardens*, late January 1913. *The Theatre*, January–February 1913. *San Gaudenzio*, *The Dance*, *Il Duro* and *John*, April 1913. Rewritten for book-publication by the autumn of 1915.

THE RAINBOW (Methuen, 1915).

Begun, as *The Sisters*, in March 1913; finished by the beginning of June (*CL* 197, 200). It was apparently written in the first person. The heroine, Ella, was closely based on Frieda (*CL* 208). The second version was begun in September (*CL* 223) and finished by January 1914 (*CL* 263). Third version begun February 1914 (*CL* 264) as *The Wedding Ring* and finished by mid-May as *The Rainbow* (*CL* 276). The fourth and final version was begun by 4 December 1914 (*CL* 295). And the decision was taken at about this time to split the material into two volumes (*CL* 306). Finished by 2 March 1915 (*CL* 327).

LOOK! WE HAVE COME THROUGH!

Spring Morning to *Song of A Man Who Has Come Through*, April 1913 to late 1913 or early 1914.

THOMAS MANN (*Blue Review*, July 1913; *Phoenix*).

Probably early 1913.

THE PRUSSIAN OFFICER (*English Review*, August 1914 as *Honour and Arms*; Duckworth, 1914).

Before 11 June 1913 (*CL* 209).

A THORN IN THE FLESH (*English Review*, June 1914 as 'Vin Ordinaire'; *The Prussian Officer*, 1914).

Probably mid-June 1913 (*CL* 209).

THE PRIMROSE PATH (*England, My England*, Seltzer, 1922).

Before 28 July 1913 (*CL* 216).

TWILIGHT IN ITALY.

Italians in Exile and *The Return Journey*, September–October 1913.

THE MORTAL COIL (*Seven Arts*, July 1917).

Written before the war in Italy, probably in the spring of 1914 when Sir T. D. Dunlop, from whom Lawrence received the story in 1916, was typing for him. Rewritten early October 1916 (*CL* 480).

Lawrence and Frieda returned to England in June 1914.

39

STUDY OF THOMAS HARDY (*Phoenix*).

Conceived by mid-July 1914 (*CL* 287). Begun by 5 September (*CL* 290). Finished in November. On 18 December, Lawrence wrote of his intention to rewrite it 'still another time' (Moore, *The Intelligent Heart*, 172).

LOOK! WE HAVE COME THROUGH!

From *One Woman to All Women* to *Elysium*, June 1914–July 1915.

RHYMING POEMS (*New Poems*, Secker, 1918).

From *Noise of Battle* to *Narcissus*, late 1914 and 1915.

THE CROWN (*The Signature*, 4 and 18 October, 4 November 1915; *Reflections on the Death of a Porcupine*, Centaur Press, Philadelphia, 1925).

Apparently a rewriting of an earlier work called *Le Gai Savaire* (*CL* 324). Begun by 2 March 1915 (*CL* 327), now to be called *The Signal* or *The Phoenix*. Abandoned by 19 March (*CL* 330). Begun again by 8 April (*CL* 331); finished by mid-May. Begun again, as *Morgenrot*, on 3 June (AH 237). 7 July—'broken down in the middle of my philosophy' (AH 240). On 12 July, Lawrence states his intention to write it yet again (*CL* 353). The MS for the first number of *The Signature* was sent off on 20 September 1915 (AH 257).

ENGLAND, MY ENGLAND (*English Review*, October 1915; Seltzer, 1922).

By September 1915 (*CL* 308). Rewritten in December 1921.

THE THIMBLE (*Seven Arts*, March 1917).

October 1915 (*CL* 372). This story has been described as an early version of *The Ladybird* (cf. Roberts's Bibliography, p. 61), but is, in fact, quite different.

GOATS AND COMPASSES.

The prospectus for Rainbow Books and Music, issued in February 1916, advertised as a possible future publication 'Mr Lawrence's philosophical work, *Goats and Compasses*' (Carswell, *The Savage Pilgrimage*, 44). The work was never published, but was certainly completed. Cecil Gray, who read the typescript in 1916, has described it as 'a bombastic, pseudo-mystical, psycho-philosophical treatise dealing largely with homosexuality' (*Peter Warlock*, p. 114). Of the two copies which existed, Lawrence destroyed one and Philip Heseltine the other. On 13 January 1916, Lawrence wrote: 'I'm doing my philosophy. It's come at last. I am satisfied, and as sure as a lark in the sky' (*CL* 414). On 25 February he wrote, also to Lady Ottoline Morrell: 'I send you now the first, the destructive half of my philosophy' (*CL* 437). The second half is to deal with the 'new world' that lies ahead.

DEMOCRACY (*Phoenix*).

The above quotations may refer to *Democracy* which Mrs Lawrence has placed in the Cornwall period (Tedlock 133). Revised in Italy, 1920–1.

3

THE PERFECT MEDIUM
1913–1914

The Rainbow

The novel is a perfect medium for revealing to us the changing rainbow of our living relationships (*Phoenix* 532).

For me the rainbow interprets this (as well as hope), the glory shining between every two people which can exist only between them. Each human relationship should be a glorious rainbow (Nehls III, 133).

§1

IN reading Lawrence's letters of 1913–14 we can make no distinction between his thinking about life and about art. His own marriage is the anvil on which he fettles a new art and a new life. Four of these letters, two to Ernest Collings and two to Edward Garnett, are crucial.

17 January 1913
My great religion is a belief in the blood, the flesh, as being wiser than the intellect. We can go wrong in our minds. But what our blood feels and believes and says, is always true. The intellect is only a bit and a bridle. What do I care about knowledge. All I want is to answer to my blood, direct, without fribbling intervention of mind, or moral, or what-not. I conceive a man's body as a kind of flame, like a candle flame, forever upright and flowing: and the intellect is just the light that is shed on to the things around. And I am not much concerned with the things around—which is really mind —but with the mystery of the flame forever flowing, coming God knows how from out of practically nowhere, and being *itself*, whatever there is around it, that it lights up...
    The real way of living is to answer to one's wants. Not 'I want to light up with my intelligence as many things as possible' but 'For the living of my full flame—I want that liberty, I want that woman, I want that pound of peaches, I want to go to sleep, I want to go to the pub and have a good time, I want to look beastly swell today, I want to kiss that girl, I want to insult that man' (*CL* 180).

We saw Lawrence, in *Daughters of the Vicar*, beginning to move in this direction:

He saw some collier lurching straight forward without misgiving, pursuing his own satisfactions, and he envied him. Anything, he would have given for this spontaneity and this blind stupidity which went to its own satisfaction direct (*Stories* 1, 165).

It represents, of course, his reaction against the mother. And that in the father which had seemed mere 'blind stupidity' at the time, Lawrence now hails as 'spontaneity', selfhood. The images of blood and flame are used here as if they were synonymous, as, of course, they can be; it is the blood which draws the flame, the current, through the body, a fountain of life. It is in this sense that we take, at the end of *The Rainbow* (where the flame is now transmuted into the rainbow image itself), these words: 'the rainbow was arched in their blood and would quiver to life in their spirit'. The danger, however, is that the blood in its narrower connotations of unbridled passion will usurp both spirit and flame.

The Foreword to *Sons and Lovers*, written at the same time as the Collings letter, exemplifies the danger, for this pseudo-biblical paean to the flesh 'in its unquestionable sincerity' leads Lawrence to this logical and appalling conclusion:

But if in my passion I slay my neighbour, it is no sin of mine, but it is his sin, for he should not have permitted me (AH 98).

But while the balance holds, Lawrence's beliefs have the authentic discipline of a great religion:

I know how hard it is. One needs something to make one's mood deep and sincere. There are so many little threats that prevent our coming at the real naked essence of our vision. It sounds boshy, doesn't it? I often think one ought to be able to pray, before one works—and then leave it to the Lord. Isn't it hard, hard work to come to real grips with one's imagination,— throw everything overboard. I always feel as if I stood naked for the fire of Almighty God to go through me—and it's rather an awful feeling. One has to be so terribly religious, to be an artist (*CL* 189).

'He has not submitted himself to any discipline', said Muir, echoing the common cry. Lawrence replied:

Try, Mr Muir *et al.*, putting your little iron will into abeyance for one hour daily, and see if it doesn't need a harder discipline than this doing of your 'daily dozen' and all your other mechanical repetitions (*Phoenix* 802).

Muir had meant, of course, the formal disciplines, whose absence can indeed be disabling when the current is off (in *Kangaroo*, for example), but whose presence would be equally disabling in the great early novels. Again, Frieda was the first to understand, writing to Garnett in September 1912:

> I have heard so much about 'form' with Ernest; why are you English so keen on it? Their own form wants smashing in almost any direction, but they can't come out of their snail-house. I know it's so much safer. That's what I love Lawrence for, that he is so plucky and honest in his work, he dares to come out into the open and plants his stuff down bald and naked; really he is the only revolutionary worthy of the name, that I know; any new thing must find a new shape, then afterwards one can call it 'art' (*Frieda* 185).

To come out of the snail-house of preconceived form; to refuse to imitate; to abandon all 'rules of construction' and let the content give birth to its own unique formal 'characteristics'—this is the most rigorous of disciplines.

Like almost everyone else, Garnett shared Muir's assumptions. Lawrence sent *The Sisters* to him, in bits, as he finished them. But Garnett's criticisms were not always acceptable to the 'revolutionary':

22 April 1914
You know how willing I am to hear what you have to say, and to take your advice and to act on it when I have taken it. But it is no good unless you will have patience and understand what I *want* to do. I am not after all a child working erratically. All the time, underneath, there is something deep evolving itself out in me. And it is *hard* to express a new thing, in sincerity. And you should understand and help me to the new thing...But primarily I am a passionately religious man, and my novels must be written from the depth of my religious experience (*CL* 273).

In his next letter but one to Garnett, Lawrence analyses more fully the 'different attitude' to his characters in the work in progress. 'That which is physic—non-human, in humanity', he claims, interests him more 'than the old-fashioned human element—which causes one to conceive a character in a certain moral scheme and make him consistent'. The moral scheme (nearly always the same scheme) is 'dull, old, dead'. The use of the words 'physic' and 'element' here indicates that Lawrence is now going so far as to try to indicate, by scientific analogy, the very substance of the soul (as, in the Psychoanalysis books, he tries to indicate its location). 'Whatever our souls are made of,' said Cathy of Heathcliff, 'his and mine are the same; and Linton's is as different as a moonbeam from lightning, or frost from fire.'

Emily Brontë and Lawrence both care less about analysing what a woman feels than about grasping what she *is* ('inhumanly, physiologically, materially...as a phenomenon').

You mustn't look in my novel for the old stable *ego*—of the character. There is another ego, according to whose action the individual is unrecognizable, and passes through, as it were, allotropic states which it needs a deeper sense than any we've been used to exercise to discover are states of the same single radically unchanged element. (Like as diamond and coal are the same pure single element of carbon. The ordinary novel would trace the history of the diamond—but I say, 'Diamond, what! This is carbon.' And my diamond might be coal or soot, and my theme is carbon) (*CL* 282).

At times he writes of his people as if they were, literally, material phenomena:

He was like a gleaming, bright pebble, something bright and inalterable. He did not think. He sat there in his hard brightness and did not speak...He lay awake for many hours, hard and clear and unthinking, his soul crystallising more inalterably...It was as if his soul had turned into a hard crystal (*The Rainbow* 121–2).

Lawrence's new language sometimes degenerates into jargon. But this is only one of several ways the novel discovers of penetrating beneath appearances, personalities (diamond, coal or soot) to being (carbon). For the most part, the characters we see revealed in their elemental state we have already lived with in the world of the immediately recognisable. In *The Rainbow*, at least, the new modes are used not to replace traditional characterisation, but to take over from it when it reaches the limits of its resources.

Perhaps more important even than characterisation is the 'rhythmic form' of the novel which is no longer 'to follow the lines of certain characters':

The characters fall into the form of some other rhythmic form, as when one draws a fiddle-bow across a fine tray delicately sanded, the sand takes lines unknown.

I find it difficult to imagine what lines a fiddle-bow might leave on a sanded tray. But if we think of the spore of a snake on sand, or the delicate precise ripples of sand often left by the sea itself, we have an image which applies equally well to the rhythms of Lawrence's prose, the movement from episode to episode within a chapter, from chapter to chapter, or the great sweep of the whole novel over its three generations.

§2

It is from *Sons and Lovers* that we get the clue (if any clue is needed) to the basic structure of *The Rainbow*:

He talked to her endlessly about his love of horizontals: how they, the great levels of sky and land in Lincolnshire, meant to him the eternality of the will, just as the bowed Norman arches of the church, repeating themselves, meant the dogged leaping forward of the persistent human soul, on and on, nobody knows where; in contradiction to the perpendicular lines and to the Gothic arch, which, he said, leapt up at heaven and touched the ecstasy and lost itself in the divine (177).

In *The Rainbow* Lawrence uses the horizontal, the great levels of sky and land, the agricultural, the rural, to symbolise that which is natural, unconscious, pre-industrial. The perpendicular Gothic arch, associated with traditional religion, is spiritual aspiration. The Norman arch becomes the rainbow symbol itself, beckoning towards the 'unknown', the 'beyond', the 'finer, more vivid circle of life', and offering, ultimately, some kind of fulfilment, of blessedness.

From the first paragraph, the Brangwens are clearly associated with the fields and the horizontal land. They have been there 'for generations'. Their moods correspond to the changes in the weather. Their lives are directed by the rhythms of the seasons. The rhythm flowing from nature into the blood of the Brangwens corresponds to the pulsing rhythm of Lawrence's prose:

The young corn waved and was silken, and the lustre slid along the limbs of the men who saw it. They took the udder of the cows, the cows yielded milk and pulse against the hands of the men, the pulse of the blood of the teats of the cows beat into the pulse of the hands of the men. They mounted their horses, and held life between the grip of their knees, they harnessed their horses at the wagon, and, with hand on the bridle-rings, drew the heaving of the horses after their will (2).

The imagery too is heavily sexual:

But heaven and earth was teeming around them, and how should this cease? They felt the rush of the sap in spring, they knew the wave which cannot halt, but every year throws forward the seed to begetting, and, falling back, leaves the young-born on the earth. They know the intercourse between heaven and earth, sunshine drawn into the breast and bowels, the rain sucked up in the daytime, nakedness that comes under the wind in autumn, showing the birds' nests no longer worth hiding. Their life and interrelations were such; feeling the pulse and body of the soil, that opened to their furrow for the grain, and became smooth and supple after their ploughing, and clung to their feet with a weight that pulled like desire, lying hard and unresponsive when the crops were to be shorn away (2).

The richness and heat and pulse, the fusion with fecund nature is pre-urban, pre-conscious, almost pre-natal. They have harnessed the horses to their purposes, but they are in turn on nature's leading stresses:

The limbs and the body of the men were impregnated with the day, cattle and earth and vegetation and the sky (2).

And this is the very limit of their existence. Their senses are flooded to the drowning of consciousness:

The men sat by the fire and their brains were inert, as their blood flowed heavy with the accumulation from the living day (2).

They 'faced inward to the teeming life of creation, which poured unresolved into their veins' (3).

There is a sluggishness in their lives corresponding to the sluggish twisting of the Erewash through their meadows. Marsh farm, the name implies, is liable to flooding, and is, in fact, finally inundated, drowning the drunken Tom, the Brangwen patriarch, who had been 'afraid of the unknown in life':

And the unconscious, drowning body was washed along in the black, swirling darkness, passively (244).

The sensuous knowledge of warmth and generating also includes knowledge of pain and death. It is all the same to help the cow in labour and to break the back of a rabbit with a sharp knock of the hand. The rain which fertilises is also the rain which drowns.

Before his death, Tom Brangwen had made a great step towards the 'unknown', despite his fear of it. The Brangwens were aware of 'verticals', of other values than those associated with the land:

Whenever one of the Brangwens in the fields lifted his head from his work, he saw the church-tower at Ilkeston in the empty sky. So that as he turned again to the horizontal land, he was aware of something standing above him and beyond him in the distance (1).

Canal and railway and mine are signs of another era, another life-activity about to break in upon the farming community. But

so much warmth and generating and pain and death did they know in their blood, earth and sky and beast and green plants, so much exchange and interchange they had with those, that they lived full and surcharged, their senses full fed, their faces always turned to the heat of the blood, staring into the sun, dazed with looking towards the source of generation, unable to turn round (3).

It was left to the woman to look outwards, to strive towards some kind of awareness and resolution:

She stood to see the far-off world of cities and governments and the active scope of man, the magic land to her, where secrets were made known and desires fulfilled. She faced outwards to where men moved dominant and creative, having turned their back on the pulsing heat of creation, and with this behind them, were set out to discover what was beyond to enlarge their own scope and range and freedom...She strained her eyes to see what man had done in fighting outwards to knowledge, she strained to hear how he uttered himself in his conquest, her deepest desire hung on the battle that she heard, far off, being waged on the edge of the unknown. She also wanted to know, and to be of the fighting host (2–3).

The first generation of women cannot see beyond board school, church, and hall. The vicar and the squire had 'the power of thought and comprehension', a power the women yearned for and strove for through their children:

Why must they remain obscure and stifled all their lives, why should they suffer from lack of freedom to move? How should they learn the entry into the finer, more vivid circle of life? (4).

This is a question which dominates the structure of the novel. Each generation takes up the struggle afresh. Each has a different starting-point and different conscious objectives. But on and on, perceiving clearly at last the rainbow which is the unattainable goal—

> Effort and expectation and desire
> And something evermore about to be.

Tom, the youngest child of a large family, was his mother's favourite and carried the burden of her hopes. At twelve she sent him away to grammar school; but he could not force his unintellectual nature to fit her conception. Mentally, he was almost a fool, but 'more sensuously developed, more refined in instinct' than the other boys. Like Louisa, in *Daughters of the Vicar*, he had a spontaneous recognition of real things, and, centrally, a knowledge 'at the bottom of his soul' that 'the business of love was...the most serious and terrifying of all' (14). He rejects the 'reality' of Cossethay, with its drinking and wenching, by holding firm to this saving knowledge:

47

The via media to being, for man or woman, is love, and love alone (*Study of Thomas Hardy*; *Phoenix* 398).

To preserve and develop his own individuality he must acknowledge and cherish the 'fragile reality' of his intuitions—'That's her', he said involuntarily (24) as he passed the strange woman in the street. His 'curious certainty' about her was not in his mind.

In his breast, or in his bowels, somewhere in his body, there had started another activity (33).

Already the image of rebirth suggests itself to Lawrence for this experience—the birth of a new self within the known and acknowledged self—an image which is to grow, without changing its meaning, into a religious ritual with its literal resurrection of the flesh.

Queer little breaks of consciousness seemed to rise and burst like bubbles out of the depths of his stillness. 'It's got to be done', he said as he stopped to take the shirt out of the fender, 'it's got to be done, so why balk it?'...He did not think of anything, only knew that the wind was blowing (36–7).

We are never aware of Tom taking any decisions, exerting his will in any way. He does nothing. Rather things happen to him. He does not belong to himself, but is given over to 'the greater ordering'. The suspension of his will leaves a 'deep stillness' at the centre of him, a surety. There is a corresponding stillness in the woman and child seen through the lighted kitchen window. We do not merely have Lawrence's word for the 'greater ordering'; it is physically present in the roaring wind, the fecund darkness, the 'starry multiplicity of the night'. The wind is the hero of this passage. It bears Tom on his little journey as it bears the stars on 'some eternal voyage'. His inner stillness is a condition of submitting wholly to it. The identical experience is recorded in *Song of a Man Who Has Come Through*:

Not I, not I, but the wind that blows through me!
A fine wind is blowing the new direction of Time.
If only I let it bear me, carry me, if only it carry me!
If only I am sensitive, subtle, oh, delicate, a winged gift!
If only, most lovely of all, I yield myself and am borrowed
By the fine, fine wind that takes its course through the chaos of the world...

Oh, for the wonder that bubbles into my soul,
I would be a good fountain, a good well-head,
Would blur no whisper, spoil no expression.

And the knocking at the door in the night is interpreted, in this poem, as the three strange angels (the angels who brought the promise of a child to Abraham and Sarah).

The language in the novel draws heavily on the Bible:

As he worked alone on the land, or sat with his ewes at lambing time, the facts and material of his daily life fell away, leaving the kernel of his purpose clean. And then it came upon him that he would marry her and she would be his life (35).

The image of the kernel falling from its shell is a version of the resurrection theme which is to be given more and more weight. Lawrence draws no distinction between the life which roams abroad in the universe and the life within each being. The darkness of the night is also the darkness of the unconscious. What emerges from the shell is selfhood:

They are people each with a real, vital, potential self. . .and this self suddenly bursts the shell of manner and convention and commonplace opinion, and acts independently, absurdly, without self-knowledge or acquiescence (*Phoenix* 410).

This is not quite true of Tom, who does acquiesce. He also is able to recognise and respect the selfhood and impenetrable otherness of the woman, who will always be a stranger to him, and, for that very reason, a strange angel, all the unknown opening out behind her.

At times, after their marriage, when Lydia in her foreignness and womanly otherness seems unattainable, Tom feels like 'a broken arch thrust sickeningly out from support' (60). At other times he experiences a confirmation, in gladness and peace:

When her pains began afresh, tearing her, he turned aside, and could not look. But his heart in torture was at peace, his bowels were glad. He went downstairs and to the door, outside, lifted his face to the rain, and felt the darkness striking unseen and steadily upon him. The swift, unseen threshing of the night upon him silenced him and he was overcome. He turned away indoors, humbly. There was the infinite world, eternal, unchanging, as well as the world of life (76).

The sense of this 'other world' is even more vividly created when, during this same confinement, Tom takes Anna out to the barn to quieten her:

They were in another world now. The light shed softly on the timbered barn, on the whitewashed walls, and the great heap of hay; instruments cast their shadows largely, a ladder rose to the dark arch of a loft. Outside there was the driving rain, inside, the softly-illuminated stillness and calmness of the barn.

The rhythm of his movements as he fills the pan and 'carefully balancing the child on one arm, the pan in the other hand' feeds each beast, soothes the distraught child: 'A new being was created in her for the new conditions' (74). The passage is one of Lawrence's finest. The barn (just the place where a man would take his sobbing child on such a night, and invested with a full life of its own, with colours and shadows, sounds and smells), simultaneously corresponds to and indicates the nature of the serenity at the heart of Tom's suffering in which he is able to shelter Anna, and which deepens as Tom and Lydia discover new fulfilment in sexual love after two years of marriage. They come through to a new recognition and acceptance of each other, which removes a great weight and responsibility from the child:

Her father and her mother now met to the span of the heavens, and she, the child, was free to play in the space beneath, between (92).

This is the first realisation of the rainbow symbol. But it is presented as the creation of an environment in which Anna can grow rather than as an ultimate fulfilment in the parents, though at first it seems to be that too:

It was the entry into another circle of existence, it was the baptism to another life, it was the complete confirmation. Their feet trod strange ground of knowledge, their footsteps were lit-up with discovery. Wherever they walked, it was well, the world re-echoed round them in discovery. They went gladly and forgetful. Everything was lost, and everything was found. The new world was discovered, it remained only to be explored. They had passed through the doorway into the further space, where movement was so big, that it contained bonds and constraints and labours, and still was complete liberty. She was the doorway to him, he to her...They did not think of each other—why should they? Only when she touched him, he knew her instantly, that she was with him, near him, that she was the gateway and the way out, that she was beyond, and that he was travelling in her through the beyond. Whither?—What does it matter? (91).

But Tom and Lydia do not go on to explore the new world. The question 'Whither?' is passed to the next generation, and the novel begins to shift its focus towards Anna. The progenitors have achieved what fulfilment is open to them.

Was his life nothing? Had he nothing to show, no work? He did not count his work, anybody could have done it. What had he known, but the long, marital embrace with his wife? Curious, that this was what his life amounted to! At any rate, it was something, it was eternal. He would say so to anybody, and be proud of it. He lay with his wife in his arms, and she was still his fulfilment, just the same as ever. And that was the be-all and the end-all. Yes, and he was proud of it (124).

'There's very little else on earth but marriage', says Tom at Anna's wedding. And that is the first generation's limitation and achievement.

He felt himself tiny, a little upright figure on a plain circled round with the immense, roaring sky: he and his wife, two little, upright figures walking across this plain, whilst the heavens shimmered and roared about them. When did it come to an end? In which direction was it finished? There was no end, no finish, only this roaring vast space...What was sure but the endless sky? But that was so sure, so boundless...How rich and splendid his own life was, red and burning and blazing and sporting itself in the dark meshes of his body: and his wife, how she glowed and burned dark within her meshes! Always it was so unfinished and unformed! (131).

'The great living experience for every man is his adventure into the woman', Lawrence wrote to Russell in 1915.

The man embraces in the woman all that is not himself, and from that one resultant, from that one embrace, comes every new action (CL 324).

Tom Brangwen experiences the embrace and the adventure, but no new action results; his 'social passion' remains unsatisfied:

For I go to a woman to know myself, and to know her. And I want to know myself, that I may know how to act for humanity (CL 318).

We do not yet realise why Tom Brangwen's life is 'unfinished and unformed'; but these standards are to be applied more and more explicitly to Will Brangwen and Skrebensky.

§3

After Anna's wedding, the men of the former generation gather outside the honeymoon cottage to sing a Christmas hymn which is, at the same time, an epithalamium, a celebration of the sanctity of marriage, epitomising the achievement of Tom and Lydia. Anna and Will are obliged to make a successful marriage before they can go on to new explorations of experience. During the honeymoon, Will and Anna lose track of time:

It was even irritating the way the church-clock kept on chiming: there seemed no space between the hours, just a moment, golden and still, whilst she traced his features with her finger-tips (141).

51

Their bed is a hub for the wheeled universe. At the still centre they lie 'complete and beyond the touch of time or change':

They found themselves there, and they lay still, in each other's arms: for their moment they were at the heart of eternity, whilst time roared far off, for ever far off, towards the rim. Then gradually they were passed away from the supreme centre, down the circles of praise and joy and gladness, further and further out, towards the noise and the friction. But their hearts had burned and were tempered by the inner reality, they were unalterably glad (141).

Much of this section of the novel is to deal with this 'inner reality', with a battle of 'carbon' wills which are not at all sub-servient to laws of cause and effect, consistency, time or place. In paragraphs beginning: 'And ever and again',...'And ever and again',...'Then all this passed away', the timeless, psychic drama moves with its rhythms, lulls and climaxes, behind the daily lives and personal loves of the characters, sometimes in peace and gladness, more often in bitter strife. Actions in the surface drama derive from causes in the psychic drama—Will's destruction of his carving, Anna's refusal to sleep with him because he puts 'a pressure' on her head:

However her pity might give way for moments, she was hard and cold as a jewel. He must be put off from her, she must sleep alone. She made him a bed in the small room. And he lay there whipped, his soul whipped almost to death, yet unchanged (185).

At first Will had seemed to offer an answer to Anna's 'whither?':

In him the bounds of her experience were transgressed: he was the hole in the wall, beyond which the sunshine blazed on an outside world (109).

This is what Anna passionately desires. But is it what Will really offers?

And the land seemed to be covered with a vast, mystic church, reserved in gloom, thrilled with an unknown Presence. Almost it hurt her, to look out of the window and see the lilacs towering in the vivid sunshine. Or was this the jewelled glass? (108).

He offers a 'very real experience', half mystical, half aesthetic; but scarcely sunshine blazing on an outside world. His passion is for church architecture. His world is enclosed and dim within the jewelled arch, his substitute for the rainbow:

Spanned round with the rainbow, the jewelled gloom folded music upon silence, light upon darkness, fecundity upon death, as a seed folds leaf upon leaf, and silence upon the root and the flower, hushing up the secrets of all between its parts (198).

The imagery reveals the extent to which his experience in Lincoln Cathedral is a substitute for sensual experience, a sublimation of his whole affective life:

Here the stone leapt up from the plain of earth, leapt up in a manifold, clustered desire each time, up, away from the horizontal earth, through twilight and dusk and the whole range of desire, through the swerving, the declination, ah, to the ecstasy, the touch, to the meeting and consummation, the meeting, the clasp, the close embrace, the neutrality, the perfect, swooning consummation, the timeless ecstasy. There his soul remained, at the apex of the arch, clinched in the timeless ecstasy, consummated.

And there was no time nor life nor death, but only this, this timeless consummation, where the thrust from earth met the thrust from earth and the arch was locked on the keystone of ecstasy. This was all, this was everything (199).

In Lincoln Cathedral Anna is impressed, as by something unworldly, but she is not transported:

But even in the dazed swoon of the cathedral, she claimed another right. The altar was barren, its lights gone out. God burned no more in that bush. It was dead matter lying there. She claimed the right to freedom above her, higher than the roof (200).

She catches at the grotesque faces of the gargoyles, which 'jeered their mockery of the Absolute, and declared for multiplicity, polygeny' (*Phoenix* 454).

Anna succeeds in breaking down Will's absolute:

He listened to the thrushes in the gardens and heard a note which the cathedrals did not include: something free and careless and joyous. He crossed a field that was all yellow with dandelions, on his way to work, and the bath of yellow glowing was something at once so sumptuous and so fresh, that he was glad he was away from his shadowy cathedral (202).

When his soul can no longer live in the darkness and mystery and abstraction of churches, Will finds that he can live only in Anna. Without her he is 'only half alive':

Was he then like the old man of the sea, impotent to move, save on the back of another life? Was he impotent, or a cripple, or a defective, or a fragment? (184).

The self which should blossom in warmth and tenderness and assurance is the self he can never bring to birth. Her father, sneers Anna, could put ten of him in his pipe and push them down with his little finger. Her lack of respect for him is related to his failure to embody for her any significance beyond the personal relationship. He has no vocation:

She did not care for what he represented in himself. It is true, he did not know himself what he represented. But whatever it was she did not really honour it. She did no service to his work as a lace-designer, nor to himself as bread-winner. Because he went down to the office and worked every day— that entitled him to no respect or regard from her, he knew. Rather she despised him for it (167).

Sexually he is all will—a poised hawk, a coiled snake, a tiger lying in the darkness, a creature 'that lies hidden and excites its will to the destruction of the free-running creature'. Yet he depends on her, as the predator depends on his prey.

When Will's search for religious fulfilment fails, he falls back on sex, and, in an orgy of sensual indulgence with Anna, burns out much of his shame, makes possible some further unfolding of his personality. He discovers physical beauty:

He had always, all his life, had a secret dread of Absolute Beauty. It had always been like a fetish to him, something to fear, really. For it was immoral and against mankind. So he had turned to the Gothic form, which always asserted the broken desire of mankind in its pointed arches, escaping the rolling, absolute beauty of the round arch.

But now he had given way, and with infinite sensual violence gave himself to the realisation of this supreme immoral, Absolute Beauty, in the body of woman. It seemed to him, that it came to being in the body of woman, under his touch (234).

And his new-found freedom allows him to develop outside interests:

His intimate life was so violently active, that it set another man in him free. And this new man turned with interest to public life, to see what part he could take in it. This would give him scope for new activity, activity of a kind for which he was now created and released. He wanted to be unanimous with the whole of purposive mankind (235).

He teaches woodwork to the village lads two nights a week. Anna continues to bear children: 'If her soul had found no utterance, her womb had.' It is a compromise, deferring the struggle again for the coming generation. Having children is not, for Lawrence, a primary human purpose, nor even the primary purpose of the sexual act:

It is so arranged that the very act which carries us out into the unknown shall probably deposit seed for security to be left behind. But the act, called the sexual act, is not for the depositing of the seed. It is for leaping off into the unknown, as from a cliff's edge, like Sappho into the sea (*Phoenix* 441).

It is not in children, the future lies. The Red Indian mothers bore many children, and yet there *are* no Red Indians. It is the truth, the new perceived hope, that makes spring. And let them bring forth that who can: they are the creators of life. There are many enceinte widows, with a new crop of death in their wombs. What did the mothers of the dead soldiers bring forth, in childbed?—death or life? (*CL* 468).

Anna settles for 'the ring of physical considerations' (352), having had fleeting glimpses of the rainbow in the hazy distance:

She was straining her eyes to something beyond. And from her Pisgah mount, which she had attained, what could she see? A faint, gleaming horizon, a long way off, and a rainbow like an archway, a shadow-door with faintly coloured coping above it. Must she be moving thither?...Dawn and sunset were the feet of the rainbow that spanned the day, and she saw the hope, the promise. Why should she travel any further?...With satisfaction she relinquished the adventure to the unknown. She was bearing her children. There was another child coming, and Anna lapsed into vague content. If she were not the wayfarer to the unknown, if she were arrived now, settled in her builded house, a rich woman, still her doors opened under the arch of the rainbow, her threshold reflected the passing of the sun and moon, the great travellers, her house was full of the echo of journeying. She was a door and a threshold, she herself. Through her another soul was coming, to stand upon her as upon the threshold, looking out, shading its eyes for the direction to take (192).

§4

The third generation story differs from the first two in that Ursula's 'struggles against the confines of her life' take place before marriage. Her disposition is adventurous, eager, naïvely optimistic:

She wanted to read great, beautiful books, and be rich with them; she wanted to see beautiful things, and have the joy of them for ever; she wanted to know big, free people; and there remained always the want she could put no name to (406).

We see, through Ursula, what modern society offers, either masquerading as these things or as alternatives to them. Her story is of disillusion, but also of the courage which transcends it, replacing broken dreams not by cynicism or conformity, but by new, more robust and more jealously guarded dreams. Her faith in life is never shaken. If life seems to thwart her, it must be that she has sought the wrong things; rather than ask for less, she will ask even more of it.

Tom and Lydia were rooted at Marsh Farm, where the Brangwens had lived 'for generations'. They lived in the past—the mellow past of the yeoman farmer—unaffected by the distant sounds of pit and railway. Ursula's first suitor, Anthony Schofield, is very like the young Tom. He offers Ursula a return to the 'horizontal' world. Ursula 'cannot' accept. It is a question of consciousness:

She turned away, she turned round from him, and saw the east flushed strangely rose, the moon coming yellow and lovely upon a rosy sky, above the darkening, bluish snow. All this so beautiful, all this so lovely. He did not see it. He was one with it. But she saw it, and was one with it. Her seeing separated them infinitely...She was a traveller on the face of the earth, and he was an isolated creature living in the fulfilment of his own senses (417).

As the first generation had taken the rhythm of its life from the seasons, the natural cycles of birth, death and fruition, pagan, with only the first glimmer of spiritual aspiration, so the second generation lives within the rhythms of the Church year, and Ursula's young life gladly responds to this cycle, each week turning about the precious Sunday, and each year on Christmas and Easter:

So the children lived the year of christianity, the epic of the soul of mankind. Year by year the inner, unknown drama went on in them, their hearts were born and came to fulness, suffered on the cross, gave up the ghost, and rose again to unnumbered days, untired, having at least this rhythm of eternity in a ragged, inconsequential life (279).

But the great drama, at this moment of history, is becoming mechanical, tawdry; it goes the way of Ursula's earlier passion for Romance and her later passion for Knowledge, failing, like them, to match the realities of her experience.

The Brangwen farmers had been only dimly aware of church and hall and school in the distance, always on the perimeter of their consciousness holding out a promise their consciousness could never fully grasp. Will and Anna had set up house in Cossethay, in close proximity to church and school. Later, when Will became Art and Handwork Instructor to the County of Nottingham, they moved to Beldover—'new red-brick suburbia in a grimy, small town' (421). Ursula faces the problems of adjustment and emancipation in a specifically urban and twentieth-century environment. She has to grow into a world which offers no communal fulfilment or aspiration, no civilised life-effort worth taking part in. The first danger is that she will be beaten down by the system; but the second and even greater danger is that she will seek her absolute within her own ego, exploiting others to serve her lusts. Ursula is emancipated and uprooted: she is free as her parents and grandparents were not, but free as a man overboard without a lifebelt is freer than those trapped aboard a sinking ship. In which direction shall she strike out?

How to act, that was the question? Whither to go, how to become oneself? One was not oneself, one was merely a half-stated question. How to become oneself, how to know the question and the answer of oneself, when one was merely an unfixed something-nothing, blowing about like the winds of heaven, undefined, unstated (282).

Is she an island unto herself alone; or must she find, outside herself, someone or something worthy of service? It is a specifically modern dilemma, which few of us face with Ursula's honesty and courage.

Ursula is the first 'free soul' in the English novel. The structure of this novel must change to accommodate her desperate search for bearings. In the first generation Tom had to extend the boundaries of the inherited life, which had become oppressive. In the second generation values clashed and modified each other, ending in a compromise and withdrawal from the struggle. Ursula doggedly persists, veering away from that from which her soul recoils, moving into unknown territory with no better guide than the principle of trial and error, a deep sense of responsibility for her own life, and an indestructible faith, at the very centre of her, surviving all disillusions, in a world of 'absolute truth and living mystery' within the everyday world, within herself and all living things. In adolescence, she thinks of this as the Sunday world, over which the weekday world quickly triumphs, superficially.

Like Ellie in Shaw's *Heartbreak House*, Ursula is looking for 'life with a blessing', which is what the rainbow specifically symbolises. Before she finds her true rainbow at the end of the novel, she must follow several false rainbows—loves and allegiances which do not bring the liberation she seeks. Her love for Christ, she realises, is merely a substitute for loving and being loved in the flesh. Yet physical love in its turn, in the person of Skrebensky, proves unable to satisfy her: 'Between them was the

57

compact of his flesh with hers, in the hand-clasp' (295). But Skrebensky is not a son of God, not an incarnation of the mystery, so the sensual compact with him is not also the covenant with God.

To the girlish Ursula, Skrebensky brings 'a strong sense of the outer world': 'She laid hold of him at once for her dreams' (290). But the want that Ursula could put no name to is not to be satisfied by Skrebensky. He is a soldier, responding, in peace time, to such dead ideals as 'nation' and 'property'. He serves 'the highest good of the community', meaning material prosperity. He is 'just a brick in the whole great social fabric':

His life lay in the established order of things...At the bottom of his heart, his self, the soul that aspired and had true hope of self-effectuation lay as dead, still-born, a dead weight in his womb (327).

A man must conceive his own soul, bring his self to birth. Ursula herself has come far enough on this road to recognise Skrebensky as a nonentity:

'It seems to me as if you weren't anybody—as if there weren't anybody there, where you are. Are you anybody, really? You seem like nothing to me' (309).

Lawrence has set himself a difficult enough task in describing the inner core of a character. But when that core is absent, where the penetrating vision reveals a mere void, the task is virtually impossible unless other modes of presentation are also drawn on. Here expanses of intrusive direct comment from the author and repetitive and overwritten symbolic passages draw out interminably the breaking of this butterfly. A negative character can be substantial, as Gerald is to be in *Women in Love*. Skrebensky seems to be a first sketch for Gerald. But he hardly carries his weight in *The Rainbow*.

The incomplete personality can never be the complete lover or husband. The 'unknown' is excluded from Skrebensky's worldview, as it is from the 'passion' he offers Ursula:

It was magnificent self-assertion on the part of both of them, he asserted himself before her, he felt himself infinitely male and infinitely irresistible, she asserted herself before him, she knew herself infinitely desirable, and hence infinitely strong. And after all, what could either of them get from such a passion but a sense of his or her own maximum self, in contradistinction to all the rest of life? Wherein was something finite and sad, for the human soul at its maximum wants a sense of the infinite (301).

We are invited at the outset to compare this relationship with the previous generations. Ursula walks

where her grandfather had walked with his daffodils to make his proposal, and where her mother had gone with her young husband, walking close upon him as Ursula was now walking upon Skrebensky (298).

We remember the moonlit stooking scene, where the rhythm of the work carried Will and Anna ever closer until they met 'as the sheaves that swish together' (118). Will's 'steadied purpose' was more profound than his consciousness and made his proposal part of a wider pattern of creativeness and fruition. The first coming together of Ursula and Skrebensky initiates Ursula only into the release of her own desires and an awareness 'of what a kiss might be' (298). His five senses are to be gratified. And she uses him as a mere vehicle for her lust, 'a fierce, white, cold passion', which is really a relationship between Ursula and Aphrodite. She annihilates him as a person. He is the necessary medium for her self-contained, uncreative, corrosive lust, burning, poisonous, deadly. They perform a dance of death under the all-pervading moonlight. Ursula, glorying in her triumph, 'felt she had now all licence'. 'Her sexual life flamed to a kind of disease within her', and Skrebensky existed 'in her own desire only'.

In Skrebensky's absence Ursula turns to the lights and crowds of the town as a haven of tangible values outside the chaos of her own uncreated consciousness:

All this stir and seethe of lights and people was but the rim, the shores of a great inner darkness and void. She wanted very much to be on the seething, partially illuminated shore, for within her was the void reality of dark space (339).

But 'seethe' as opposed to 'glow' in Sons and Lovers is a word which the novel is to define, negatively, through Ursula's consciousness:

The stupid, artificial, exaggerated town, fuming its lights. It does not exist really (453).

Ursula's disillusion comes largely through her relationship with Winifred Inger, a scientific humanist:

Winifred had had a scientific education. She had known many clever people. She wanted to bring Ursula to her own position of thought. In philosophy she was brought to the conclusion that the human desire is the criterion of all truth and all good. Truth does not lie beyond humanity, but is one of the products of the human mind and feeling (340–1).

59

Sexually and educationally, her influence is equally perverted and deadly. Winifred marries Uncle Tom, a colliery-owner from the mining village of Wiggiston. Tom believes that 'living human beings must be taken and adapted to all kinds of horrors' (346). Life is a squalid heap of side-shows round the pit, the *raison d'être* of all. After the nightmare experience of Wiggiston, Ursula is able to reject the God of the Machine, worshipped by both Uncle Tom and Winifred (in her case 'the impure abstraction and mechanisms of matter').

This experience does not deter Ursula from striving to connect herself 'with the outer, greater world of activity, the man-made world' (360). Her parents become very real barriers. She is already transcending their values. They shatter her dream of teaching at Kingston-on-Thames and condemn her to Brinsley Street School, Ilkeston. There 'everything was as in hell, a condition of hard, malevolent system'. Ursula's 'responsive, personal self' is out of place where teachers must be 'hard, insentient things, that worked mechanically, according to a system' (395). 'The whole situation was wrong and ugly' (388). The education system is part of a subtle death spreading through society. The boy Williams has a 'half-transparent unwholesomeness, rather like a corpse' (402). His mother has a 'sense of being unpleasant to touch, like something going bad inside'. Ursula is shut in with 'unliving spectral people'. She must break away from this sunless, lifeless, enclosed form of life. But she will not retreat 'into her fields where she was happy'. She will continue to fight for 'joy, happiness, and permanency' within modern industrial society:

She must have her place in the working world, be a recognised member with full rights there. It was more important to her than fields and sun and poetry, at this time. But she was only the more its enemy (410).

Ursula's new identity as Standard Five Teacher gives her independence from her parents:

In coming out and earning her own living she had made a strong, cruel move towards freeing herself (406).

It is not a matter of female emancipation:

She had within her the strange, passionate knowledge of religion and living far transcending the limits of the automatic system that contained the vote. But her fundamental organic knowledge had as yet to take form and rise to utterance...She felt that somewhere, in something, she was not free. And she wanted to be. She was in revolt. For once she were free she could get somewhere. Ah, the wonderful, real somewhere that was beyond her, the somewhere that she felt deep, deep inside her (406).

Lawrence makes this 'somewhere' take form and rise to utterance in the closing pages.

Another disillusionment awaits Ursula at the University, where 'the religious virtue of knowledge was become a flunkey to the god of material success' (435).

Always the shining doorway ahead; and then, upon approach, always the shining doorway was a gate into another ugly yard, dirty and active and dead. Always the crest of the hill gleaming ahead under heaven: and then, from the top of the hill only another sordid valley full of amorphous, squalid activity (436).

Her movement is restricted, her growth stunted, her horizons close in.

Anna had been satisfied to hold on to the wide sky and sunlit land as her absolute. This landscape, richly invested with values, remains, nevertheless, the real landscape which is the physical setting of the novel, just as Will's absolute remained incarnate in the solid masonry of cathedrals. But Ursula comes to perceive that 'the world in which she lived was like a circle lighted by a lamp':

...Nevertheless the darkness wheeled round about, with grey shadow-shapes of wild beasts, and also with dark shadow-shapes of the angels, whom the light fenced out, as it fenced out the more familiar beasts of darkness (437–8).

This is no longer the physical setting, but a psychic landscape which Ursula's soul explores:

'What do you think you are?' her soul asked of the professor as she sat opposite him in class. 'What do you think you are, as you sit there in your gown and your spectacles? You are a lurking, blood-sniffing creature with eyes peering out of the jungle darkness, snuffing for your desires' (448).

She recognises the darkness of her own unconscious not only as the home of hyena and wolf, but of angels 'lordly and terrible and not to be denied'. The gleam in the eye of the wild beast, the flash of fangs, is also the flash of the sword of angels, for the gleam is the very quick of life. Miraculously, Lawrence brings us back from the psychic drama to the narrative analogy by letting

Ursula at college see the same gleam through her microscope as she examines a living cell:

She looked at the unicellular shadow that lay within the field of light, under her microscope. It was alive. She saw it move—she saw the bright mist of its ciliary activity, she saw the gleam of its nucleus, as it slid across the plane of light. What then was its will? If it was a conjunction of forces, physical and chemical, what held these forces unified, and for what purpose were they unified?

For what purpose were the incalculable physical and chemical activities nodalised in this shadowy, moving speck under her microscope? What was the will which nodalised them and created the one thing she saw? What was its intention? To be itself? Was its purpose just mechanical and limited to itself?

It intended to be itself. But what self? Suddenly in her mind the world gleamed strangely, with an intense light, like the nucleus of the creature under the microscope. Suddenly she had passed away into an intensely-gleaming light of knowledge. She could not understand what it all was. She only knew that it was not limited mechanical energy, nor mere purpose of self-preservation and self-assertion. It was a consummation, a being infinite. To be oneself was a supreme, gleaming triumph of infinity (441).

But *how* to be oneself?

Despite her earlier dissection of him in the vain hope of finding some intact core, she still holds on to Skrebensky as the key to this puzzle, the next shining doorway:

She would not admit to herself the chill like a sunshine of frost that came over her. This was he, the key, the nucleus to the new world (442).

It was again 'as if she were a blank wall in his direction, without windows or outgoings' (355). They are enemies come together in a sensual truce.

Every movement and word of his was alien to her being...He seemed made up of a set of habitual actions and decisions. The vulnerable, variable quick of the man was inaccessible. She knew nothing of it. She could feel the dark, heavy fixity of his animal desire...He wanted something that should be nameless...The same iron rigidity, as if the world were made of steel, possessed her again. It was no use turning with flesh and blood to this arrangement of forged metal (443).

She sees that Skrebensky is to be associated rather with Doctor Frankstone than with the nucleus, and with Mr Harby, and Winifred and Uncle Tom, and all other mechanical wills she has met and rejected. At last Ursula has to recognise that love as a matter of personal gratification, as an end in itself, is not enough for her:

Love—love—love—what does it mean—what does it amount to?...As an end in itself, I could love a hundred men, one after the other. Why should I end with a Skrebensky? (475).

Frieda, who helped to write *The Rainbow* and on whom Ursula is largely based, comments:

In the end the man fails Ursula because he has no ideal beyond the old existing state, it does not satisfy her nor him. For perfect love you don't only have two people, it must include bigger, universal connection. An *idea*, something outside themselves, and it is really against individualism (*Frieda* 211–12).

The crisis comes when, in alliance with a full, dazzling moon, she challenges him to satisfy her. But the unknown does not emerge from this experience. Ursula comes no nearer to the male mystery, to the wonder and reverence of love, to the religious dimension. The experience is death to the relationship. In the Foreword to *Sons and Lovers* Lawrence describes a similar relationship as blasphemous and doomed to sterility:

But if a man shall say 'This woman is flesh of my flesh', let him see to it that he be not blaspheming the Father. For the woman is not flesh of his flesh by the bidding of the Word; but it is of the Father. And if he take a woman, saying in the arrogance of the Word, 'The flesh of that woman is goodly', then he has said, 'The flesh of that woman is goodly as a servant unto the Word, which is me', and so hath blasphemed the Father, by which he has his being, and she hath her being. And the flesh shall forsake these two, they shall be fabric of Word. And their race shall perish (AH 98).

Skrebensky marries another and goes to India, leaving Ursula pregnant and ill with despair and self-doubt:

She had been wrong, she had been arrogant and wicked, wanting that other thing, that fantastic freedom, that illusory, conceited fulfilment which she had imagined she could not have with Skrebensky. Who was she to be wanting some fantastic fulfilment in her life?...Suddenly she saw her mother in a just and true light. Her mother was simple and radically true. She had taken the life that was given. She had not, in her arrogant conceit, insisted on creating life to fit herself (483–4).

But accepting the given life and creating a life to fit yourself are not the only alternatives. A third way is dramatised in the episode of the horses. The imagery which reaches its climax here has been present throughout the novel—in the heaving of the horses the Brangwens held between their thighs; in the darkness which was 'passionate and breathing with immense, unperceived heaving' (316); in the 'triumphant, flaming, overweening heart of the intrinsic male', which would never beat again in Skrebensky (321); in the body of the earth which 'seemed to stir its powerful flank beneath her as she stood' (322). The action here, like so much of *Women in Love*, is purely an analogy for the inner conflict of the characters. The symbolism is explained at some length in *Fantasia of the Unconscious*:

A man has a persistent passionate fear-dream about horses. He suddenly finds himself among great, physical horses, which may suddenly go wild. Their great bodies surge madly round him, they rear above him, threatening to destroy him. At any minute he may be trampled down...Examining the emotional reference we find that the feeling is sensual, there is a great impression of the powerful, almost beautiful physical bodies of the horses, the nearness, the rounded haunches, the rearing (167-8).

He goes on to conclude that the horse represents 'the great sensual male activity' which is normally repressed and therefore seen as a menace to the soul's automatism—

Whereas the greatest desire of the living spontaneous soul is that this very male sensual nature, represented as a menace, shall be actually accomplished in life. The spontaneous self is secretly yearning for the liberation and fulfilment of the deepest and most powerful sensual nature (167-8).

The rhythm of the horses as they approach, then sheer off, circle, regroup, approach again, closely resembles the strange rhythm of a mind struggling with its deepest problems and moving, unconsciously, towards a resolution:

The mind makes curious swoops and circles. It touches the point of pain or interest, then sweeps away again in a cycle, coils round and approaches again the point of pain or interest. There is a curious spiral rhythm, and the mind approaches again and again the point of concern, repeats itself, goes back, destroys the time-sequence entirely, so that time ceases to exist, as the mind stoops to the quarry, then leaves it without striking, soars, hovers, turns, swoops, stoops again, still does not strike, yet is nearer, nearer, reels away again, wheels off into air, even forgets, quite forgets, yet again turns, bends, circles slowly, swoops and stoops again, until at last there is the closing-in, and the clutch of a decision or a resolve (*Phoenix* 249-50).

The urgent, massive fire locked within the flanks of the horses (differing only in scale from the gleam of the nucleus under the microscope) can never be put out:

Far back, far back in our dark soul the horse prances. He is a dominant symbol: he gives us lordship: he links us, the first palpable and throbbing link with the ruddy-glowing Almighty of potence: he is the beginning even of our god-head in the flesh. And as a symbol he roams the dark underworld meadows of the sou!. He stamps and threshes in the dark fields of your soul and mine (*Apocalypse* ch. 10).

Ursula tries to get back to 'the highroad and the ordered world of man'. But she cannot evade the extinction to which the horses subject her. Her fall from the oak tree is the breaking of all her connections with 'the old, hard, barren form of by-gone living' which must precede the issuing of the 'naked, clear kernel' of herself, like an acorn bursting from its shell.

The threshing in Ursula's soul is succeeded by a great peace in which she sees a rainbow spanning the landscape (simultaneously psychic and physical).

§5

Towards the end of the novel such words as religion and God appear with great frequency. We must ask what, precisely, Lawrence means by these words, whether he can be said to be writing, here, within the Christian faith, or whether he is merely exploiting Christian terminology in an attempt to confer a spurious transcendence on what is essentially a pantheistic position. In February 1915 Lawrence wrote to Lady Ottoline Morrell:

The strong soul must put off its connection with this society and go naked with its fellows, weaponless, armourless, without shield or spear, but only with naked hands and open eyes. Not self-sacrifice, but fulfilment, the flesh and the spirit in league together, not in arms against one another. And each man shall know that he is part of the greater body, each man shall submit that his own soul is not supreme even to himself...but that all souls of all things do but compose the body of God (*CL* 312).

At first glance the final clause would seem to be a classic statement of pantheism; but it does not, in fact, exclude the possibility that there might also be a soul of God not incarnate in 'things'. Life itself is presented in the novel as something infinite and eternal, hardly to be transcended. But whence, if God means Life, the benevolence and purpose to which a man can submit in utter trust and nakedness? Surely Lawrence was well aware of the objections to Wordsworthian pantheism which Aldous Huxley exposed so trenchantly in *Wordsworth in the Tropics*? The ending of *St Mawr* is the ultimate realisation of Huxley's point. But in

The Rainbow there is no sense of the senseless universe which nineteenth-century rationalism had discovered and which had determined the form of Hardy's late novels.

The rainbow symbol reappears in *Kangaroo* as 'a pledge of unbroken faith, between the universe and the innermost'. By 1922 Lawrence had stopped using the word God in more or less Christian contexts and was beginning to talk about his 'dark gods'. But a 'universe' which is capable of pledging faith seems to be in the sort of personal and benevolent relationship with mankind which we associate with the Christian God. The symbol derives, of course, from Genesis ix. 12–15, which is quoted in full in the novel and kept before us throughout:

And God said: This is the token of the covenant which I make between me and you and every living creature that is with you, for perpetual generations; I do set my bow in the cloud, and it shall be a token of a covenant between me and the earth. And it shall come to pass, when I bring a cloud over the earth, that a bow shall be seen in the cloud; And I will remember my covenant, which is between me and you and every living creature of all flesh, and the waters shall no more become a flood to destroy all flesh (323).

The Rainbow is Lawrence's Isaiah, a reaffirmation of Noah's covenant 'from generation to generation'.

The basic form of the novel, spread over three generations, is not designed to allow Lawrence to present a social and cultural history of English civilisation in the manner of George Eliot, nor even to allow him to explore the psychological implications of heredity and environment in the manner of Emily Brontë. He does both these things, but incidentally. The structure shows how the Brangwens, beginning with the patriarch Tom, strive to keep this covenant while the society around them is devoting more and more of its energy to breaking it. To lose the relationship with God is to be in hell. But the rainbow is 'a sign that life will never be destroyed, or turn bad altogether' (502).

Lawrence uses the word 'beyond' very frequently in *The Rainbow*. At the beginning it seems to mean unknown areas of experience within society (areas of which school and rectory and hall are tokens). In Ursula's adolescence it comes to signify also the darkness outside the area lit by the arc-lamp of man's civilised consciousness—both the elemental forces of nature and the sub-conscious forces in man. Thirdly, and in its most vivid realisa-tions, it is the gleam at the centre of the living cell, the fire in the

66

breasts of the horses, the rainbow arched in the blood of men, the God who is to be approached only by 'a deeper immersion in existence' (Kierkegaard) and by 'an openness to the holy, the sacred, in the unfathomable depths of even the most secular relationship' (Robinson):

Who was she to have a man according to her own desire? It was not for her to create, but to recognise a man created by God. The man should come from the Infinite and she should hail him. She was glad she could not create her man. She was glad she had nothing to do with his creation. She was glad that this lay within the scope of that vaster power in which she rested at last (493).

What the Christian calls grace, Lawrence calls fulfilment.

In 1924 (*Books*) Lawrence wrote of his attitude to Christianity in terms which clearly refer to *The Rainbow*. It is a little-known passage worth quoting at length:

During the Dark Ages...the flood of barbarism rose and covered Europe from end to end.

But, bless your life, there was Noah in his Ark with the animals. There was young Christianity. There were the lonely fortified monasteries, like little arks floating and keeping the adventure afloat. There was no break in the great adventure in consciousness. Throughout the howlingest deluge, some few brave souls are steering the ark under the rainbow...

Once all men in the world lost their courage and their newness, the world would come to an end...

So we begin to see where we are. It's no good leaving everything to fate. Man is an adventurer, and he must never give up the adventure...

I know the greatness of Christianity: it is a past greatness. I know that, but for those early Christians, we should never have emerged from the chaos and hopeless disaster of the Dark Ages. If I had lived in the year 400, pray God, I should have been a true and passionate Christian. The adventurer.

But now I live in 1924, and the Christian venture is done. The adventure is gone out of Christianity. We must start on a new venture towards God (*Phoenix* 733-4).

There is a sense in which Tom Brangwen, at the beginning of *The Rainbow*, did leave things to fate; and even Ursula, at the end, though she has made certain conscious rejections, is leaving her future fulfilment to fate. Rupert Birkin's 'new venture towards God' is to be of a radically different character, and largely accounts for the very different formal characteristics of *Women in Love*. There is a sense in *The Rainbow* that human purposes, when they are not mechanical and deadly, subserve an evolutionary process which is God-given. We feel that each generation, even when, exhausted, it lapses from the adventure, is still held within a divine matrix. The creative process is not complete within the individual life, but is carried forward generation after generation, wave after wave, towards the shores of the unknown. Ursula's wave is borne forwards on the residue of desire from her parents and grandparents.

The rainbow is a symbol of this reality—'new heaven and earth', 'a whole new world', 'all that is to be'. The novel is 'the voyage of discovery towards the real and eternal and unknown land' (AH 240). It is not romantic escapism, for the voyage is into and through the known, the surface realities. This is the sense in which Lawrence defines poetry:

The essential quality of poetry is that it makes a new effort of attention, and 'discovers' a new world within the known world (*Phoenix* 255).

The creative imagination is here in close alliance with evolution, as Lawrence understands it, in striving always towards greater and greater distinctiveness and clarity:

So on and on till we get to naked jelly, and from naked jelly to enclosed and separated jelly, from homogeneous tissue to organic tissue, on and on, from invertebrates to mammals, from mammals to man, from man to tribesman, from tribesman to me: and on and on, till, in the future, wonderful, distinct individuals, like angels, move about, each one being himself, perfect as a complete melody or a pure colour (*ibid.* 432).

Whether we move any further towards the angels or sink into a new sort of savagery depends on the quality of our vision:

The unspeakable inner chaos of which we are composed we call consciousness, and mind, and even civilisation. But it is, ultimately, chaos, lit up by visions, or not lit up by visions. Just as the rainbow may or may not light up the storm. And, like the rainbow the vision perisheth (*ibid.* 255).

§6

These wearisome sickening little personal novels! After all, they aren't novels at all. In every great novel, who is the hero all the time? Not any of the characters, but some unnamed and nameless flame behind them all...In the great novel, the felt but unknown flame stands behind all the characters, and in their words and gestures there is a flicker of the presence. If you are *too personal, too human*, the flicker fades out, leaving you with something awfully lifelike, and lifeless as most people are ('The Novel'. *SLC* 69).

Lawrence's growing contempt for the too personal, for 'social beings' and the world of appearances ('no clarity of being anywhere, only a stinking welter of sensations', *CL* 508) had led him to evolve a style which, at first, he could hardly himself understand:

> I am doing a novel which I have never grasped. Damn its eyes, there I am at page 145, and I've no notion what it's about. I hate it. F. says it is good. But it's like a novel in a foreign language I don't know very well—I can only just make out what it is about (*CL* 203).

It is hardly surprising that the work was unintelligible to most of its first readers. But the technical difficulty of the novel is hardly sufficient to account for the tone of almost hysterical defensiveness to be found in so many of the reviews and, in a very pure and revealing form, in the letter which John Galsworthy sent to J. B. Pinker in the autumn of 1915:

Wingstone
Manaton
Devon

My dear Pinker,

I've read 'The Rainbow', & will send it back to you in a day.

Frankly—I think it's aesthetically detestable. Its perfervid futuristic style revolts me. Its reiterations bore me to death. And—worse than all—at the back of its amazing fecundity—what is there? What real discovery, what of the spirit, what that is touching, or even true? There is a spurious creativeness about it all, as of countless bodies made with tremendous gusto, and not an ounce of soul within them, in spite of incredible assertions and pretence of sounding life to its core. It's a kind of portent; a paean of the undisciplined shallow fervour that passes with the young in these days for art. It has no time-resisting quality whatever. Brittle as glass, and with something of its brilliance.

As to the sexual aspect. The writer forgets—as no great artist does—that by dwelling on the sexual side of life so lovingly he falsifies all the values of his work—for this reason if for no other: the sexual instinct is so strong in all of us that any emphasis upon it drags the whole being of the reader away from seeing life steadily, truly, & whole; drags it away from the rest of the book, stultifies the writer's own efforts at the presentation of human life and character.

I much prefer a frankly pornographic book to one like this. That at all events achieves what it sets out to do; and does not leave on one the painful impression of a man tragically obsessed to the ruin of his gifts.

I am a pagan; but this is not paganism, it is fever. A grievous pity—so much power, & vision (up to a point) run so young to seed. I don't see him getting back now—he will go on, & become more and more perfervid, seeing less and less the wood for the trees. And the worst of it is he will lead away those who think that what glitters must be gold.

I'm sorry, the first part of *Sons & Lovers* was so good.

Yours always,
JOHN GALSWORTHY

I hope I have demonstrated that the art of *The Rainbow* is very far from 'undisciplined shallow fervour', and that what Galsworthy took for brittle surface brilliance is, in fact, the very life of the novel.

The essential point at issue is not, of course, merely formal or aesthetic, as Galsworthy's paragraph on sex reveals. What kind of pagan is it who can claim to be able to present human life and character whole without any emphasis upon the sexual side of life? Lawrence would have claimed that evasion of it drags the whole being of the reader away from seeing life steadily, truly and whole. It all depends on what you mean by 'human character'. In his letter of the previous year to Edward Garnett, Galsworthy revealed that his preference for the first half of *Sons and Lovers* was also a matter of sex:

The body's never worth while, and the sooner Lawrence recognizes that, the better—the men we swear by—Tolstoy, Turgenev, Tchekov, Maupassant, Flaubert, France—knew that great truth, they only use the body, and that sparingly, to reveal the soul (Marrot, *Life and Letters of John Galsworthy*, Heinemann, 1935, p. 724).

To Lawrence this would have seemed a blasphemy against life, and crippling to the art of any writer who really believed it. Lawrence swore by other men: from Galsworthy's pantheon only Tolstoy is to be found in Lawrence's.

In his scrutiny of *John Galsworthy* (1927) Lawrence uses Galsworthy's 'social beings' against which to set the life at the core of the great figures both of history and literature:

It is the essential innocence and naïvete of the human being, the sense of being at one with the great universe-continuum of space-time-life, which is vivid in a great man, and a pure nuclear spark in every man who is still free (*Phoenix* 541).

Hardy's characters, not caring very much for money or self-preservation, 'are struggling hard to come into being':

And it is this quality Hardy shares with the great writers, Shakespeare, Sophocles or Tolstoy, this setting behind the small action of his protagonists the terrific action of unfathomed nature; setting a smaller system of morality, the one grasped and formulated by the human consciousness within the vast, uncomprehended and incomprehensible morality of nature or of life itself, surpassing human consciousness (*ibid.* 419).

This is also, clearly, what Lawrence himself was trying to do in *The Rainbow* and *Women in Love*.

§7

The nineteenth-century vision had certainly perished in the hands of Galsworthy, Bennett and Wells. Lawrence breaks out simultaneously from the nineteenth-century aesthetic and metaphysic to new shapes and new patterns of perception, thought and feeling. But however much we talk about the originality of *The Rainbow*, an amazing and far-reaching originality, we must not lose sight of the fact that it would still be among the greatest English novels without that originality (something which could not be said for *Women in Love*, where the original elements take over almost all the functions). It is a realistic novel, perhaps even, where human relationships are concerned, *the* realistic novel. Lawrence's mature prose gives us the tangible presence, the visible aura of real life, together with his own deep perception of inner realities and subtle relationships, so that the total presentation of the courtship of Tom and Lydia, the childhood of Anna, her honeymoon, the childhood and adolescence of Ursula, is more real than anything we experience in the actual world except in the rarest moments. Whole episodes have the life-enhancing quality of such moments. Here Lawrence gives us the very consciousness of the unintellectual farmer, the wilful child, the pregnant woman, the adolescent girl; the very quality of living—in the fastnesses of the inviolable self, in the straining intimacies of family relationships, in the pressures of an authentic environment—region, class, tradition, change; above all the poignancy of the real, possible (indeed *normal*) innocence, beauty, gladness and fearful strife of love.

Throughout the novel, but particularly in the first half, this framework is filled with the flesh and sinew of Lawrence's best prose, prose of such immediacy and potency that it continually provokes our almost vocal assent. The rightness of scene can be broken down to a rightness of phrase and cadence. The object or experience is rendered so completely that the intensely personal vision finds language of impersonal vividness and actuality. The chosen words are, moreover, charged with overtones and resonances from the rest of the novel (and from the Bible), carrying over the accumulated sanctions and relationships.

Towards the end of the book there are a few scenes where these verbal resources are exploited without the enclosing and vitalising dramatic realisation. The symbol escapes its dramatic context and seeks to impose form from without, as the rainbow symbol itself does in the ending. The horizontals of the first generation are organic, hardly to be called symbolic at all; the land the Brangwens work justifies its presence naturalistically. Similarly, the verticals of the second generation are real features of the churches which capture Will's imagination. But the arched is concretely embodied only in the rainbow, which has no business in the novel except as a symbol—its symbolic accretions being literary and external rather than organic.

'I have no longer the joy in creating vivid scenes, that I had in *Sons and Lovers*', Lawrence wrote to Garnett in 1914 (*CL* 263). We can think of many scenes just as vivid as anything in *Sons and Lovers*. It is only because the early chapters were so rich in such scenes that we feel dissatisfied with some of the less fully realised episodes of the later chapters, where Lawrence, losing interest, lapses occasionally into his Carlylean essay-style.

Also, as the novel progresses, 'action' gives way to 'being' as the writer's preoccupation. The pressure, towards the end, is to sacrifice range for depth, to approach the wider public themes through the symbolism of the individual psyche. The perfection of this technique will make possible a wholly new kind of structure in *Women in Love*.

CHAPTER 4

CHRONOLOGY

LOOK! WE HAVE COME THROUGH!
From *Manifesto* to *Craving for Spring*, March 1916–October 1917.

RHYMING POEMS (*Bay*, Beaumont Press, 1919).
From *Tommies on the Train* to *Nostalgia*, 1916–17.

WOMEN IN LOVE (privately printed, N.Y. 1920; Secker, 1921).
Begun as *The Sisters* in April 1916 (AH 348). Finished in June (*CL* 457).
Revision and expansion continued until November.

THE HORSE DEALER'S DAUGHTER (*English Review*, April 1922; *England, My England*, Seltzer, 1922).
Written in November 1916 as *The Miracle* (AH 378, 380).

The Lawrences planned to leave England for America in February 1917, but were refused passports.

SAMSON AND DELILAH (*English Review*, March 1917; *England, My England*).
Written before March 1917.

THE REALITY OF PEACE.
Seven essays written by 7 March 1917 (AH 401), four of which were published in *Phoenix*. The others are lost.

AT THE GATES.
By 27 July 1917 the *Reality of Peace* essays had been expanded into a little book. This is lost (*CL* 519; AH 414).

STUDIES IN CLASSSIC AMERICAN LITERATURE (Seltzer, 1923).
Lawrence was reading American literature regularly throughout the Cornwall years. He conceived the set of essays in January 1917 (AH 394) and began them in August, as *The Transcendental Element in American Literature* (AH 414). The final essay, on 'Whitman' was completed in June 1918 (AH 444). The seven essays published in the *English Review* were expanded to twelve by February 1919. The essays were rewritten in the winter of 1922–3. The earlier versions are published as *The Symbolic Meaning*, Centaur Press, 1962.

LOVE, LIFE (*English Review*, January, February 1918; *Phoenix*).
These essays were sent to Pinker in the autumn of 1917, but had apparently been written some time earlier.

4

ARTICULATE EXTREMITY
1915–1916

Women in Love

I know it is true, the book. And it is another world, in which I can live apart from this foul world which I will not accept or acknowledge or even enter. The world of my novel is big and fearless—yes, I love it, and love it passionately...I shall call my novel I think The Latter Days...But everybody will hate it, save me—most people won't even be able to read it (*CL* 477).

§1

THE third and penultimate version of *The Rainbow* was completed at Fiascherino in May 1914. The following month the Lawrences returned to England. Lawrence was walking in Westmorland with Koteliansky and two other friends when war was declared. 'The War finished me', he wrote to Lady Cynthia Asquith six months later (*CL* 309). He felt, he said, as if he had spent those months in the tomb. It was at this time that Lawrence conceived his 'pet scheme'—Rananim:

I want to gather together about twenty souls and sail away from this world of war and squalor and found a little colony where there shall be no money but a sort of communism as far as necessaries of life go, and some real decency (*CL* 307).

The final version of *The Rainbow* was begun in December and carried through on a burst of new hope which lasted from the end of January to the beginning of March 1915:

I couldn't tell you how fragile and tender this hope is—the new shoot of life. But I feel hopeful now about the War...I know we shall all come through, rise again and walk healed and whole and new in a big inheritance, here on earth (*CL* 310).

The brief friendships with E. M. Forster and Bertrand Russell date from these months, and the more lasting friendship with Lady Ottoline Morrell, who offered buildings at Garsington as a centre for Rananim:

Tomorrow Lady Ottoline is coming again and bringing Bertrand Russell...
We are going to struggle with my Island idea—Rananim—But they say, the
island shall be England, that we shall start our new community in the midst
of this old one, as a seed falls among the roots of the parent. Only wait, and
we will remove mountains and set them in the midst of the sea (*CL* 314).

Having discovered a new world in his fiction, Lawrence felt that
he must make that world real, not only for Frieda and himself, or
even for a small select community (though that would be a start),
but, ultimately, for humanity:

If I know that humanity is chained to a rock, I cannot set forth to find it new
lands to enter upon...Because an explorer is one sent forth from a great body
of people to open out new lands for their occupation. But my people cannot
even move—it is chained—paralysed (*CL* 318).

In this context the function of art must be destructive:

Only satire is decent now. The rest is a lie (*CL* 317).

But more important than art is direct political action:

So a vision of a better life must include a revolution of society. And one must
fulfil one's vision as much as possible (*CL* 324).

The letter to Bertrand Russell of 12 February 1915 is Lawrence's
most committed statement of revolutionary socialism:

But we shall smash the frame. The land, the industries, the means of com-
munication and the public amusements shall all be nationalised. Every man
shall have his wage till the day of his death, whether he work or not, so long
as he works when he is fit. Every woman shall have her wage till the day of
her death, whether she works or not, so long as she works when she is fit—
keeps her house or rears her children.
    Then, and then only, shall we be able to *begin* living (*CL* 320).

At the end of February, Lawrence's revolutionary enthusiasm
was at its strongest. 'It makes me quite glad to think how
splendid it will be, when more and more of us fasten our hands on
the chains, and pull, and pull, and break them apart' (*CL* 325).
He planned to form a revolutionary party, and hoped to recruit
some of the Cambridge intellectuals to whom Russell was to
introduce him on the weekend of 6–8 March:

Also I feel frightfully important coming to Cambridge—quite momentous
the occasion is to me. I don't want to be horribly impressed and intimidated,
but am afraid I may be. I only care about the revolution we shall have
(*CL* 328).

He also planned to begin publishing weekly pamphlets—'my initiation of the great and happy revolution' (*CL* 328). The Cambridge weekend, on which, for Lawrence, the future of Western civilisation hinged, was the first of many deep disappointments of that year:

When I saw Keynes that morning in Cambridge it was one of the crises of my life. It sent me mad with misery and hostility and rage... (David Garnett, *Flowers of the Forest*).

The whole Cambridge set seemed to him 'done for forever'. The connection with Russell was maintained, and a joint lecture-programme planned, but when it came to examining Russell's proposed contributions, in July, Lawrence found himself compelled to cover the manuscript with huge NO!s. Lawrence's letter to Russell of 14 September begins 'The article you send me is a plausible lie, and I hate it', and ends 'Let us become strangers again, I think it better' (*CL* 366). In April the Garsington project had fallen through. At the beginning of November *The Rainbow* was suppressed. Lawrence consoled himself that he would be in America in a short time:

We are all ready to go to America. I cannot live here any more; and I am sure I cannot do any more work for this country. I know America is bad, but I think it has a future. I think there is no future for England: only a decline and fall. That is the dreadful and unbearable part of it: to have been born into a decadent era, a decline of life, a collapsing civilisation (*CL* 383).

The *Rainbow* proceedings delayed departure, and in December he learned that he would not be allowed to leave the country after all. He had finished *The Rainbow* in March and written nothing since but *The Crown* and a few other bits of 'philosophy'. Worse than all the more personal disappointments was the increasing impingement on Lawrence's conscience through 1915 of the war—not only the carnage at the front, but the moral debacle at home.

Seven years later, in the 'Nightmare' chapter of *Kangaroo*, he looked back on that year as the end of an era:

It was in 1915 the old world ended. In the winter of 1915–1916 the spirit of the old London collapsed; the city, in some way, perished, perished from being a heart of the world, and became a vortex of broken passions, lusts, hopes, fears, and horrors. The integrity of London collapsed, and the genuine debasement began, the unspeakable baseness of the press and the public voice, the reign of that bloated ignominy, *John Bull* (220).

It was Lawrence's thirtieth year, the end of his youth, and the end of his faith in democracy:

No man who has really consciously lived through this can believe again absolutely in democracy (220).

When the people chose Bottomley, it really seemed that the covenant of *The Rainbow* had broken, that life had gone bad altogether:

Humanity in Europe fell horribly into a hatred of the living soul, in the war. There is no gainsaying it. We all fell. Let us not try to wriggle out of it. We fell into hideous depravity of hating the human soul; a purulent small-pox of the spirit we had. It was shameful, shameful, shameful, in every country and in all of us. Some tried to resist and some didn't. But we were all drowned in shame. A purulent small-pox of the vicious spirit, vicious against the deep soul that pulses in the blood (Introd. to *Memoirs of the Foreign Legion by M.M.* 90).

The world of humanity, which Birkin wishes could be swept away, became a hell for Lawrence:

It isn't my disordered imagination. There is a wagtail sitting on the gate-post. I see how sweet and swift heaven is. But hell is slow and creeping and viscous and insect-teeming: as is this Europe now, this England (*CL* 338).

That it was not, indeed, his disordered imagination can be established with reference to many other testimonies, such as those of Forster and Shaw (in the preface to *Heartbreak House*), and to the poetry which the war produced even from men who had approached it in the spirit of Rupert Brooke. But the prose of Lawrence's letters carried its own guarantee of sanity in such passages as this to Lady Ottoline Morrell on 30 April 1915:

The death of Rupert Brooke fills me more and more with a sense of the fatuity of it all. He was slain by bright Phoebus' shaft—it was in keeping with his general sunniness—it was the real climax of his pose. I first heard of him as a Greek god under a Japanese sunshade, reading poetry in his pyjamas, at Grantchester upon the lawns where the river goes. Bright Phoebus smote him down. It is all in the saga. O God, O God, it is all too much of a piece: it is like madness (*CL* 337).

The world seemed to be, indeed was, 'one colossal madness, falsity, a stupendous assertion of not-being' (*CL* 446). Lawrence had to write another novel to create a world in which his sanity could live and breathe:

I have got a long way with my novel. It comes rapidly and is very good. When one is shaken to the very depths, one finds reality in the unreal world. At present my real world is the world of my inner soul, which reflects on to the novel I write. The outer world is there to be endured, it is not real—neither the outer life (*CL* 453).

If *The Rainbow* is Lawrence's Genesis or Isaiah, *Women in Love* is his Jeremiah:

It [*The Rainbow*] was a kind of working up to the dark sensual or Dionysic or Aphrodysic ecstasy, which does actually burst the world, burst the world-consciousness in every individual. What I did through individuals, the world has done through the war. But alas, in the world of Europe I see no Rainbow. I believe the deluge of iron rain will destroy the world here, utterly: no Ararat will rise above the subsiding iron waters. There is a great *consummation* in death, or sensual ecstasy, as in *The Rainbow*. But there is also death which is the rushing of the Gadarene swine down the slope of extinction. And this is the war in Europe. We have chosen our extinction in death, rather than our Consummation. So be it: it is not my fault.

There is another novel, sequel to *The Rainbow*, called *Women in Love*... This actually does contain the results in one's soul of the war: it is purely destructive, not like *The Rainbow*, destructive-consummating (*CL* 519).

The problem Birkin wrestles with throughout the novel is: what must the individual do to be saved when he finds himself living in an age of renewed chaos, of dissolution? Does he go with the current, or does he fight against it? The imagery of waves moving onwards towards the shores of the unknown would no longer be appropriate in *Women in Love*. The new image is the ebb and flow of the sea—cycles of creation and decay which are indifferent to human life. Yet humanity is somehow responsible for what is happening to it. There is a loss, in so many men, of that integrity 'which alone keeps life real' (*Kangaroo* 216). The animals and plants are integrated with nature in a way man is not. Man should, then, be swept away until some new evolutionary cycle is ready to begin. Or perhaps the cycles are not natural but historical. Perhaps there is within man something corresponding to the integrity of Bismarck (a rabbit) which can be asserted against historical processes. Integrity, or 'truth in being', manifests itself in personal, especially sexual relationships; its presence guarantees creativeness, its absence reduction, disintegration. Birkin and Ursula move towards distinctiveness and selving through their coming together. Gerald and Gudrun resolve back towards inanimate matter, symbolised in the novel by ice and snow.

Birkin assumes that God does not exist (51). Lawrence's own position in 1916 is stated at length in a letter to Catherine Carswell of 16 July. Here he continues to use the word God, though he apologises for it, but the word which is now carrying all the weight is 'desire', with its complement 'fulfilment'. 'God in me is my desire', he claims, but the existence of God outside human desires now receives only token gestures.

The great Christian tenet must be surpassed, there must be something new: neither the war, nor the turning the other cheek.

What we want is the fulfilment of our desires, down to the deepest and most spiritual desire. The body is immediate, the spirit is beyond: first the leaves and then the flower: but the plant is an integral whole: therefore *every* desire, to the very deepest. And I shall find my deepest desire to be a wish for pure, unadulterated relationship with the universe, for truth in being. My pure relationship with one woman is marriage, physical and spiritual: with another, is another form of happiness, according to our nature. And so on for ever.

It is this establishing of pure relationships which makes heaven, wherein we are immortal, like the angels, and mortal, like men, both. And the way to immortality is in the fulfilment of desire (*CL* 467).

The new belief which Birkin seems to me to embody, that a human being can himself generate creativeness, and must do so if he is not to be swept along into spiritual death, is implied in a later passage of the same letter, which also relates the theme of *Women in Love* closely to Lawrence's own marriage:

Frieda's letter is quite right, about the *difference* between us being the adventure, and the true relationship established between different things, different spirits, this is creative life. So that act of love, which is a pure thrill, is a kind of friction between opposites, interdestructive, an act of death. There is an extreme self-realisation, self-sensation, in this friction against the really hostile, opposite. But there must be an act of love which is a passing of the self into a pure relationship with the other, something new and creative in the coming together of the lovers, in their creative spirit, before a new child can be born: a new *flower* in us before there can be a new seed of a child (*CL* 468).

The relationship between Gerald and Gudrun is deadly because it always involves exploitation of the other. If Gerald were able to experience a pure relationship with a woman, or with Birkin, he would no longer be able to function as industrial magnate, for this, too, involves the using of others. It is the same mentality as that of the commander who sent his men over the top into barbed wire and machine-gun fire. The public and private themes meet in Gerald, who accepts the extant social form, the class hegemony, the cash nexus. The needs and perversions of his private life follow from this. In order to preserve his integrity Birkin has to throw up his job and build an ark of marriage against the flood.

§2

Though Gudrun and Gerald never go through any formal ceremony, what we are given is, in effect, two marriages, one sacramental, the other licentious. The novel opens with a discussion on marriage between the sisters. Gudrun advocates marriage as 'an experience'. She has been 'living a studio life' for several years, and has come to feel that 'everything withers in the bud'. Her desire to force some sort of blossoming—to pull open the bud before it withers—manifests itself in her craving for a man: 'a highly attractive individual of sufficient means'. Her stridency at this point betrays her failure to 'lay hold on life', and contrasts with Ursula's 'sensitive expectancy', her ability to hold herself in reserve until some man elicits a natural response. The moral ambiguity of Gudrun's desires is hinted at by her 'strange grimace, half sly smiling, half anguish', her 'long, slow look of knowledge', which frightens Ursula.

Our introduction to Gerald is even more foreboding:

There was something northern about him that magnetised her. In his clear northern flesh and his fair hair was a glisten like sunshine refracted through crystals of ice. And he looked so new, unbroached, pure as an arctic thing. Perhaps he was thirty years old, perhaps more. His gleaming beauty, maleness, like a young, good-humoured, smiling wolf, did not blind her to the significant sinister stillness in his bearing, the lurking danger of his unsubdued temper (9).

Her 'knowledge' of him is like a sharp inoculation that changes her blood. 'Blood' carries associations of both lust and death. It is revealed that Gerald had killed his brother. Birkin accuses him of having a lurking desire to cut everybody's throat, and to have his own gizzard slit. He also relates Gerald's death-wish to his position in society and his deference to convention:

He saw the perfect good-humoured callousness, even strange, glistening malice, in Gerald, glistening through the plausible ethics of productivity (49).

Gerald's malice, his domineering will and almost sadistic sexual pride, reveals itself in his treatment of the Arab mare. As in the later episode of the rabbit, it is the sight of blood which draws Gudrun and Gerald together:

Gudrun looked and saw the trickles of blood on the sides of the mare, and she turned white. And then on the very wound the bright spurs came down, pressing relentlessly. The world reeled and passed into nothingness for Gudrun, she could not know any more... Gudrun was as if numbed in her mind by the sense of indomitable soft weight of the man, bearing down into the living body of the horse: the strong, indomitable thighs of the blond man clenching the palpitating body of the mare into pure control; a sort of soft white magnetic domination from the loins and thighs and calves, enclosing and encompassing the mare heavily into unutterable subordination, soft-blood-subordination, terrible (104, 106).

There is no sinister stillness in Birkin's bearing. Rather an endearing restlessness and energy. At the beginning, however, he is groping rather wildly for standards. He knows intuitively what is wrong with the world and with people like Gerald and Hermione, and he can be articulate in his disapproval. But when it comes to formulating his positive values, he tends to preach, to contradict or parody himself.

At the beginning of the novel Birkin is prepared to advocate the destruction of the whole human race. Life, in its purer, non-human forms, will continue. Meanwhile, he will seek his own satisfaction in sensuality—

the great dark knowledge you can't have in your head—the dark involuntary being. It is death to one's self—but it is the coming into being of another... When the mind and the known world is drowned in darkness—everything must go—there must be the deluge. Then you find yourself in a palpable body of darkness, a demon (36).

Gerald also thinks of himself as a sensualist, and Birkin has great difficulty in distinguishing, even to himself, between his own position which, though demonic, is a way to wholeness and sanity, and Gerald's which he sees to be suicidal. Gerald interrupts his thoughts about the destruction of Sodom to discuss accommodation in Soho and the morals of the London bohemians he is to meet. To enter their world is 'a real death' for Birkin. Gerald blithely denies that it makes him feel like one of the damned.

The African carving at Halliday's seems to Birkin to convey 'a complete truth':

Pure culture in sensation, culture in the physical consciousness, mindless, utterly sensual. It is so sensual as to be final, supreme (72).

Even Gerald feels that the statue is, in fact, profoundly opposed to Birkin's best self, and extracts from him the admission 'this isn't everything'. 'Ultimate marriage' is Birkin's catch-phrase, but it is not clear wherein the ultimacy lies if not in sensuality. The novel is much less ambivalent than Birkin about the carving. Western European culture cannot go back to this. The attempt would bring only such corruption as Minette typifies. She has lapsed almost to the level of the carving, the face 'void, peaked, abstracted almost into meaninglessness by the weight of sensation beneath', which Gerald had seen immediately before going to bed with her.

The Gerald–Gudrun relationship is very delicately developed. Birkin tells Gerald about Gudrun's art, of which there are examples in Hermione's boudoir which Gerald has seen and mistaken, significantly, for savage carving. The 'Coal-Dust' chapter gives us considerable insight into the affinities which draw them together. A group of miners make suggestive remarks as Gudrun passes, and this pruriency is linked to the ugliness of the whole industrial environment—an ugliness overlaid with the beauty of the sunset, which stupefies Gudrun with a 'thick, hot attraction':

It seemed to envelop Gudrun in a labourer's caress (108).

She finds the air surcharged with a 'glamorous thickness of labour and maleness', given off by the 'thousands of vigorous, underworld, half-automatised colliers'. It goes to her brain and heart 'awakening a fatal desire, a fatal callousness...She craved to get her satisfaction of it':

Now she realised that this was the world of powerful, underworld men who spent most of their time in the darkness. In their voices she could hear the voluptuous resonance of darkness, the strong, dangerous underworld, mindless, inhuman. They sounded also like strange machines, heavy, oiled. The voluptuousness was like that of machinery, cold and iron...They aroused a strange, nostalgic ache of desire, something almost demoniacal, never to be fulfilled (108).

The glamour and potency, coupled with callousness and mechanism, refer us to Gerald; the underworld voluptuousness and prurience to Minette; the mindless, inhuman, demoniacal, *nostalgic* desire, to the obscene carving at Halliday's. Beldover is as much a part of the underworld as Bohemia. For this is the quality of a whole civilisation, and all who subscribe to it are damned. The evil is pervasive in art, industry, human relationship:

The same secret seemed to be working in the souls of all alike, Gudrun, Palmer, the rakish young bloods, the gaunt, middle-aged men. All had a secret sense of power, and of inexpressible destructiveness, and of fatal half-heartedness, a sort of rottenness in the will (110).

The next chapter 'Sketchbook' translates the same themes into new symbols of disintegration, *fleurs du mal*:

What she [Gudrun] could see was mud, soft, oozy, watery mud, and from its festering chill, water-plants rose up, thick and cool and fleshy, very straight and turgid, thrusting out their leaves at right-angles, and having dark lurid colours, dark green and blotches of black-purple and bronze. But she could feel their turgid fleshy structure as in a sensuous vision, she knew how they rose out of the mud, she knew how they thrust out from themselves, how they stood stiff and succulent against the air (111).

Set against this is a passage embodying the health, vitality, purity and colour of Ursula's world and life:

Ursula was watching the butterflies, of which there were dozens near the water, little blue ones suddenly snapping out of nothingness into a jewel-life, a large black-and-red one standing upon a flower and breathing with his soft wings, intoxicatingly, breathing pure, ethereal sunshine; two white ones wrestling in the low air; there was a halo round them; ah, when they came tumbling nearer they were orange-tips, and it was the orange that had made the halo. Ursula rose and drifted away, unconscious like the butterflies (111).

The butterflies 'are a sign that pure creation takes place' (120). Their very distinctiveness and selfhood constitutes a heaven of existence, far transcending the uncreate mess of mud from which life struggled all those aeons ago. Gudrun's *nostalgie de la boue* is a symptom of her unconscious desire to lapse back from the struggle for selfhood towards man's first slime.

But the imagery so far associated with Birkin ('underworld', 'dark', 'inhuman', 'demoniacal', etc.) seems much nearer to Gudrun's world than Ursula's. To some extent the fact that Birkin had felt obliged to use this kind of imagery indicates the extent to which he was himself caught up in the destructive process until Hermione's crushing blow jolts him free of the old world, the old ethic. His new-found self-sufficiency is a necessary starting-point for a healthy approach to human relationships: Afterwards, he 'knew where he belonged' and could return to the world without being drawn into its madness, implicated in its purposes and values. Sunshine, bird-song and flowers form the setting of his next meeting with Ursula:

The afternoon was full of larks' singing. On the bright hillsides was a subdued smoulder of gorse. A few forget-me-nots flowered by the water. There was a rousedness and glancing everywhere (115).

This is not to say that Birkin abandons his demonic sensualism. But he holds it in abeyance now, turning to his new image of 'star-equilibrium'.

The relationship he now seeks with Ursula is 'freedom together'. Ursula calls this 'purely selfish' and demands 'love'.

'But it isn't selfish at all. Because I don't *know* what I want of you. I deliver *myself* over to the unknown, in coming to you, I am without reserves or defences, stripped entirely, into the unknown. Only there needs the pledge between us, that we will both cast off everything, cast off ourselves even, and cease to be, so that that which is perfectly ourselves can take place in us... What I want is a strange conjunction with you—not meeting and mingling;— you are quite right:—but an equilibrium, a pure balance of two single beings:—as the stars balance each other' (138, 139).

Ursula does not trust him when he drags the stars in. His position is still too insistent and theoretical. He is too guarded. He has not the abandon, and spontaneity, the tenderness of Ursula. But gradually we see them coming together. The initial victory is to Ursula, who finally draws from him a declaration of love.

Birkin's fear of love is related to all the symbolic themes of the novel, particularly the Aphrodite theme, which will come into the foreground in the chapter 'Moony'. It is first introduced in 'Water-Party', where Birkin expounds at some length his vision of ultimate evil, embracing the whole of western civilisation and moving towards 'universal nothing—the end of the world':

We always consider the silver river of life, rolling on and quickening all the world to a brightness, on and on to heaven, flowing into a bright eternal sea, a heaven of angels thronging. But the other is our real reality...that dark river of dissolution. You see it rolls in us just as the other rolls—the black river of corruption. And our flowers are of this—our sea-born Aphrodite, all our white phosphorescent flowers of sensuous perfection, all our reality, nowadays...She is the flowering mystery of the death-process...When the stream of synthetic creation lapses, we find ourselves part of the inverse process, the blood of destructive creation. Aphrodite is born in the first spasm of universal dissolution—then the snakes and swans and lotus—marsh-flowers—and Gudrun and Gerald—born in the process of destructive creation (164).

The theme is to be enacted on the level of plot, as Gerald and Gudrun engage in deadly combat:

'You have struck the first blow', he said at last.
'And I shall strike the last', she retorted involuntarily, with confident assurance (162).

The last blow is struck in an explicitly end-of-the-world setting—'the infolded navel of eternal snow'. One of the fruits of the perverse alliance between Gudrun and Loerke is a terribly specific account of the impending debacle:

As for the future, that they never mentioned except one laughed out some mocking dream of the destruction of the world by a ridiculous catastrophe of man's invention: a man invented such a perfect explosive that it blew the world in two, and the two halves set off in different directions through space, to the dismay of the inhabitants: or else the people of the world divided into two halves, and each half decided *it* was perfect and right, the other half was wrong and must be destroyed; so another end of the world. Or else, Loerke's dream of fear, the world went cold, and snow fell everywhere, and only white creatures, Polar bears, white foxes, and men like awful white snow-birds, persisted in ice-cruelty (444).

Birkin does not know how far he is himself implicated in the destructive process. He doesn't feel that he and Ursula are altogether *fleurs du mal*—'there ought to be some roses, warm and flamy'. But if the end of the world is desirable, as making way for a new creative cycle to begin, then he and Ursula must be of it: 'It means a new cycle of creation after, but not for us.' Part of Birkin wants death, as an end to the process of dying, wants love which is a kind of death, an escape from the world and the obligations of humanity. Ursula insists that she is a rose of happiness. She demands a more passionate and affirmative love. But her passion Birkin interprets as essentially domineering and possessive, like Hermione's, assuming the man to be an incomplete, fragmentary being until fulfilled by the woman. Birkin rejects this:

We are not broken fragments of one whole. Rather we are the singling away into purity and clear being, of things that were mixed. Rather the sex is that which remains in us of the mixed, the unresolved. And passion is the further separating of this mixture, that which is manly being taken into the being of the man, that which is womanly passing to the woman, till the two are clear and whole as angels, the admixture of sex in the highest sense surpassed, leaving two single beings constellated together like two stars (192-3).

§3

The pressure in Birkin all the time is to find another world. He believes that two exceptional people might make such a world, and, after his disillusionment with Ursula, he turns to Gerald. But Gerald is too limited, unfree:

Gerald could never fly away from himself, in real indifferent gaiety. He had a clog, a sort of monomania (199).

He is defined in his own eyes by his social and economic function:

Gerald himself, who was responsible for all this industry, was he a good director? If he were, he had fulfilled his life. The rest was by-play (215).

The chapter 'The Industrial Magnate' shows Gerald's assertion, against the antiquated liberal-humanism of his father, of the pure instrumentality of mankind and the godhead of the productive machine. At the water-party, for the first time in his life, Gerald withdraws his will, relaxes out of his habitual mechanism:

Now he had let go, imperceptibly he was melting into oneness with the whole. It was like pure, perfect sleep, his first great sleep of life (170).

But everything at Shortlands is dependent on his will. His world, without the imposition of a systematic, mechanical control, drifts straight into catastrophe: his sister and her would-be rescuer are drowned in his absence.

And once or twice lately, when he was alone in the evening and had nothing to do, he had suddenly stood up in terror, not knowing what he was (224).

He fears that his face in the mirror is a mask, that his eyes are bubbles that will 'burst in a moment and leave clear annihilation'. His life, dedicated to output, is sterile. 'His centres of feeling were drying up' (225). When Gudrun finally breaks his will, Gerald himself drifts into annihilation.

What little 'quick sufficiency in life' Gerald retains, derives from his contact with Birkin, whose life seems to contain 'the quintessence of faith'. But Gerald cannot relate Birkin's words to 'the real outside world of work and life'. This is not surprising, for Birkin himself has not yet found a way of life appropriate to his faith, and is never to do so completely in all his subsequent metamorphoses in Lawrence's novels. Gerald seeks relief with women. But even 'a debauch with some desperate woman' can no longer give him the illusion of being alive. His mind must be stimulated too. He needs to bring into full consciousness the obscenity of his desires and to share with a woman this recognition. Birkin offers a friendship whereby both men can combine resources, their reserves of sanity and hope, in mutual trust and commitment. The quality of the relationship offered is 'there' in the 'clear, happy eyes of discovery' with which Birkin looks at Gerald, in the 'luminous pleasure' with which his face shines, and in the 'fine living hand' he extends. Faith and gaiety and wholeness are offered—the same 'freedom together' that Birkin had offered Ursula—without the bondage of a 'personal' union of 'love', without the eternal struggle against 'cursed Syria Dea'.

The rainbow was arched in the blood of men and quivering to life in their spirit at the end of *The Rainbow*. Birkin is the prophet and pioneer of this renascence, though he is not yet aware of this. His blood, which he metaphorically offers to Gerald, would have been a saving, quickening transfusion from the bright river of life. Gerald is unable to give himself, to let go. Instead we see him enter into an obscene blood-pact with Gudrun, a blasphemous inversion of the blood-brotherhood Birkin offered, hellish and cruel, a mutual commitment to the river of corruption which flows in Gudrun's veins:

The long, shallow red tip seemed torn across his own brain, tearing the surface of his ultimate consciousness, letting through the forever unconscious, unthinkable red ether of the beyond, the obscene beyond (235).

Gerald and Gudrun penetrate to the depths of each other with unspoken suggestiveness:

'God be praised we aren't rabbits', she said in a high, shrill voice. The smile intensified a little on his face.

'Not rabbits?' he said, looking at her fixedly. Slowly her face relaxed into a smile of obscene recognition. 'Ah, Gerald', she said in a strong, slow, almost man-like way. 'All that, and more.' Her eyes looked up at him with shocking nonchalance (235).

They are implicated in abhorrent mysteries. But the mystery of life, of incarnation, is dead in them, and they are blind to the normality and sanity of the rabbit—'a sickening fool', 'most decidedly mad':

And suddenly the rabbit, which had been crouching as if it were a flower, so stil˙ and soft, suddenly burst into life. Round and round the court it went, as if shot from a gun, round and round like a furry meteorite, in a tense hard circle that seemed to bind their brains. They all stood in amazement, smiling uncannily, as if the rabbit were obeying some unknown incantation. Round and round it flew, on the grass under the old red walls like a storm.

And then quite suddenly it settled down, hobbled among the grass, and sat considering, its nose twitching like a bit of fluff in the wind. After having considered for a few minutes, a soft bunch with a black, open eye, which perhaps was looking at them, perhaps was not, it hobbled calmly forward and began to nibble the grass with that mean motion of a rabbit's quick eating (235).

'As if it were a flower', 'like a furry meteorite', 'like a storm'— these similes place Bismarck in a universe to which he belongs, whose incantations he obeys. His singleness of being is without reference to them or to the only 'life' they understand. They are baffled by him. Is he looking at them or not? 'That's what it is to be a rabbit.'

It is essential to the budding relationship between Birkin and Ursula that it should not be a fixed thing, that they should never finally 'know' each other, as Hermione had wanted to 'know' Birkin. Each acknowledges the mystery and uniqueness of the other. Each has an 'odd mobility and changeableness'. Each can 'fly away from himself in real, indifferent gaiety', like Bismarck 'because it is so mysterious—'.

Without Birkin, the world lapses into nothingness for Ursula, leaving only her self 'a tiny little rock'. Her self is a hard definite core, isolated and indifferent, as Birkin had been after the blow from Hermione. And this is a prerequisite in the movement towards the relationship she and Birkin are to accomplish. In Birkin's absence there is nothing for Gerald to fall back on:

And there were only three things left that would rouse him, make him live. One was to drink or smoke hashish, the other was to be soothed by Birkin, and the third was women. And there was no one for the moment to drink with. Nor was there a woman. And he knew Birkin was out. So there was nothing to do but to bear the stress of his own emptiness (258-9).

Birkin's fear of Aphrodite breaks out dramatically in the chapter 'Moony'. The inviolable incandescent white moon, re-asserting itself with strange insidious triumph, reminds us of Gudrun's taunting of the Highland cattle at the water-party:

Gradually the fragments caught together re-united, heaving, rocking, dancing, falling back as if in panic, but working their way home again persistently, making semblance of fleeing away when they had advanced, but always flickering nearer, a little closer to the mark (240).

Gudrun, with her arms outspread and her face uplifted, went in a strange palpitating dance towards the cattle, lifting her body towards them as if in a spell, her feet pulsing as if in some little frenzy of unconscious sensation, her arms, her wrists, her hands stretching and heaving and falling and reaching and reaching and falling, her breasts lifted and shaken towards the cattle, her throat exposed as in some voluptuous ecstasy towards them, whilst she drifted imperceptibly nearer, an uncanny white figure, towards them, carried away in its own rapt trance, ebbing in strange fluctuations upon the cattle, that waited, and ducked their heads a little in sudden contraction from her, watching all the time as if hypnotised, their bare horns branching in the clear light, as the white figure of the woman ebbed upon them, in the slow, hypnotising convulsion of the dance. She could feel them just in front of her, it was as if she had the electric pulse from their breasts running into her hands. Soon she would touch them, actually touch them. A terrible shiver of fear and pleasure went through her. And all the while Ursula, spellbound, kept up her high-pitched thin, irrelevant song, which pierced the fading evening like an incantation. Gudrun could hear the cattle breathing heavily with helpless fear and fascination (159).

Aphrodite is also Ursula at this point, her 'female ego' that she wants Birkin to worship. Birkin demands that she should let herself go:

I want you not to care about yourself, just to be there and not to care about yourself, not to insist—be glad and sure and indifferent (243).

Birkin must find out what he really wants. Does he want 'a further sensual experience'? Here, at the very heart of the book, we have Birkin's most direct positive statement. His initial reaction to the African statuettes at Halliday's had been one of uneasy praise, with the proviso 'This isn't everything'. Now he completely rejects the 'inverted culture' they represent:

The goodness, the holiness, the desire for creation and productive happiness must have lapsed, leaving the single impulse for knowledge in one sort, mindless progressive knowledge through the senses, knowledge arrested and ending in the senses, mystic knowledge in disintegration and dissolution, knowledge such as the beetles have, which live purely within the world of corruption and cold dissolution (245-6).

The Northern races have simply taken a different route to the same death:

It would be done differently by the white races. The white races, having the Arctic north behind them, the vast abstraction of ice and snow, would fulfil a mystery of ice-destructive knowledge, snow-abstract annihilation (246).

89

The moon, Aphrodite, 'the queen of the senses', represents, as in *Twilight in Italy*, the sensual aspect of this knowledge:

She is the gleaming darkness, she is the luminous night, she is goddess of destruction, her white, cold fire consumes and does not create...The flesh, the senses, are now self-conscious. They know their aim. Their aim is in supreme sensation. They seek the reduction of the flesh, the flesh reacting upon itself, to a crisis, an ecstasy, a phosphorescent transfiguration in ecstasy (*Twilight in Italy* 35).

Birkin's reaction is to shy away from ecstasy altogether: 'But I hate ecstasy, Dionysic or any other. It's like going round in a squirrel cage' (243). But the imagery is gradually salvaging certain terms for his later reclamation, gradually separating out the two kinds of sensuality or darkness. Aphrodite's darkness is, paradoxically, gleaming, luminous, white; her fire is cold. There remains an unselfconscious darkness which is rich and warm, a creative, invigorating demon to be released.

Gerald, on the other hand,

was one of these strange white wonderful demons from the north, fulfilled in the destructive frost mystery. And was he fated to pass away in this knowledge, this one process of frost-knowledge, death by perfect cold? Was he a messenger, an omen of the universal dissolution into whiteness and snow? (246–7).

Birkin chooses another way, 'the way of freedom':

There was the paradisal entry into pure, single being, the individual soul taking precedence over love and desire for union, stronger than any pangs of emotion, a lovely state of free proud singleness, which accepted the obligation of the permanent connection with others, and with the other, submits to the yoke and leash of love, but never forfeits its own proud individual singleness, even while it loves and yields (247).

Without this singleness of being, Gerald is not free to choose any genuine union:

And marriage was the seal of his condemnation. He was willing to be sealed thus in the underworld, like a soul damned but living for ever in damnation. But he would not make any pure relationship with any other soul. He could not. Marriage was not the committing of himself into a relationship with Gudrun. It was a committing of himself in acceptance of the established world, he would accept the established order, in which he did not livingly believe, and then he would retreat to the underworld for his life. This he would do.

The other way was to accept Rupert's offer of alliance, to enter into the bond of pure trust and love with the other man, and then subsequently with the woman. If he pledged himself with the man he would later be able to pledge himself with the woman: not merely in legal marriage, but in absolute, mystic marriage.
Yet he could not accept the offer (345).

Gerald chooses not to ally himself to Birkin and take his life-direction from him, but to drift aimlessly down the river of corruption. He is not actively, wilfully destructive, perverse, like Loerke, the leader rat: he has not, for all his executive talents, the insight, the consciousness of a leader. He is an agent of evil, not a creator of it. It is not Loerke who dies of spiritual inanition.

'Blasphemous living' is the phrase Lawrence uses in a letter to Gertler of September 1916. The following month Gertler sent him a photograph of one of his paintings, in which Lawrence saw all the 'terrible and soul-tearing obscenity', the 'ghastly, utterly mindless human intensity of sensational extremity', which he had tried to portray in the destruction of Gerald. He could, he says, 'sit down and howl beneath it...in soul-lacerating despair'. It is a 'real and ultimate revelation' nevertheless. 'I must say, I have, for you, in your work, reverence, the reverence for the great articulate extremity of art' (*CL* 477–8).

§4

Birkin, however, is a leader, a creator, and recognises himself as such—a little Jesus. He feels a moral obligation to 'strive for a coherent, satisfied life'; he is 'damned and doomed to the old effort at serious living'. But Birkin is still willing to come to terms with the death-process. He will not yet affirm that the end of the world is not as good as the beginning. Ursula calls him 'a whited sepulchre'. She convinces him that his own position is untenable, without converting him to her own.

The overt conflict between Gerald and Gudrun conceals an essential likeness which is briefly recognised, for example, in the rabbit episode. The conflict is deadly. The conflict between Birkin and Ursula is much more thorough-going, more real. It is a conflict which changes both parties, which moves towards a resolution. It clears away that which is inessential and allows their real selves to come into being and to recognise each other. What they are both able to hold on to finally, is 'the reality of beauty, the reality of happiness in warm creation', of which the rings are tokens. And the actual communion has (as so often in Lawrence) a flower as its token:

She came up and stood before him, hanging her head.

'See what a flower I found you', she said, wistfully holding a piece of purple-red bell-heather under his face. He saw the clump of coloured bells, and the tree-like tiny branch: also her hands with their over-fine, over-sensitive skin.

'Pretty!' he said, looking up at her with a smile, taking the flower. Everything had become simple again, quite simple, the complexity gone into nowhere. But he badly wanted to cry: except that he was weary and bored by emotion.

Then a hot passion of tenderness for her filled his heart. He stood up and looked into her face. It was new, and oh, so delicate in its luminous wonder and fear. He put his arms round her, and she hid her face on his shoulder.

It was peace, just simple peace, as he stood folding her quietly there on the open lane. It was peace at last. The old, detestable world of tension had passed away at last, his soul was strong and at ease (302).

From this relationship 'the goodness, the holiness, the desire for creation and productive happiness' has not lapsed. The flower imagery persists:

He stood on the hearth-rug looking at her, at her face that was upturned exactly like a flower, a fresh, luminous flower, glinting faintly golden with the dew of the first light... Her face was now one dazzle of released, golden light, as she looked up at him and laid her hands full on his thighs, behind, as he stood before her. He looked down at her with a rich bright brow like a diadem above his eyes. She was beautiful as a new marvellous flower opened at his knees, a paradisal flower she was, beyond womanhood, such a flower of luminousness (304-5).

The implications are not allowed to become wholly mystical. Ordinary human health and joy and richness and normality are there in the informal ceremony at the tea-table:

They were glad, and they could forget perfectly. They laughed and went to the meal provided. There was a venison pasty, of all things, a large broad-faced cut ham, eggs and cresses and red beetroot, and medlars and apple-tart, and tea. 'What *good* things!' she cried with pleasure. 'How noble it looks!—shall I pour out the tea?—' She was usually nervous and uncertain at performing these public duties, such as giving tea. But to-day she forgot, she was at her ease, entirely forgetting to have misgivings. The tea-pot poured beautifully from a proud slender spout. Her eyes were warm with smiles as she gave him his tea. She had learned at last to be still and perfect.

'Everything is ours', she said to him (306-7).

Immediately the problem arises of finding a context for their happiness. Birkin wants to wander 'away from the world's somewheres, into our own nowhere'. He seeks 'freedom together'—together not only with Ursula but with a 'few other people'. 'We've got to take the world that's given—because there isn't any other', says Ursula. But Birkin has now acquired the faith to believe that they can create their own new world. Ursula feels that she has already reached her destination, fulfilled her purposes. But for Birkin it is only the beginning of a search which carries him beyond the confines of this novel.

It is striking that the next chapter should be called 'Death and Love'. The equilibrium which Gerald seeks is the opposite of the star-polarity of the Birkin–Ursula love. It is a desperate need, a dependence. Gerald has nothing to set against death. He is in danger of caving in unless he can 'use' Gudrun as a support:

> He wanted to put his arm round her. If he could put his arm round her and draw her against him as they walked, he would equilibrate himself. For now he felt like a pair of scales, the half of which tips down and down into an indefinite void. He must recover some sort of balance (321).

So that, in a literal sense, Gudrun is 'everything' to him. 'I care for nothing on earth, or in heaven, outside this spot where we are' (322). Ursula and Birkin surrendered to the mystery of otherness to achieve peace. Gudrun and Gerald strain for knowledge of each other, and, hence, power over each other.

Dependence, exploitation, violation and murder, are the developing implications of this relationship, implications which are set against Birkin's principle of 'star-equilibrium', 'polarity', with its corollaries—individual self-sufficiency and wholeness, mutual respect, tenderness, unforced spontaneous sensuality, and, ultimately, the relating of the achieved sexual harmony to larger purposes, to wider forms of civilised human activity. But Birkin's principles are formulated gradually, modulate with his experiences, cohere only towards the end, and then with a question-mark remaining. He is far from being a mouthpiece for a pre-existing Lawrentian philosophy. We live through his processes of discovery.

The dénouement takes place in 'a blind valley, the great cul-de-sac of snow and mountain peaks'. It is a shrine of death-worship. The theme of death-by-snow comes, once more, from *Twilight in Italy*:

There, it seemed, in the glamorous snow, was the source of death, which fell down in great waves of shadow and rock, rushing to the level earth. And all the people of the mountains, on the slopes, in the valleys, seemed to live upon this great, rushing wave of death, of breaking-down, of destruction.

The very pure source of breaking-down, decomposition, the very quick of cold death, is the snowy mountain-peak above. There, eternally, goes on the white foregathering of the crystals, out of the deathly cold of the heavens; this is the static nucleus where death meets life in its elementality. And thence, from their white, radiant nucleus of death in life, flows the great flux downwards, towards life and warmth. And we below, we cannot think of the flux upwards, that flows from the needle-point of snow to the unutterable cold and death (153).

Ursula cannot stand the place:

Suddenly she wanted to go away. It occurred to her like a miracle, that she might go away into another world. She had felt so doomed up here in the eternal snow, as if there were no beyond.

Now suddenly, as by a miracle she remembered that away beyond, below her, lay the dark fruitful earth, that towards the south there were stretches of land dark with orange trees and cypress, grey with olives, that ilex trees lifted wonderful plumy tufts in shadow against a blue sky. Miracle of miracles!— this utterly silent, frozen world of the mountain-tops was not universal! One might leave it and have done with it. One might go away.

She wanted to realise the miracle at once. She wanted at this instant to have done with the snow world, the terrible, static ice-built mountain-tops. She wanted to see the dark earth, to smell its earthy fecundity, to see the patient wintry vegetation, to feel the sunshine touch a response in the buds.

She went back gladly to the house, full of hope (425).

Her mother had reacted similarly in Lincoln Cathedral, fleeing from the jewelled gloom into the space and light and warmth and movement of a concrete, sensuous, temporal world.

Gerald and Gudrun continue to torture each other in a cage of nervous, furtive ecstasies. They flirt with death tobogganing, and Gudrun flirts with Loerke. The Gerald who bids goodbye to Birkin and Ursula has lapsed out of life almost completely:

'There's something final about this. And Gudrun seems like the end to me. I don't know—but she seems so soft, her skin like silk, her arms heavy and soft. And it withers my consciousness, somehow, it burns the pith of my mind.' He went on a few paces, staring ahead, his eyes fixed, looking like a mask used in ghastly religions of the barbarians. 'It blasts your soul's eye', he said, 'and leaves you sightless. Yet you *want* to be sightless, you *want* to be blasted, you don't want it any different.' He was speaking as if in a trance, verbal and blank (430-1).

He and Gudrun are now completely isolated, cut off from life, enclosed in the cold mechanical world of knowledge and sensationalism. Loerke offers Gudrun something more subtly suggestive than Gerald, a still further reduction, a myriad subtle thrills. Nothing else has any meaning for her. Her head 'ticks like a clock, with a very madness of dead mechanical monotony and meaninglessness' (455-6).

All life, all life resolved itself into this: tick-tack, tick-tack, tick-tack; then the striking of the hour; then the tick-tack, tick-tack, and the twitching of the clock-fingers. Gerald could not save her from it. He, his body, his motion, his life—it was the same ticking, the same twitching across the dial, a horrible mechanical twitching forward over the face of the hours. What were his kisses, his embraces. She could hear their tick-tack, tick-tack (456).

As she has broken up mentally, Gerald breaks up physically. Singleness of being is violated by any 'love', sensual or spiritual, which demands merging or uses compulsion. The drowned Diana had her arms locked round the neck of the young man who had tried to save her in an earlier image of such deadly compulsion. Gerald tries to strangle Gudrun, but his will breaks and he wanders off to his own death by merging. The moon is another symbol of this consuming 'love':

A small bright moon shone brilliantly just ahead, on the right, a painful brilliant thing that was always there, unremitting, from which there was no escape (464).

And Gerald's conviction that he is about to be murdered is brought into consciousness by the sight of a half-buried crucifix. Sacrifice and murder are both extremes to which the love which merges or compels can lead, extreme forms of the violation and disintegration of self and soul. Gerald's corpse becomes 'cold, mute Matter'. Birkin remembers 'the beautiful face of one whom he had loved'

and who had died still having the faith to yield to the mystery. That dead face was beautiful, no one could call it cold, mute, material. No one could remember it without gaining faith in the mystery, without the soul's warming with new, deep life trust (471).

Gerald's 'tragedy' is 'a stupendous assertion of not-being' (*CL* 446)—a lapsing of trust in life, with its consequent loss of purpose, direction, coherence, and, ultimately, humanity and being.

§5

We are never allowed to forget that Gerald is the representative and embodiment of European industrial civilisation and its associated values. His death by freezing is symbolic of the failure of that civilisation to preserve any contact with the life-source, with warmth and colour, through spontaneity, movement, interchange:

Who can do it? Nobody. Yet we have all got to do it, or else suffer ascetic tortures of starvation and privation or distortion and overstrain and slow collapse into corruption. The whole of life is one long, blind effort at an established polarity with the outer universe, human and non-human; and the whole of modern life is a shrieking failure. It is our own fault (*Psychoanalysis and the Unconscious* 119).

But if 'nobody' can do it, if the 'whole' of modern life is a shrieking failure, where do Birkin and Ursula fit in? Where do they find sustenance in this waste land?

Birkin and Ursula enact at least the first two stages of the process that Lawrence desiderates and are left, at the end, still grappling with the third stage.

Stage 1. The isolate self in proud singleness of being.

Stage 2. The polarity, the equipoise of an achieved sexual harmony.

Stage 3. A conscious purpose in life, a coordinated effort towards a society which will embody life-values—'A number of people united...to fulfil collectively the highest truth known to them' (*CL* 462).

'The extant social world', of which Gerald and Gudrun are representative, groans on the brink of the bottomless pit, and finally topples. We notice, almost peripherally at this stage, that Birkin and Ursula have managed to cling to the edge. They are left isolated, wandering, Ursula satisfied to have Birkin, but Birkin groping for some further bearings, for a social context in which to struggle, for something beyond their marriage to get into relationship with, for a purpose for which the sexual achievement is merely a precondition.

Civilisation is corrupt, putrefying. The individual is within society; we 'roam in the belly of our era'. If the novel is to be about what is, and not about the end of the rainbow, it must concern itself with characters trying to live within this context of disintegration. For this reason Birkin and his values can have no 'social objectification', no presentable context in action within the world of the novel, which is still the real world—'social England' at a specific point in history, a moment of debacle. Where society is death, life can only be found outside any given social context. The struggle to find identity, relationship and purpose takes place in a vacuum. In cutting themselves off from society, Birkin and Ursula are, in a sense, cutting themselves off from the novel. Hence the evasions and mystifications of the writing at points.

The success of Gerald depends partly on the fulness of his presentation as a social personality (coal and diamond) and partly on the complex ice-imagery which, metaphorical at first, grows by the ending into a myth—symbol and narrative fusing in the enactment of the psychic dissolution. Birkin's crucial image is star-equilibrium, but Lawrence fails to work this into the story in any other form than in Birkin's own set-speeches. Consequently it fails to become an organic part of the novel. And even the death-by-snow myth is worked in a little too consciously, so that the moon-stoning or the excursion to the Alps, brilliantly done as they are, seem a little arbitrary. If we contrast Gerald's death with Cathcart's in *The Man Who Loved Islands*, we see that in the later story we can respond to the snow as snow and the symbolism looks after itself. Whereas, in *Women in Love*, we have to be conscious throughout that snow has a whole complex of meaning. We have to remember all the contexts in which the word (and such associated words as ice, white, cold, Northern, etc.) has appeared. The meaning we should attach to the word outside the novel is almost lost sight of under its symbolic accretions. In the late works the images are rarer, less complex and insistent.

Nor can we be altogether happy about Birkin. He is almost pure carbon. He descends on Ursula at the beginning more like a *deus ex machina* than a ministry inspector. He has no relations. Apart from his affair with Hermione, he has no past. He remains elusive throughout. His inscrutability is finally passed off as 'immemorial potency'.

The failures are marginal but significant. The pervasive mis-anthropy gives the clue to the rather tenuous quality of the book's positives. The social context is much less rich than it was in *The*

Rainbow, and scarcely exists in the second half of the novel, where the world is virtually reduced to five characters. H. M. Daleski has perceptively noted the social significance of these lives:

> Birkin and Ursula, clinging to the life preserver of their own 'unison in separateness', abandon ship; Gerald and Gudrun, by trying to destroy each other, symbolically prefigure in themselves the desire for death of those who do not attempt to leave the ship—a desire, it is implied, which is to achieve its shattering consummation in the general wreck that lies ahead. There is, therefore, no internal division in the book between the social and the personal, for all the 'social scenes' are designed to evoke that background of impending ruin against which the personal drama is enacted, and in relation to which it derives its ultimate meaning (*The Forked Flame*, 128).

Birkin and Ursula, despite the relative success of their marriage, have already begun that movement away from all other relationships and commitments (even the commitment to 'creation and productive happiness') which is to give *Aaron's Rod* its peculiar sense of demoralisation.

CHAPTER 5

CHRONOLOGY

In June 1917 Lawrence was called up for his second medical examination, but was rejected. In October 1917 he and Frieda were expelled from Cornwall on suspicion of spying.

AARON'S ROD (Seltzer, 1922).

Begun by December 1917 (*CL* 655). First draft finished in September 1919 (Nehls I, 505). Taken up again in July 1920 and finished in May 1921 (*CL* 655).

MOVEMENTS IN EUROPEAN HISTORY (Oxford, 1921).

Lawrence was approached by a representative of the Oxford University Press at the beginning of July 1918, and began work immediately (AH 449, 450). The work dragged over the last months of 1918, but was finished by January 1919 (AH 467). The text was revised in April 1919 (*CL* 585) and a new chapter added on Italian Unification in November 1920 (*CL* 636). An epilogue was added in September 1924 (*CL* 810).

TOUCH AND GO (C. W. Daniel, London, 1920; *Plays*, 1933; *Complete Plays*, 1965).

On 5 November 1918, Lawrence wrote to Amy Lowell that he had recently finished this play (Moore, 246).

THE BLIND MAN (*English Review*, July 1920; *England, My England*, Seltzer, 1922).

Finished by 21 November 1918 (*CL* 566).

EDUCATION OF THE PEOPLE (*Phoenix*, 1936).

Four essays intended for *The Times Educational Supplement*, written in November and early December 1918 (*CL* 566, 570).

THE FOX (*Dial*, May–August 1922; *The Ladybird*, Secker, 1923).

The first version (*A D. H. Lawrence Miscellany*) was written in November 1918 (*CL* 566). The story was rewritten in the summer of 1919 and a new ending added in mid-November 1921 (Tedlock 94).

FANNIE AND ANNIE (*Hutchinson's Magazine*, 21 November 1921).

YOU TOUCHED ME (*Land and Water*, 29 April 1920).

WINTRY PEACOCK (*Metropolitan*, August 1921).

MONKEY NUTS (*Sovereign*, August 1922).

TICKETS PLEASE (*Strand*, April 1919).

These stories from *England, My England* were probably written in the winter of 1918–19.

THE WHISTLING OF BIRDS (*Athenaeum*, 11 April 1919; *Phoenix*).

ADOLF (*Dial*, September 1920; *Phoenix*).

Written for Murry as editor of the *Athenaeum* in March 1919 (*CL* 581, 584).

'ALL THINGS ARE POSSIBLE' BY LEO SHESTOV (Secker, 1920).

In the summer of 1919 Lawrence completely revised Koteliansky's translation (*CL* 591) and added a foreword by 24 September (*CL* 594).

PREFACE TO THE AMERICAN EDITION OF 'NEW POEMS' (Huebsche, N.Y., 1920).

August 1919 (*CL* 591).

FOREWORD TO 'WOMEN IN LOVE' (Gelber, Lilienthal, San Francisco, 1936).

12 September 1919.

On 14 November 1919 the Lawrences left England for Italy, never to reside here again.

PSYCHOANALYSIS AND THE UNCONSCIOUS (Seltzer, 1921).

Begun December 1919 (*CL* 599) and finished in January 1920 (*CL* 618).

THE LOST GIRL (Secker, 1920).

The final version was begun on 12 February 1920 and finished on 5 May (Tedlock 90) as *Mixed Marriage*.

MR NOON (*A Modern Lover*, Secker, 1934).

Begun 7 May 1920, finished by 22 February 1921 (Tedlock 48).

REX (*Dial*, February 1921; *Phoenix*).

Probably written in June 1920 (Tedlock 90).

AMERICA, LISTEN TO YOUR OWN (*New Republic*, 15 December 1920; *Phoenix*).

September–October 1920.

SEA AND SARDINIA (Seltzer, 1921; the first and third sections first appeared in the *Dial*, October–November 1921).

February–March 1921 (*CL* 645).

A HISTORY OF ITALIAN PAINTING FOR CHILDREN.

Lawrence was asked to do a history of painting for children by De Grey on behalf of the Medici Society. Starting to plan the book in June 1921, Lawrence decided that the supply of illustrations was unsatisfactory, and suggested that he should restrict himself to Italian painting, for which the illustrations were adequate (*CL* 657). Apparently the scheme fell through in July.

FANTASIA OF THE UNCONSCIOUS (Seltzer, 1922).

May–July 1921.

'THE GENTLEMAN FROM SAN FRANCISCO' BY I. A. BUNIN (*Dial*, January 1922; Hogarth Press, Richmond, 1922).

Lawrence began to revise Koteliansky's translation in June 1921 (*CL* 656) and finished it by the beginning of October (Nehls II, 80).

THE CAPTAIN'S DOLL (*The Ladybird*, Secker, 1923).

Begun in October 1921 (*CL* 670), finished by 15 November (*CL* 675).

THE LADYBIRD (Secker, 1923).

Written in December 1921 (*CL* 680).

5

THE WITHERING VISION
1917–1921

Aaron's Rod
The Lost Girl
The Fox

I find things, both in general and in particular, very exasperating. In the first place, I am at the dead end of my money, and can't raise the wind in any direction. Do you think you might know of somebody who would give us something to keep us going a bit. It makes me swear—such a damned, mean, narrow-gutted, pitiful, crawling, mongrel world, that daren't have a man's work and won't even allow him to live...

Still I wait for the day when this foul tension of war and pot-bellied world will break, when we can meet in something like freedom and enjoy each other's company in something like decency. Nowadays one can do nothing but glance behind to see who now is creeping up to do something horrible to the back of one's neck (*CL* 541).

The hot, blind, anguished voice of a man who has seen too much, experienced too much, and doesn't know where to turn...a hot, blind, mesmerised voice, going on and on, mesmerised by a vision that the soul cannot bear (*Aaron's Rod* 108–9).

§1

I DO not wish to devote a great deal of space to negative criticism. Yet we must judge Lawrence's work by his own best standards; and in comparison with what came before and after, the works of the period between the war and Lawrence's arrival in America are clearly of a lower order. It is widely accepted that the full-length novels of the period—*The Lost Girl*, *Aaron's Rod* and *Kangaroo*—are inferior to *The Rainbow* and *Women in Love* in lacking the form, coherence, range and density of those works. They are episodic: the pressure of immediate experience breaks down the form instead of tightening the imaginative grasp and controlling vision. There are many fine things in these novels: one would not be without them. But it is not on them that Lawrence's claim to greatness rests, still less his claim to have made of the novel a finer instrument than it had been before. It is significant, I think, that the works of this period were unusually staggered. The first half of *The Lost Girl* was written in the first three months of 1913. It was not completed until 1920. *Aaron's Rod*, begun in 1917 'very spasmodically', was not finished until 1921. *The Fox* was first written in December 1918, was rewritten in the summer of 1919, and had a new ending added in November 1921. Some of the major novels were, of course, written several times over, but normally in a single creative drive, without long periods of inactivity or turning to something else. But during the period in question it seems that the creative drive would frequently fail to carry Lawrence through to the completion of the work.

After finishing *Women in Love* in July 1916, Lawrence's demoralisation took the form of acute, almost homicidal misanthropy:

I must say I hate mankind—talking of hatred, I have got a perfect androphobia. When I see people in the distance, walking along the path through the fields to Zennor, I want to crouch in the bushes and shoot them silently with invisible arrows of death. I think truly the only righteousness is the destruction of mankind, as in Sodom. Fire and brimstone should fall down.
But I don't want even to hate them—I only want to be in another world than they. Here, it is almost as if one lived on a star, there is a great space of sky and sea in front, in spirit one can circle in space and have the joy of pure motion. But they creep in, the obstructions, the people, like bugs they creep invidiously in, and they are too many to crush. I see them—fat men in white flannel trousers—*père de famille*—and the *familles* passing along the field-path and looking at the scenery. Oh, if one could but have a great box of insect powder, and shake it over them, in the heavens, and exterminate them. Only to clear and cleanse and purify the beautiful earth, and give room for some truth and pure living (Letter to Koteliansky, 4 September 1916; *Encounter*, December 1953, p. 31).

Persecution and poverty were to deepen Lawrence's distress in the next years—experiences he was still scarcely able to write about in 1922 (the 'Nightmare' chapter of *Kangaroo*). You cannot make fiction out of hatred for humanity unless your conception of art is radically different from Lawrence's. Of Thomas Mann he had written in 1913:

And so, with real suicidal intention, like Flaubert's, he sits, a last too-sick disciple, reducing himself grain by grain to the statement of his own disgust, patiently, self-destructively, so that his statement at least may be perfect in a world of corruption (*Phoenix* 312).

Lawrence's androphobia never threatened to drive him in this direction, as the last-quoted sentence from the Koteliansky letter clearly indicated. Rather, he moved away from fiction altogether:

Philosophy interests me most now—not novels or stories. I find people ultimately boring: and you can't have fiction without people. So fiction does not, at bottom, interest me any more. I am weary of humanity and human things. One is happy only in the thoughts that transcend humanity (*CL* 514).

The years 1917–19 produced only two full-length works, neither of them fiction—*Studies in Classic American Literature* and *Movements in European History*. Both must have involved a great deal of reading and research. We cannot doubt that they would have been set aside had any imaginative work demanded attention. *Aaron's Rod* Lawrence describes to his friends with much less enthusiasm than any earlier novel:

February 21st 1918

I am doing some philosophic essays, also, very spasmodically, another daft novel. It goes slowly—very slowly and fitfully, but I don't care (*CL* 543).

By June 1918 Lawrence had lost interest in all writing:

I have finished up all the things I am writing at present—have a complete blank in front of me—feel very desperate, and ready for anything, good or bad. I think something critical will happen this month—finally critical. If it doesn't I shall bust (*CL* 558).

The armistice possibly saved Lawrence from doing something really rash:

Well, my dear Kot, I am at the end of my line. I had rather be hanged or put in prison than endure any more. So now I shall move actively, personally, do what I can. I am a desperado (*CL* 563).

In response to the peace Lawrence was able to salvage from beneath this desperation a grain of hope for a 'new world of spring':

We may not choose the world. We have hardly any choice for ourselves. We follow with our eyes the bloody and horrid line of march of extreme winter, as it passes away. But we cannot hold back the spring. We cannot make the birds silent, prevent the bubbling of the wood-pigeons. We cannot stay the fine world of silver-fecund creation from gathering itself and taking place upon us. Whether we will or no, the daphne tree will soon be giving off perfume, the lambs dancing on two feet, the celandines will twinkle all over the ground, there will be a new heaven and new earth (*Phoenix* 4).

But post-war Europe turned out to be quite capable of holding back the spring indefinitely, and Lawrence's desperation soon returned.

§2

The essays and theoretical works continue to hold out the hope of a new world built on 'the old passion of deathless friendship between man and man':

In the great move ahead, in the wild hope which rides on the brink of death, men go side by side, and faith in each other alone stays them. They go side by side. And the extreme bond of deathless friendship supports them over the edge of the known and into the unknown (*Phoenix* 665).

But first he must forge from his relationship with the woman a proud singleness of being:

Men, being themselves made new after the act of coition, wish to make the world new. A new, passionate polarity springs up between men who are bent on the same activity...It is now daytime, and time to forget sex, time to be busy making a new world...Primarily and supremely man is always the pioneer of life, adventuring onward into the unknown, alone with his own temerarious, dauntless soul (*Fantasia of the Unconscious*).

This is the position Birkin has reached at the end of *Women in Love*, and we might expect the hero of the next novel to be a Birkin-figure moving out from the success of his marriage to take his place among the pioneers.

But Aaron's leap into the unknown is made from very different ground. His marriage has failed, and we are given no hint that it has ever been satisfactory. He leaps because he is at the end of his tether. He is like a stray dog, broken loose, and looking for a new master. Aaron's rod is his only guide through uncharted experience:

Allons, there is no road yet, but we are all Aarons with rods of our own (*Fantasia of the Unconscious* 18).

Aaron Sissons's rod is his independent spirit, his self-sufficiency. In so far as it might bud, it is his hope of fulfilment. It is also the phallus, which he hopes will be the vehicle of that fulfilment. And finally it is his flute which gives voice to the creative impulse foiled in its human contacts. The flute corresponds to the spontaneous bird-song of *The Whistling of Birds*, which 'we cannot prevent'. But Aaron's 'sixteenth-century Christmas melody, very limpid and delicate', is prevented by something in the very air:

As he sat he was physically aware of the sounds of the night: the bubbling of water in the boiler, the faint sound of the gas, the sudden crying of the baby in the next room, then noises outside, distant boys shouting, distant rags of carols, fragments of voices of men. The whole country was roused and excited (8).

But the excitement is far from the religious awe which had characterised Christmas Eve for the Brangwen girls. Aaron's daughters love the Christmas-tree decorations so possessively that the loveliest is wilfully broken with the first of a whole series of explosions which punctuate the novel. The carol singers do 'vocal violence' to their music. The Christmas excitement and hilarity is purely nervous, masking a deadness which in turn masks a real hysteria and homicidal madness:

It was Christmas Eve. Also the war was over, and there was a sense of relief that was almost a new menace. A man felt the violence of the nightmare released now into the general air (1).

The war has been a great explosion of society and all its forms and assumptions, a sundering of men, like bits of shrapnel flying apart from each other out into a void and there drifting:

He had only flown loose from the old centre-fixture...He swung wildly about from place to place, as if he were broken (158).

He was breaking loose from one connection after another: and what for? Why break every tie? Snap, snap, snap went the bonds and ligatures which bound him to the life that had formed him, the people he had loved or liked. He found all his affections snapping off, all the ties which had united him with his own people coming asunder. And why? In God's name, why? What was there instead? (174).

Had Lawrence been one for epigraphs, he might have taken these lines from *The Second Coming*, Yeats's vision of the same nightmare, published the year before *Aaron's Rod*:

Things fall apart; the centre cannot hold;
Mere anarchy is loosed upon the world,
The blood-dimmed tide is loosed, and everywhere
The ceremony of innocence is drowned;
The best lack all conviction, while the worst
Are full of passionate intensity.

Throughout *Aaron's Rod* things break, people separate, presenting a cumulative image of social disintegration, so that Lilly can comment on the news of a broken engagement: 'World coming to pieces bit by bit.' The whole structure of the novel is centrifugal.

Having failed to achieve Birkin's polarity in his marriage, Aaron recoils from the dominance of the 'female impulse' in his domestic life, the impulse towards inertia and routine, and responds to his own deepest 'male impulse'—'centrifugal... fleeing abroad, away from the centre, outward to infinite vibration' (*Phoenix* 457). He drifts to London, then to Italy, vaguely seeking Lilly, who seems to offer the only hope of a meaningful relationship. But Lilly is absent for most of the book. All Aaron's other relationships fail to blossom; and all the relationships he observes between others are revealed as futile. Aaron certainly lacks all conviction; and he is terrified by the passionate intensity both of the women who love him and the political mobs, bolshevists and anarchists, which he hates. Lilly finally convinces him that love and hate are both manifestations of bullying:

The anarchist, the criminal, the murderer, he is only the extreme lover acting on the recoil. It flies back, the love-urge, and becomes a horror (285).

Unlike Yeats, Lilly has no nostalgia for the order of the pre-war world, the country-house life of the leisured class. 'The house where all's accustomed, ceremonious' that Yeats prays (in 1919) that his daughter's bridegroom will bring her to, would have seemed to Lilly/Lawrence just the sort of Heartbreak House in which the seeds of violence were sown. There is no adult innocence which is not the product of bitter experience; and the forms of any class or culture are valuable only to push off from in the certainty that wherever integrity (which is both innocence and fulfilment) is to be found, it is not there. The ceremony of innocence is gently but thoroughly punctured by Lawrence in the person of Corinna Wade, an elderly, cultured English authoress:

She was charming in her old-fashioned manners too, as if the world were still safe and stable, like a garden in which delightful culture, and choice ideas bloomed safe from wind and weather. Alas, never was Aaron more conscious of the crude collapse in the world than when he listened to this animated, young-seeming lady from the safe days of the seventies. All the old culture and choice ideas seemed like blowing bubbles...Aaron listened spellbound, watching the bubbles float round his head, and almost hearing them go pop (261).

Shaw's preface to *Heartbreak House*, written in 1919, is a highly relevant document, with much of the courage and sanity of Lawrence's analysis of the war and immediate post-war hysteria. Of the inhabitants of the country houses of Europe Shaw writes:

They took the only part of our society in which there was leisure for high culture, and made it an economic, political, and, as far as practicable, a moral vacuum; and as Nature, abhorring the vacuum, immediately filled it up with sex and with all sorts of refined pleasures, it was a very delightful place at its best for moments of relaxation. In other moments it was disastrous.

Lawrence introduces us to three such Heartbreak Houses—the Bricknell home in Beldover, the Franks home at Novara in Northern Italy, and the del Torre home in Florence—each of them fits Shaw's description: 'The same nice people, the same utter futility.' In the play itself Shaw's primary symbols are also Lawrence's—drifting without a rudder, and explosion. Shaw even compares the explosions to orchestral music, and has Randall play his flute while the Home Counties burn. As the bombers approach, the occupants of Heartbreak House turn on all the lights and stand out in the garden. They think of setting fire to the house themselves. They hope the bombers will return the following night. The Bricknell set in *Aaron's Rod* have the same lust for a violent debacle: a civil war would be even better than fighting Germans:

'You'd feel you were doing something, in a civil war.'
'Pulling the house down,' said Lilly.
'Yes,' she cried. 'Don't you hate it, the house we live in—London—England—America!...
What I should really like more than anything would be an end of the world...a great big upheaval—and then darkness...' (56, 62).

Shotover is Shaw's Lilly, his leader-figure with all the answers. Shotover's answer is navigation (sane government); but first he must wrest by violence the power of life and death from the insane.

Lilly's answer is ambivalent:

Why can't they submit to a bit of healthy human authority? (91)

at one moment—

A man should remain himself, not try to spread himself over humanity. He should pivot himself on his own pride (92) the next. The division of humanity into those who have sufficient 'living pride' to pivot on, and those who must, in the absence of it, submit, is partly racial, and the passage in question (92) has often provided ammunition for those accusing Lawrence of Fascist tendencies. The penultimate chapter furnishes more such ammunition. There Lilly rejects every idea and ideal European civilisation has produced as dead and stinking:

> The ideal of love, the ideal that it is better to give than receive, the ideal of liberty, the ideal of the brotherhood of man, the ideal of the sanctity of human life, the ideal of what we call goodness, charity, benevolence, public spiritedness, the ideal of sacrifice for a cause, the ideal of unity and unanimity—all the lot (271).

When accused of nihilism and challenged to produce his alternative, Lilly replies:

> You've got to have a sort of slavery again. People are not *men*: they are insects and instruments, and their destiny is slavery. They are too many for me, and so what I think is ineffectual. But ultimately they will be brought to agree—after sufficient extermination—and then they will elect for themselves a proper and healthy and energetic slavery...I mean a real committal of the life-issue of inferior beings to the responsibility of a superior being...It is written between a man's brows which he is (272).

This programme strikes his hearers (as Lawrence knows it must strike his readers), as 'the preposterous pretentiousness of a megalomaniac...criminal-imbecile pretensions' (273). At this point Lilly turns on his critic with a smile:

> Bah, Levison—one can easily make a fool of you. Do you take this as my gospel?...
> Why, I'll tell you the real truth. I think every man is a sacred and holy individual, *never* to be violated. I think there is only one thing I hate to the verge of madness, and that is *bullying*. To see any living creature *bullied*, in *any* way, almost makes a murderer of me. That is true. Do you believe it—? (273).

We have seen in Lilly's relationship with Aaron his utter refusal to put any kind of pressure on Aaron, to take any responsibility for his life or deprive him of the least fraction of his freedom. Obviously this second credo is true; and obviously the former one was a deliberately provocative overstatement or caricature, tongue-in-cheek. But there is a grain of truth in it which the second statement does not altogether invalidate.

In the next and last chapter Lilly is able to return to the leadership theme in all seriousness and with no sense of inconsistency. The ambivalence in the penultimate chapter is resolved not by words, but by symbolic action; for before Lilly can be driven to define his position more fully, the conversation is brutally terminated by the novel's last and greatest explosion as a bomb bursts in the café, producing an 'awful gulfing whirlpool of horror in the social life' (273). Later Aaron finds his flute smashed to pieces among the debris. When he first arrived in the city soldiers had deliberately jostled him and taken his wallet:

If they had stabbed him it could hardly have had a greater effect on him... For surely a very ugly evil spirit had struck him, in the midst of that gang of Italian soldiers. He knew it—it had pierced him. It had *got* him (225–6).

In Milan before that he had sensed 'a curious vacancy in the city —something empty and depressing in the great human centre' (177). The emptiness and tension had foreboded senseless violence, two inexplicable shots in the street, as if the vacuum at the heart of the city had suddenly imploded. In this context, the final bomb outrage, of which no explanation is offered, has the same kind of symbolic rightness and richness as the breaking string in *The Cherry Orchard*. Aaron must now acknowledge that his rod will never blossom; his selfhood has suffered the final violation. Being himself has meant no more than following his nose, running in ever-increasing circles:

If he had to yield his wilful independence, and give himself, then he would rather give himself to the little, individual *man* than to any of the rest. For to tell the truth, in the man was something incomprehensible, which had dominion over him, if he chose to allow it (280).

He acknowledges Lilly as 'his mind's hero':

Aaron looked at Lilly, and saw the same odd, distant look on his face as on the face of some animal when it lies awake and alert, yet perfectly at one with its surroundings. It was something quite different from happiness: an alert enjoyment of rest, and intense and satisfying sense of centrality (283).

Lilly here seems to have found a 'true relationship' with everything, which has so far eluded Aaron. The scene is not clinching, because it is the only scene in the book where Lawrence has allowed himself the luxury of a rural scene with sunshine and silence—an environment it is not difficult to be at one with. We need to know how Lilly keeps himself 'life-central' in relation to the incipient violence and madness of urban life.

Something of this has, I think, been given to us in the crucial early chapter 'The War Again'. 'It is written between a man's brows', Lilly tells Aaron, whether he is a heroic soul or not. In the earlier chapter we were told of Captain Herbertson that 'between his brows there was a tension like madness'. His soul has failed to awake from the nightmare of the war:

'In—let me see—1916—the German guns were a lot better than ours. Ours were old, and when they're old you can't tell where they'll hit: whether they'll go beyond the mark, or whether they'll fall short. Well, this day our guns were firing short, and killing our own men. We'd had the order to charge, and were running forward, and I suddenly felt hot water spurting on my neck—' He put his hand to the back of his neck and glanced round apprehensively.

'It was a chap called Innes. Oh, an awfully decent sort—people were in the Argentine. He'd been calling out to me as we were running, and I was just answering. When I felt this hot water on my neck, and saw him running past me with no head—he'd got no head, and he went running past me. I don't know how far, but a long way...Blood, you know. Yes, well...' (109–10).

Lilly's response to this is to assert that

it never happened...Not to me or to any man, in his own self. It took place in the automatic sphere, like dreams do. But the *actual man* in every man was just absent—asleep—or drugged—inert—dream-logged.

There was a wakeful, self-possessed bit of me which knew that the war and all that horrible movement was false for me. And so I wasn't going to be dragged in. The Germans could have shot my mother or me or what they liked: I wouldn't have joined the *war*. I would like to kill my enemy. But become a bit of that huge obscene machine they called the war, that I never would, no, not if I died ten deaths and had eleven mothers violated.

No man who was awake and in possession of himself would use poison gasses: no man. His own awake self would scorn such a thing (113–14).

Men like Herbertson had displayed plenty of death-courage, but no life-courage:

We'll *never* get anywhere till we stand up man to man and face *everything* out, and break the old forms, but never let our own pride and courage of life be broken (115–16).

The war had revealed the essential sterility of all the old ideals. Loving and sacrificing, and their complements 'anarchising and throwing bombs', are all evasions of this basic responsibility to the only stable centre 'the Holy Ghost which is inside you, your own soul's self'. The anarchy and flying asunder of the era is good if it makes for a 'clearance' and frees the individual from the clutter of irrelevant ties and allegiances. The dead leaves must be shaken from the tree before it can put forth new buds.

In the final chapter Lilly takes up the argument again. The love-urge is exhausted. Lilly proposes life in a new mode, the power-mode:

It is a vast dark source of life and strength in us now, waiting either to issue into true action, or to burst into cataclysm...It urges from within, darkly, for the displacing of the old leaves, the inception of the new (288).

The power-urge is, then, simply the principle of growth from the living centre, without reference to any God or goal outside the self. Once life in the love-mode is abandoned, the souls of women will wish to yield themselves to men, and the mass of men will wish to submit 'to the heroic soul in a greater man'. The argument at this stage is not convincing, and Aaron, despite the need to yield which he acknowledges, is not convinced: 'You'll never get it.' The sceptical note on which the novel ends leaves the leadership issue in the air, to be taken up again, more frontally, in *Kangaroo*.

The reader, it seems certain, is intended, at the end of *Aaron's Rod*, to feel that Aaron ought to submit to Lilly. But, though we can see what Lilly has to offer as friend, or even guide, the novel presents few of his credentials as leader. Indeed, his insistence on going about his own business without reference to the social world would seem to preclude such pretensions. It does not help us, at the end, to be told that his face 'was like a Byzantine eikon'.

Even in the overtly political novel, *Kangaroo*, the leadership issue is translated by Lawrence into a personal, almost physical relationship between two men, Somers and Jack at first, Somers and Kangaroo later; in the first case Somers as leader, in the second as follower. It is the same with Lilly and Aaron as it was with Birkin and Gerald. And the common factor in all these relationships is the pressure away from leadership as a form of social organisation towards what looks very much more like a homosexual relationship. The Birkin–Gerald relationship is much less overtly homosexual in the published *Women in Love*, despite the wrestling scene, than it seems from early drafts was originally intended:

It satisfied him (Birkin) to have to do with Gerald Crich, it fulfilled him to have this other man, this hard-limbed traveller and sportsman, following implicitly, held as it were consummated within the spell of a more powerful understanding. Birkin felt a passion of desire for Gerald Crich, for the clumsier, cruder intelligence and the limited soul, and for the striving, unenlightened body of his friend. And Gerald Crich, not understanding, was transfused with pleasure. He did not even know he loved Birkin (*Texas Quarterly*, Spring 1963, 101).

Lilly does not quite succeed in transforming this kind of relationship into the sort of political programme outlined in *Fantasia of the Unconscious*:

The leaders must stand for life, and they must not ask the simple followers to point out the direction. When the leaders assume responsibility they relieve the followers forever of the burden of finding a way. Relieved of this hateful incubus of responsibility for general affairs, the populace can again become free and happy and spontaneous, leaving matters to their superiors. No newspapers—the mass of the people never learning to read. The evolving once more of the great spontaneous gestures of life.

We can't go on as we are. Poor, nerve-worn creatures, fretting our lives away and hating to die because we have never lived. The secret is to commit into the hands of the sacred few the responsibility which now lies like torture on the mass. Let the few, the leaders be increasingly responsible for the whole. And let the mass be free: free, save for the choice of leaders. Leaders —this is what mankind is craving for. But men must be prepared to obey, body and soul, once they have chosen the leader. And let them choose the leader for life's sake only. Begin then—there is a beginning (84).

I have said that the structure of the novel is centrifugal. It might be argued that this is almost to say that it is structureless. Relationships scarcely develop. New characters come in for a chapter or two, then disappear. The scene changes with similar rapidity and seeming inconsequence. The only thing Aaron moves towards is Lilly:

He had perhaps a faint sense of Lilly ahead of him: an impulse in that direction: or else merely an illusion (174).

But Lilly is absent for most of the book, and is not a very tangible figure when present. Lawrence does not avoid the great danger that the novel itself, like the society it depicts, will be hollow at the centre. Indeed, the central chapters XIII–XV are among Lawrence's worst, full of offhand smugness of the kind which vitiates *Mr Noon*, self-conscious apologies to the reader, untransmuted essay material. In *The Rainbow* and *Women in Love*

Lawrence had developed the appropriate artistic resources to cope with this kind of probing below the day-time consciousness of a character. He cannot draw on these resources in *Aaron's Rod* because the novelist himself to a large extent shares the doubts and vacillations of his characters. The vision of disintegration has overwhelmed the integrity of the artist, which cannot create firm values out of the chaos he contemplates. The authenticity of that vision stands, eliciting our admiration that the artist can maintain even a shaky sanity.

§3

Lawrence is now beginning to associate his leader-figure with the demons of the underworld, the gods of darkness. But in this phase of spiritual sickness he cannot decide whether that darkness is a rich source of life and health, or whether it is the darkness of total annihilation.

The exploration of darkness continues in *The Lost Girl*. The darkness of the pit has become part of Lawrence's mythology, an underworld where human contact is by touch and knowledge is intuition. Alvina's visit down the mine opens her eyes to the fact that the ordinary day-world is but the surface of the darkness:

The miners seemed to her to loom tall and grey, in their enslaved magic. Slaves who would cause the superimposed day-order to fall. Not because, individually, they wanted to. But because, collectively, something bubbled up in them, the force of darkness which had no master and no control. It would bubble and stir in them as earthquakes stir the earth. It would be simply disastrous, because it had no master. There was no dark master in the world. The puerile world went on crying out for a new Jesus, another Saviour from the sky, another heavenly superman. When what was wanted was a Dark Master from the Underworld (49).

What was this secret knowledge they brought with them from the darkness? Alvina is forced into awareness of her own secret urges, the attraction of forbidden experiences:

There was a thickness in the air, a sense of dark, fluid presence in the thick atmosphere, the dark, fluid, viscous voice of the collier making a broad-vowelled, clapping sound in her ear. He seemed to linger near her as if he knew—as if he knew—what? Something for ever unknowable and inadmissible, something that belonged purely to the underground: to the slaves who work underground: knowledge humiliated, subjected, but ponderous and inevitable (48).

Cicio inhabits the mysterious world below consciousness, a mindless, savage world, into which he summons Alvina. Mrs Tuke calls him an animal and Alvina atavistic for responding to him, for subjecting her individuality to 'forces', prostituting herself. Alvina herself feels like a sacred prostitute; but the word 'sacred' indicates the gulf between her own position and Mrs Tuke's. We can sympathise with Alvina when she says:

There are good life-forces. Even the will of God is a life-force...You should have faith in life...Perhaps life itself is something bigger than intelligence (291–2).

She denies that Cicio is just an animal; he is 'something else'. But the novel is hardly more convincing than Alvina in defining that something:

Was he just stupid and bestial? The thought went clean through her. His yellow eyes watched her sardonically. It was the clean modelling of his dark, other-world face that decided her—for it sent the deep spasm across her (185).

How much further does the word 'spasm' take us? We hear about his 'demon quality', his 'strange mesmeric power over her, as if he possessed the sensual secrets, and she was to be subjected' (297). We can find nothing in him for her to yield to except his sexual potency, which is asked to stand for life itself, health, sanity. In Katherine Mansfield's words, 'this is the doctrine of mindlessness'. Alvina loses herself in the dark void at the centre of him, becomes, like him, 'inhumanly regardless', so that her own humanity succumbs without resistance to the savage spirit of Califano:

It stole away the soul of Alvina. She felt transfigured in it, clairvoyant in another mystery of life. A savage hardness came into her heart. The gods who had demanded human sacrifice were quite right, immutably right. The fierce, savage gods who dipped their lips in blood, these were the true gods (325).

Alvina is 'not morally lost', Lawrence assures us. But we are surely justified in beginning to question his own moral bearings.

§4

Human sacrifice is also involved in some of the shorter fiction of this period, including the two most impressive stories, *The Fox* and *The Captain's Doll*. In the latter we are apparently meant to feel that a human life is a small price to pay for the hero's fulfilment. The physical presence of the captain's wife, Mrs Hepburn (itself hardly necessary and certainly not central), is an obstacle in the development of the relationship between Hepburn and Hannele. Lawrence conveniently drops her out of her bedroom window and glosses over the little incident with a comic tone:

> And then a dreadful thing happened: really a very dreadful thing.

Hepburn proposes to take Hannele to East Africa to get three thousand acres under control and write a book on the moon. Is this really an end to justify such callous means?

The case of Banford in *The Fox* is altogether more complex. Banford, a 'warm, generous soul' with March's own interests always at heart, even if mistakenly, is never established as a merely deadly, life-consuming creature like Granny in *The Virgin and the Gypsy*. She is no more responsible than March herself for the failure of the farming enterprise. Admittedly her animus against Henry derives in part from a crude sense of his social inferiority and in part from her selfish desire to keep March for herself; but there is also a much sounder case:

> I'd no more trust him than I'd trust a cat not to steal. He's deep, he's deep, and he's bossy, and he's selfish through and through, as cold as ice. All he wants is to make use of you (35).

The imagery throughout has established Henry as the hunter, indeed the fox, with Banford and March both in their different ways his victims. It is all along March's submission which he seeks, putting a spell on her:

> ...there is a strange battle, like mesmerism. Your own soul, as a hunter, has gone out to fasten on the soul of the deer...It is your own will which carries the bullet into the heart of your quarry. The bullet's flight home is a sheer projection of your own fate into the fate of the deer (20–1).
>
> But then his spell began to take hold of her. The dark, seething potency of him, the power of a creature that lies hidden and exerts its will to the destruction of the free-running creature...gradually began to take effect on her.

The second passage here is not from *The Fox* at all. It is from *The Rainbow* and describes Will Brangwen's battle with his wife

Anna in the first months of their marriage. And although the imagery is almost identical to that of *The Fox*, we are clearly intended to react strongly against Will and attribute his behaviour to some deep psychological lack or perversion in him:

Gradually she realised that she was being borne down by him, borne down by the clinging, heavy weight of him, that he was pulling her down as a leopard clings to a wild cow and exhausts her and pulls her down. Gradually she realised that her life, her freedom, was sinking under the silent grip of his physical will. He wanted her in his power. He wanted to devour her at leisure, to have her (182).

In *The Fox* this kind of submission in the woman to the cold, consuming fire of the man's willed passion is offered as the only salvation from her null freedom. Lawrence makes no attempt to humanise in Henry the qualities of the fox. Rather, as Ian Gregor has pointed out, he simply replaces the fox in March's consciousness—'the boy was to her the fox and she could not see him otherwise...March lapsed into the odour of the fox...for the youth sent a faint, but distinct odour into the room, indefinable, like a wild creature' (11, 15). Her sexual consciousness is rendered entirely in these terms; and Henry's sexual attraction entirely in terms of the fox with his burning brush.

It is all brilliantly done, drawing on the demonic potency of the real fox from the opening of the story, and the real void in March's psyche which the fox had filled. But the second version of the story, extending the first to three times its original length and introducing the death of Banford, uses the man/fox identification to evade the responsibilities of human consciousness altogether, and to render the taking of human life in terms morally equivalent to the fox's taking of a hen. Henry is shown responding to moral imperatives from within himself which tell him that Banford is deadly (i.e. opposed to his own purposes) and must be killed. And the reader should applaud his murderous skill as in the service of life.

The Fox is important for its development of the isolated image of the horses at the end of *The Rainbow* towards the full realised animal-symbols of *Snake* or *St Mawr*. But the version we know also illustrates the danger of seeking too close an identification between what humanity lacks and what gives splendour to the beasts.

CHAPTER 6

CHRONOLOGY

The Lawrences lived in Sicily from March 1920 to February 1922.

TORTOISES (Seltzer, 1921).

BIRDS, BEASTS AND FLOWERS (Seltzer, 1923).
The earliest poem in the collection is *The Mosquito* which was written in late April 1920. *Peace, Tropic* and *Southern Night* were probably written in June, and *Snake* in July.
Fruits, The Evangelistic Beasts and *Reptiles* date from the autumn of 1920, together with, probably, *The Revolutionary, Cypresses, Turkey Cock* and *Humming Bird*.
Bare Fig Trees and *Bare Almond Trees*, December 1920.
Almond Blossom, probably January 1921.
Hibiscus and Salvia Flowers was written on 31 January, *Purple Anemones* on 4 February and *The Ass* on 2 March.
Sicilian Cyclamens, He Goat and *She Goat* also probably date from the early months of 1921.
The Evening Land was written between April and July, *Fish* in July or August, and *Bat* and *Man and Bat* early in September 1921.
The remaining poems were written after the Lawrences left Europe.

INTRODUCTION TO 'MEMOIRS OF THE FOREIGN LEGION' BY M[AURICE] M[AGNUS] (Secker, 1924).
Probably January 1922 (Tedlock 95).

'MASTRO DON GESUALDO' BY VERGA (Seltzer, 1933).
Begun between 10 and 12 February 1922 (AH 529, *CL* 629). Half-finished by 15 February (Tedlock 95). Finished on board the *Osterley* in March (*CL* 696).

'LITTLE NOVELS OF SICILY' BY VERGA (Seltzer, 1925).
March–April 1922 (*CL* 702, Brewster 250).

'CAVALLERIA RUSTICANA' BY VERGA (Cape, 1928).
The title story, *The She Wolf, Fantasticalities* and *Jeli the Shepherd* were probably translated on board the *Tahiti* in August 1922. The remaining stories were not translated until the autumn of 1927.

6

OTHER WORLDS
1920–1921

Birds, Beasts and Flowers

We want to realise the tremendous *non-human* quality of life...it is wonderful. It is not the emotions, nor the personal feelings and attachments, that matter. These are all only expressive, and expression has become mechanical. Behind it all are the tremendous unknown forces of life, coming unseen and unperceived (*CL* 291).

I saw a most beautiful brindled adder, in the spring, coiled up asleep with her head on her shoulder. She did not hear me till I was very near. Then she must have felt my motion, for she lifted her head like a queen to look, then turned and moved slowly and with delicate pride into the bushes. She often comes into my mind again, and I think I see her asleep in the sun, like a Princess of the fairy world. It is queer, the intimations of other worlds, which one catches (*CL* 486).

§1

THE claim that Lawrence is a poet of real stature is still contentious. Very rarely in the early rhyming poems did he succeed in finding a form which did not muffle or choke back the utterance of his 'demon'. Partly the trouble had been fear of his demon, the natural reticence and conformity of the 'young man'. But mainly it had been his inability to hear formal rhythms. ' I don't write for your ear', he had written to Edward Marsh in 1913:

I can't tell you what *pattern* I see in any poetry, save one complete thing (*CL* 244).

In an earlier letter to Marsh, Lawrence had written:

I have always tried to get an emotion out in its own course, without altering it. It needs the finest instinct imaginable, much finer than the skill of the craftsmen (*CL* 221).

It was, unfortunately, a rather hit-or-miss method. It works, perhaps, in *First Morning*, which is in free verse, and in one or two other poems from *Look! We Have Come Through!*, such as

Green and *Gloire de Dijon*, short lyrics where rhyme is handled, for Lawrence, quite deftly. Usually Lawrence's utter ineptitude with rhyme was even more disabling than his rhythmic flabbiness. The heart sinks on every rhyme-word. Just as a poem begins to spread its wings, the first rhyme will bring it to the ground with a dull thud. Hopkins can use the most outlandish rhymes and convince us that no other word could possibly have served. With Lawrence we feel that almost any other word would have been better than the word he rhymes on:

> The risen lord, the risen lord
> has risen in the flesh,
> and treads the earth to feel the soil
> though his feet are still nesh.

In *A Doe at Evening* we can see how a poem which begins lamely rhyming frees itself in the last two stanzas from this restraint, and achieves a poise we are not to meet again until *Birds, Beasts and Flowers*.

Lawrence wrote very few poems between 1917 and 1920, and none he thought worth collecting. But he did read a great deal of Whitman, whose influence on all Lawrence's subsequent poetry can hardly be overestimated. Whitman released Lawrence's demon from the ethos of Georgian poetry. Lawrence has fully recorded his debt in the first version of his essay on Whitman (1918) and in the Preface to the American edition of *New Poems* (1919). We shall discuss the relationship between Lawrence and Whitman more fully in the last chapter.

§2

Hopkins wrote to Canon Dixon: 'The world is full of things and events, phenomena of all sorts that go without notice, go un-witnessed.' He records in his poems the creative meeting of poet and phenomena. *Birds, Beasts and Flowers* is also a sequence of such meetings. *Snake* is, by general agreement, the finest poem in the book. It is particularly apposite to this discussion because it is virtually a dialogue between the poet's two selves—the 'young man' and the 'demon', the voice of education and the voice of the spontaneous self. It functions on several levels, which is not to say that the encounter with the snake is allegorical, for the several meanings are not discrete but composite. For convenience of discussion we can distinguish three of these: the descriptive and dramatic narrative; the psychological analogue and the myth.

The poem justifies its place in the anthologies simply as a definitive realisation of the appearance and distinctive life-mode of a snake. The technical means (in, for example, the third stanza) are obvious without being at all facile—the sibilant, slithering alliterative s's, the slack, undulating rhythms, the whole stanza trailing through one sentence of seven long lines.

One is tempted at this point to testify yet again to Lawrence's almost occult penetration into the being of other creatures, even of fruits and flowers, his ability to look out through the eyes of a mountain lion, to be a bat flicker-splashing round a room:

> He *could* not go out,
> I also realised...
> It was the light of day which he could not enter,
> Any more than I could enter the white-hot door of a blast furnace.

(Man and Bat)

to be a fish in the waters:

> Your life a sluice of sensation along your sides,
> A flush at the flails of your fins, down the whorl of your tail,
> And water wetly on fire in the grates of your gills.   (*Fish*)

But often the deeper purpose of these poems is to reveal the sheer unknowable otherness of the non-human life. *Fish*, for example, takes us as near to the watery life of the fish as human perception and language seem ever likely to allow:

> Slowly to gape through the waters,
> Alone with the element;
> To sink, and rise, and go to sleep with the waters;
> To speak endless inaudible wavelets into the wave;
> To breathe from the flood at the gills,
> Fish-blood slowly running next to the flood, extracting fish-fire;
> To have the element under one, like a lover;
> And to spring away with a curvetting click in the air,
> Provocative.
> Dropping back with a slap on the face of the flood.
> And merging oneself!

only to continue:

> I saw, dimly,
> Once a big pike rush,
> And small fish fly like splinters.
> And I said to my heart, *there are limits*

To you, my heart;
And to the one God.
Fish are beyond me.

Other Gods
Beyond my range...gods beyond my God...

They are beyond me, are fishes.
I stand at the pale of my being
And look beyond, and see
Fish, in the outerwards,
As one stands on a bank and looks in.

The poet only wonders. He does not know. He is not the measure of creation.

In *Man and Bat* the otherness, the unbroachable barrier, is turned to comic effect:

Let the God who is maker of bats watch with them in their unclean corners...
I admit a God in every crevice,
But not bats in my room;
Nor the God of bats, while the sun shines.

The accidental confusion of worlds here, the bat having entered the indoor daylight world of man, makes the man mad and the bat obscene. At the end of the poem the bat is happily restored to its element. The consequences are more serious for the fish when he is jerked from his element on the end of a line:

And the gold-and-green pure lacquer-mucus comes off in my hand,
And the red-gold mirror-eye stares and dies,
And the water-suave contour dims.

And I, a many-fingered horror of daylight to him,
Have made him die.

The only creature described in this collection which does not receive the poet's unqualified respect is the only one which seeks a relationship with him—Bibbles.

In *Snake*, the water-trough is the neutral meeting-point of two worlds. The snake descends the earth-wall from his fissure; the man descends the steps from his doorway. Each is in need of water.

The human character, Lawrence himself, appears a little ridiculous as he stands in his pyjamas at the water-trough. The snake has priority not simply because it arrived first at the trough, but because it asserts priority in the very quality of its being. The snake looks straight through the man without recognising his existence. In that setting, against the sun, the burning earth, the great dark carob-tree, Etna, he is pathetically out of place, insignificant; whereas the snake belongs:

> Being earth-brown, earth-golden from the burning bowels of the earth
> On the day of Sicilian July, with Etna smoking.

The man feels glad and honoured. The images he chooses to describe the snake reveal his growing appreciation of its stature and significance: first, like cattle, the snake is just another creature, a beast; then, 'like a guest in quiet', he is granted a human equality; 'like a forked night on the air' (a tongue of darkness from the surrounding night flicking into the little day of human consciousness) links him to the wider forces of the cosmos; and 'like a god' exalts the whole episode to the level of a divine visitation from 'one of the lords of life'.

But against this response, calling it effeminate, cowardly, perverse, comes the voice of his education with the opposite imperative—not 'I must stand and wait', but 'He must be killed'. Golden snakes, however beautiful and noble, are dangerous; and danger must be eliminated from life. The taunt 'if you were a man' implies assumptions about manhood and humanity which the poem seeks to question. Does it not mean, in this context, 'if you had the same stereotyped, civilised responses as everyone else, if your intuitive faculty, your natural, spontaneous responses, had been killed in you'. It is the attempt to harm the snake by throwing a log at him as he withdraws which the poem sees as cowardly. He is departing 'peaceful, pacified and thankless'. The log is thrown 'now his back was turned'. The 'intense still noon' swallows up the snake unharmed, and leaves the man feeling paltry, vulgar and mean, and cursing his education.

Sun (1925) gives us a situation very like that of the poem, but a response which is wholly sane:

The child had gone a few yards down the rocky path, round the great sprawling of a cactus. She had seen him, a real gold-brown infant of the winds, with burnt gold hair and red cheeks, collecting the speckled pitcher-flowers and laying them in rows. He could balance now, and was quick for his own emergencies, like an absorbed young animal playing silent. Suddenly she heard him speaking: 'Look, Mummy! Mummy, look!' A note in his bird-like voice made her lean forward sharply. Her heart stood still. He was looking over his naked little shoulder at her and pointing with a loose little hand at a snake which had reared itself up a yard away from him, and was opening its mouth so that its forked, soft tongue flickered black like a shadow, uttering a short hiss.

'Look, Mummy!'

'Yes, darling, it's a snake!' came the slow, deep voice.

He looked at her, his wide blue eyes uncertain whether to be afraid or not. Some stillness of the sun in her reassured him.

'Snake!' he chirped.

'Yes, darling! Don't touch it, it can bite.' The snake had sunk down, and was reaching away from the coils in which it had been basking asleep, and slowly was easing its long, gold-brown body into the rocks, with slow curves. The boy turned and watched it in silence. Then he said: 'Snake going!'

'Yes! Let it go. It likes to be alone.'

He still watched the slow, easing length as the creature drew itself apathetic out of sight.

'Snake gone back', he said.

'Yes, it's gone back. Come to Mummy a moment.' He came and sat with his plump, naked little body on her naked lap, and she smoothed his burnt, bright hair. She said nothing, feeling that everything was passed. The curious soothing power of the sun filled her, filled the whole place like a charm, and the snake was part of the place, along with her and the child.

Thus the snake comes to serve as an analogue for the poet's own manhood, his real 'I' as opposed to 'voices in me', or, to reduce it to Freudian terms, the ego which seeks to mediate between the id (the spontaneous, instinctive self) and the universe. As the snake issues clear from the burning bowels of the earth, so the man must meet him with a response (gladness and humility) which issues cleanly from his own bowels without the intervention of the superego (the voices of his education). In *The Shaping Spirit*, A. Alvarez quotes, in this context, the creed which Lawrence set against Benjamin Franklin's:

That I am I.

That my soul is a dark forest.

That my known self will never be more than a little clearing in the forest.

That gods, strange gods, come forth from the forest into the clearing of my known self, and then go back.

That I must have the courage to let them come and go.

That I will never let mankind put anything over me, but that I will try always to recognize and submit to the gods in me and the gods in other men and women.   (*Studies in Classic American Literature*)

The 'fissure' above the water-trough (which itself suggests fertility), the dark door of the secret earth, clearly, if we remember the earlier poems in the collection, *Pomegranate* and *Figs* (where the word 'fissure' is specifically defined as 'the female part'), combines with the phallic snake in a sexual metaphor. When the voices of education have done their work it becomes, we notice, a 'horrid black hole'. The poet's violent, almost hysterical response to the snake's putting his head into the hole is a symptom of that horror of the sex act which Lawrence saw to be at the root of our nullity and neurosis, and for which he blamed Christianity: 'The Christians, phase by phase, set out actually to *annihilate* the sensual being in man' ('Whitman', *The Symbolic Meaning* 255). In the Christian myth the snake is, indeed, accursed and exiled to the underworld. But for Lawrence it represented 'a deep, deep life which has been denied in us, and still is denied' (Brewster 118). When the poet throws a log at the snake he destroys its dignity, it becomes a convulsed and writhing thing. The affective life, deprived of its natural beauty, dignity and joy becomes obscene and destructive as it had in Bottomley's England.

The repentant poet thinks of the albatross, the life-bringing bird which the Ancient Mariner had shot. The mariner's first punishment had been thirst. Yet still he maintained an attitude of shallow conventional disgust towards the 'slimy things with legs that crawled upon the slimy sea'. Gradually he was brought to accept that everything in nature has its appointed place. He looked at the stars:

The blue sky belongs to them, and is their appointed rest, and their native country and their own natural homes, which they enter unannounced, as lords that are certainly expected and yet there is silent joy at their arrival.

He looked on 'God's creatures of the calm' in a new way:

> Beyond the shadow of the ship,
> I watched the water-snakes;
> They moved in tracks of shining white,
> And when they reared, the elfish light
> Fell off in hoary flakes.
>
> Within the shadow of the ship
> I watched their rich attire:
> Blue, glossy green, and velvet black,
> They coiled and swam; and every track
> Was a flash of golden fire.
>
> O happy living things! no tongue
> Their beauty might declare:
> A spring of love gushed from my heart
> And I blessed them unaware.

Instead of reacting conventionally (snakes are slimy and disgusting), he allows his spontaneous feelings of love and acceptance to find expression. The snakes have their own beauty and their own place in the total God-given pattern. There is a similar passage in *Fish*:

> I saw a water-serpent swim across the Anapo,
> And I said to my heart, *look, look at him!*
> *With his head up, steering like a bird!*
> *He's a rare one, but he belongs...*

Nothing natural is to be rejected by the merely rational human consciousness, which would dam up the spring of love.

At this point the spell on the Mariner breaks and it begins to rain. Life, fertility, natural interchange resumes. We remember the rose-red bride of the opening, set against the ancient withered mariner with his death-dealing cross-bow, to take the sexual implications, too.

Lawrence takes Melville's great white whale to be an almost identical symbol:

What then is Moby Dick?—He is the deepest blood-being of the white race. He is our deepest blood-nature. And he is hunted, hunted, hunted by the maniacal fanaticism of our white mental consciousness. We want to hunt him down...The last phallic being of the white man (*Studies in Classic American Literature* 152).

In a letter to the Brewsters in 1921, Lawrence describes with great gusto how he would like to reverse the process and have the human cowards hunted down by his brightly-burning tigers:

But I don't *want* the tiger superseded. Oh, may each she-tigress have seventy-seven whelps. And may they all grow in strength and shine in stripes like day and night, and may each one eat at least seventy miserable featherless human birds, and lick red chops of gusto after it. Leave me my tigers, leave me spangled leopards, leave me bright cobra snakes, and I wish I had poison fangs and talons as good. I *believe* in wrath and gnashing of teeth and crunching of cowards' bones (*CL* 651).

It takes Lawrence four years to reach a compromise in which the human and the animal live and let live.

§3

The sequence of tortoise poems also represents the best of *Birds, Beasts and Flowers*.

The baby tortoise, 'a tiny, fragile, half-animate bean', is, mythically, taken to be the first incarnation of active, free-ranging life on earth, the prototype for all higher forms:

He is the first of creatures to stand upon his toes, and the door of his house is his heaven. Therefore it is charted out, and is the foundation of the world (Mystical Notes, *Phoenix* 67).

'Bud of the universe', the poems call him, 'pediment of life', 'brisk egg'. He is creation first asserting itself against inanimate chaos:
> And slowly pitching itself against the inertia
> Which had seemed invincible.

He moves forward with 'slow, ageless progress' impelled by the 'indomitable will and pride of the first life'. He is the prototype, too, of the human challenger, pioneer, life-adventurer, Adam, Ulysses:
> All life carried on your shoulder,
> Invincible fore-runner. (*Baby Tortoise*)

But the shell which he pitches in the midst of chaos, 'all animate creation on his shoulder', is also his doom of suffering and sex, the 'slow passion' of assertion and the 'crucifixion of desire', the complexity of an individual creature plotted out, the 'outward and visible indication of the plan within' (*Tortoise Shell*).

The arrogant triumph of his own existence—'a brisk, brindled little tortoise, all to himself'—is torn apart at adolescence by the 'crucifixion into sex'. He is:
> Doomed to make an intolerable fool of himself
> In his effort toward completion again.

Lawrence mocks himself good-humouredly in the figure of the male tortoise:
> He is much smaller,
> Dapper beside her,
> And ridiculously small...
>
> And how he feels it!
> The lonely rambler, the stoic, dignified stalker through chaos,
> The immune, the animate,
> Enveloped in isolation,
> Fore-runner.
> Now look at him! (*Lui et Elle*)

The last poem in the sequence, *Tortoise Shout*, draws on all the sources of meaning tapped in the earlier poems. Lawrence follows the tortoise 'on to the end', 'under the very edge of the farthest far-off horizon of life', through the extremity of crucifixion, to the resurrection. The scream is also a paean, the death-agony a birth-cry. The shriek tears the veil, the soul's membrane,

> ...till the last plasm of my body was melted back
> To the primeval rudiments of life, and the secret.

> The same cry from the tortoise as from Christ, the Osiris-cry of abandonment,
> That which is whole, torn asunder,
> That which is in part, finding its whole again throughout the universe.

The abandonment to life which is coition is celebrated in these poems with the same clarity and splendour as the abandonment to death in *The Ship of Death* and *Bavarian Gentians*.

§4

Cypresses, also written in the autumn of 1920, is about the same 'great secret':

> ...the secret of the long-nosed Etruscans,
> The long-nosed, sensitive-footed, subtly-smiling Etruscans,
> Who made so little noise outside the cypress groves.

The 'supple, brooding, softly-swaying pillars of dark flame', the cypresses, are said to be 'monumental' to the dead race of the Etruscans, silently speaking the lost language, darkly exuding the lost life, sinuous and flame-tall, a home still for the spirits of the lost whom Lawrence invokes

> To bring their meaning back into life again,
> Which they have taken away
> And wrapt inviolable in soft cypress-trees,
> Etruscan cypresses.

In the 'Mystical Notes' Lawrence comments: 'It is said, a disease has attacked the cypress trees of Italy, and they are all dying. Now, even the shadow of the lost secret is vanishing from earth.' For as we have banished the snake to the underworld, so in accepting the Roman verdict that the Etruscans were vicious, we share the guilt of the Romans for their extinction:

> For oh, I know, in the dust where we have buried
> The silenced races and all their abominations,
> We have buried so much of the delicate magic of life.

§5

There is a wide gulf between these poems and the prose of this period; for in the prose works there must be human characters living in the world of men:

But it is a world of Canaille; absolutely. Canaille, canaglia, Schweinhunderei, stinkpots. Pfui!—pish, pshaw, prrr! They all stink in my nostrils. That's how I feel in Taormina, let the Ionian sea have fits of blueness if it likes, and Calabria twinkle like seven jewels, and the white trumpet-tree under the balcony perfume six heavens with sweetness. That's how I feel. A curse, a murrain, a pox in this crawling, sniffling, spunkless brood of humanity (*CL* 669).

Nature is providing the standards against which humanity is judged and condemned:

But how lovely it is here! I'm sure you've forgotten: the great window of the eastern sky, seaward. I like it much the best of any place in Italy: and adore Fontana Vecchia. But my heart and my soul are broken, in Europe. It's no use, the threads are broken. I will go east, intending ultimately to go west (Brewster 27).

CHAPTER 7

CHRONOLOGY

In March 1922 the Lawrences arrived in Ceylon and
in April in Australia.

BIRDS, BEASTS AND FLOWERS.

Elephant describes incidents of 23 March 1922 (AH 540). *Kangaroo*,
summer 1922.

KANGAROO (Secker, 1923).

Begun by 3 June (Luhan 34), finished by 24 July (Brewster 59) except for
the last chapter which was added at Taos in September.

THE BOY IN THE BUSH (Secker, 1924).

Lawrence proposed recasting *The House of Ellis* to Mollie Skinner on
2 September 1923 (*CL* 751). He began to do so in October (*CL* 760), and
finished it on 14 November (AH 585).

7

THE LONG TRAVAIL

1922

Kangaroo
The Boy in the Bush

I feel as if I had a child of black fury curled up inside my bowels. I'm sure I can feel exactly what it is to be pregnant, because of the weary bowel burden of a kind of contained murder which I can't bring forth (AH 438).

§1

LAWRENCE'S fiction must suffer when it is asked merely to draw off his anger:

If I hadn't my own stories to amuse myself with I should die, chiefly of spleen (*CL* 670).

The novel which suffers most is *Kangaroo*. It also seems to have been the novel over which Lawrence spent least time and effort. Unlike most of his novels, it was, apparently, written only once, and that within a few weeks. This makes the evocation of Australian scenery and character all the more remarkable. The novel contains within it a fine travel book. The autobiographical material, apart from the 'Nightmare' chapter, focuses on the marriage between Richard Lovat Somers and Harriet, here more clearly Lawrence and Frieda than any other couple in his fiction. The perpetual cut and thrust between them is clearly far more than mere domestic bickering. It is also give and take. Harriet sees her husband not only turning his attention outwards, away from his relationship with her and excluding her, but also exposing himself to betrayal and further disillusion. He is likely to be taken in, not because of the real merits of Kangaroo and his Diggers, but because of the pressure from within to find some body of men with whom to associate himself, through whose organisation to channel his energies:

Because I feel I *must* fight out something with mankind yet. I haven't finished with my fellow men. I've got a struggle with them yet...To make some kind of an opening—some kind of a way for the afterwards...I intend to move with men and get men to move with me before I die...I have the roots of my life with you. But I want if possible to send out a new shoot in the life of mankind—the effort man makes for ever, to grow into new forms (64-5).

Harriet replies:

Send out a new shoot then. Send it out. You do it in your writing already! But getting yourself mixed up with these impudent little people won't send any shoots, don't you think it. They'll nip you in the bud again, as they always do (65).

It is not for another two or three years that Lawrence himself comes round to this view.

§2

In 1929 Lawrence wrote a pair of poems called *Retort to Whitman* and *Retort to Jesus*. The titles are interchangeable, for the poems go—

RETORT TO WHITMAN

And whoever walks a mile full of false sympathy walks to the funeral of the whole human race.

RETORT TO JESUS

And whoever forces himself to love anybody begets a murderer in his own body.

In this respect, Kangaroo seems to be an amalgam of Whitman and Christ. The sympathy is false in the sense that it is impossibly general and indiscriminate, that it is done on purpose, imposed from above, from the will, and that it does not allow for the equally healthy and necessary activity of rejection and hostility.

Somers's rejection of Kangaroo is similar to Lawrence's of Russell several years earlier:

You are simply *full* of repressed desires, which have become savage and anti-social. And they come out in this sheep's clothing of peace propaganda. As a woman said to me, who had been to one of your meetings: 'It seemed so strange, with his face looking so evil, to be talking about peace and love. He can't have *meant* what he said' (*CL* 367).

Russell's 'angel of peace' role seemed to Lawrence a 'plausible lie'. The only 'direct and honourable' course would be to bring hatred into the open, saying:

I hate you all, liars and swine, and am out to set upon you (*CL* 367).

Which is exactly what Lawrence makes Christ say in *The Risen Lord*.

The lust and cruelty and 'devilish repressions' are evident in many of Kangaroo's supporters, particularly Jack, a war hero, who wants 'a chance of keeping on being a hero':

I never knew, till the war. And I wouldn't believe it then, not for many a while. But it's *there*. Cripes, it's there right enough. Having a woman's something, isn't it? But it's a flea-bite, nothing, compared to killing your man when your blood comes up (326).

Kangaroo's pouch, in which mankind was to have nestled, contains at the end nothing more than a fatal bullet and a festering mess:

And the motion of merging becomes at last a vice, a nasty degeneration, as when tissue breaks down into a mucous slime (*The Symbolic Meaning* 259).

Somers is still groping for an alternative. He stands, he tells Kangaroo, for

the re-entry into us of the great God, who enters us from below, not from above...The god you can never see or visualise, who stands dark on the threshold of the phallic me (134).

And in the sacred dark men meet and touch, and it is a great communion. But it isn't this love. There's no love in it. But something deeper. Love seems to me somehow trivial: and the spirit seems like something that belongs to paper. It can't help it—I know another God (136).

But Somers's faith in this other God is not strong. Equally strong is his desire to be done with humanity altogether, to retreat into cold isolation, like a sea-creature.

The middle chapters seek to give us a man at the end of his tether, beating about for a new track through the bush without much success:

He left off kicking himself, and went down to the shore to get away from himself (154).

As in the centre of *Aaron's Rod*, so here, a loosening of structure and texture, a blind casting about for a new impetus, the sudden outburst of swirling black bile in 'Nightmare'. The description of Richard's inability to write comes too near to a description of Lawrence's own efforts in this part of the novel:

He tried to write, that being his job. But usually, nowadays, when he tapped his unconscious, he found himself in a seethe of steady fury, general rage (164).

Turning to the gods is itself an admission of lost faith in a human future:

Sometimes I feel I'd give anything, soul and body, for a smash up in this social-industrial world we're in. And I would. And then when I realise people—just people—the same people after it as before—why, Jaz, then I don't care any more, and feel it's time to turn to the gods (162).

The next chapter 'Harriet and Lovat at Sea in Marriage' veers from the flippancy of this:

I have not made up my mind whether she was a ship or a bark, or a schooner, technically speaking. Let us imagine her as any one of them. Or perhaps she was a clipper, or a frigate, or a brig. All I insist is that she was not a steamboat with a funnel, as most vessels are nowadays, sailing because they are stoked (173)

to the fine comic poise of the dialogue on pp. 174–6.

Somers's quarrel with Kangaroo is not presented on the same level as his quarrels with Harriet or Jack, not convincingly enacted. His position has to be stated in the form of interpolated essays.

Lawrence saw nothing of political life in Australia, which was, in any case, inert. He wanted to write about the struggle, within himself, between political allegiances, and, more important, between political involvement of any kind and withdrawal, between art as propaganda and art as autonomous thought-adventure and a rendering of real experience. He also wanted to write about Australia, the spirit of the place and people. But he did not want to stay there long. So he tried to do everything in one book.

The political theme could have given *Aaron's Rod* a backbone, in a European setting. But it conflicts with what really interests Lawrence about Australia—its un-Europeanness, the bush, the aboriginal atmosphere, the strange plants and creatures of the bush, the challenge to the settler, the shirt-sleeve brashness and carelessness of the people. Political meetings and movements are not germane to these interests. There was never any question of political involvement for him, quite the opposite:

If I stayed here six months I should have to stay for ever—there is something so remote and far off and utterly indifferent to our European world, in the very air. I should go a bit further away from Sydney, and go 'bush'—We don't know one single soul—not a soul comes to the house. And I can't tell you how I like it. I could live like that for ever: and drop writing even a letter: sort of come undone from everything (*CL* 712).

Kangaroo, for all its wonderful evocation of the Australian scene and character, is not a true Australian novel in the sense that *The Boy in the Bush* (with even better evocation of scene and character) is. The plot—the conflict between the fascist Digger movement and the Communists—is not indigenous material. It derives from Lawrence's experience of Italian politics and is merely grafted on to Australia, however skilfully. The give-away is the 'Nightmare' chapter. The Australian 'allegory' breaks down when Lawrence finds that he cannot adequately translate his personal problem into these terms. He has to drop the allegory and give us a chapter on Lawrence, no longer disguised as Richard Lovat Somers. Only a detailed account of Lawrence's war-experiences is felt to justify Somers's resistance to Kangaroo, his extreme self-reliance, his determination 'to fear one's own inward soul, and never to fear the outside world, nay, not even a single person, nor even fifty million persons'. Without this background Somers would seem to be merely rationalising some emotional blockage. It was the war, says Somers, which burst his bubble of humanity. But there is nothing within the structure and range of this novel that will serve to account for the pressure of hatred in him.

Lawrence had tried, in the *Maurice Magnus* Introduction, to look back on the war objectively:

And so it was with the war. Humanity in Europe fell horribly into a hatred of the living soul, in the war. There is no gainsaying it. We all fell. Let us not try to wriggle out of it. We fell into hideous depravity of hating the human soul; a purulent small-pox of the spirit we had. It was shameful, shameful, shameful, in every country and in all of us. Some tried to resist, and some didn't. But we were all drowned in shame. A purulent small-pox of the vicious spirit, vicious against the deep soul that pulses in the blood (90).

This last phrase reminds us of the end of *The Rainbow*. The image of the rainbow is invoked again in *Kangaroo*:

'Who is there that you feel you are with, besides me—or who feel themselves with you?' Harriet was asking.

'No one', he replied. And at the same moment he looked up and saw the rainbow fume beyond the sea. But it was on a dark background, like a coloured darkness. The rainbow was always a symbol to him—a good symbol: of this peace. A pledge of unbroken faith, between the universe and the innermost. And the very moment he said 'No one' he saw the rainbow for an answer (156).

But the answer is as insubstantial as the rainbow and fades as quickly. Lawrence, in response to irresistible pressure from within, has to go outside the framework of the novel to look his nightmare in the face and try to exorcise it from his system:

At last he had had it all out with himself, right to the bitter end. And then he realised that all the time, since the year 1918, whether he was in Sicily or Switzerland or Venice or Germany or in the Austrian Tyrol, deep in his unconsciousness had lain this accumulation of black fury and fear, like frenzied lava quiescent in his soul. And now it had burst up: the fear, then the acute remembrance. So he faced it out, trembling with shock and bitterness, every detail...

He cared for nothing now, but to let loose the hell-rage that was in him. Get rid of it by letting it out (265, 267).

The novel flounders on, with its built-in apologies to the reader:

He preached, and the record was taken down for this gramophone of a novel (286).

Chapter follows chapter, and nothing doing. But man is a thought-adventurer, and his falls into the Charybdis of ointment, and his shipwrecks on the rocks of ages, and his kisses across chasms, and his silhouette on a minaret: surely these are as thrilling as most things...We can't be at a stretch of tension *all* the time, like the E string on a fiddle. If you don't like the novel, don't read it. If the pudding doesn't please you, leave it, *I* don't mind your saucy plate. I know too well that you can bring an ass to water, etc. (289–90).

Lawrence is no longer interested in this novel. If you lose faith in men, then you lose it in your own readers, and inevitably, in your own art.

The resolution, such as it is, is in Richard's discovery of the meaninglessness of meanings. He drifts into an 'insouciant soullessness', a great pause between carings, in which only the sea-creatures, at home in the vast ocean, can impinge on his consciousness. The consciousness he seeks is 'deeper than human':

The call and the answer, without intermediary. Non-human gods, non-human human beings (349).

Again Lawrence is outside the terms of this novel, wanting to tackle the bigger theme of *The Plumed Serpent*, with its non-human gods and men.

'The long travail', Richard calls this part of his life:

The long gestation of the soul within a man, and the final parturition, the birth of a new way of knowing, a new God-influx. A new idea, true enough. But at the centre, the old anti-idea: the dark, the unutterable God. This time not a God scribbling on tablets of stone or bronze. No everlasting decalogues. No sermons on mounts, either. The dark God, the forever unrevealed. The God who is many gods to many men: all things to all men. The source of passions and strange motives. It is a frightening thought, but very liberating.

'Ah, my soul,' said Richard to himself, 'you have to look more ways than one. First to the unutterable dark of God: first and foremost. Then to the utterable and sometimes very loud dark of that woman Harriet. I must admit that only the dark god in her fighting with my white idealism has got me so clear: and that only the dark god in her answering the dark god in me has got my soul heavy and fecund with a new sort of infant. But even now I can't bring it forth. I can't bring it forth. I need something else. Some other answer' (272).

It is not only a frightening thought, it is a dangerous one. If any man can give the name of God to his passions and strange motives, we shall have some bloody gods, including Lawrence's:

To be pure in heart, man must listen to the dark gods as well as to the white gods, to the call of blood-sacrifice as well as to the eucharist (273).

§3

The criterion by which Ben Cooley is judged and found wanting is Somers's God, but Somers's God is not present in the novel. He is vaguely associated with certain qualities of the bush or the sea but as something of an afterthought. He is certainly not an Australian god as Quetzalcoatl is a Mexican god. He is a gesture merely.

The presence of God is not so necessary to the structure of *The Boy in the Bush*, but is much more strongly felt. And the dark god is clearly identified with 'one's own inward soul', what Lilly had called 'the Holy Ghost'. 'The profound unconscious of man' is his link with 'the great living darkness'. The Holy Ghost 'can scent the new tracks of the Great God across the cosmos or creation' (*Apocalypse*). The nature and purposes of a man are given, not to be willed. The purpose of consciousness is to discover them and clear a way for them. This brings the dark gods into close relation with the puritan tradition.

Jack Grant, like Lawrence himself, has had a conventional upbringing in England, but has found himself at odds with its assumptions, institutions and representatives. He escapes into the bush, an unfixed, unformulated world, where life can be confronted at its starkest, and an adult consciousness forged:

'What would my father mean, out here?' he said to himself. And it seemed as if his father and his father's world and his father's gods withered and went to dust at the thought of this bush. And when he saw one of the men on a red sorrel horse galloping like a phantom away through the dim, red-trunked, silent trees, followed by another man on a black horse; and when he heard their far, far-off yelling Coo-ee! or a shot as they fired at a dingo or a kangaroo, he felt as if the old world had given him up from the womb, and put him into a new weird grey-blue paradise, where man has to begin all over again (Penguin 104).

Being honest with himself involves acknowledging the validity of his own anger against his enemies and against what he takes to be evil:

Did these people never have living anger, like a bright black snake with unclosing eyes, at the bottom of their souls? (142).

From the Bible ('perhaps the foundation of his consciousness') he draws the moral: 'Do what seems good to you in the sight of the Lord' (157). 'The sight of the Lord' is not the sight of clergymen and church-going aunts, but 'a vast strange scope of vision in the semi-dark'. Jack can only commune with the Lord when he is absolutely alone, in 'the sanctity of his own isolation' (167). The Lord glows in the colours and lights of the bush, and utters himself in its strange sounds and cries. When Jack absorbs the pristine spirit of the bush, he is communing with the Lord and with his own real self. 'The spirit in you is God in you.' He exists only that God may act through him:

What was he for, but to show his strength to the generation, and a sign of the power of the Lord for all them that were to come (193).

He cries to his own pure heart, his deepest desires:

Lord, if you don't want me to have Monica and kill Easu, I won't. But if you want me to, I will (192).

To keep his heart pure, he must acknowledge the darkest desires. The body acting in unison with pure desire becomes a 'spiritual body', agent of the Lord, in a state of blessedness:

And when the flame came up in him, tearing from his bowels, in the sudden new desire for Monica, this was his spiritual body, the body transfigured with fire. And that steady dark vibration which made him want to kill Easu—Easu seemed to him like the Antichrist—that was his own spiritual body. And when he had hit Easu with his broken left hand, and the white sheet of flame going through him had made him scream aloud, leaving him strange and distant but super-conscious and powerful, this, too, was his spiritual body. When he drank from the burning right hand of the Lord, and wanted Monica in the same fire, it was his body spiritual burning from the right hand of the Lord. And when he knew he must destroy Easu, in the sheet of white pain, it was his body spiritual transfigured from the left hand of the Lord. And when he ate and drank and the food tasted good, it was the dark cup of life he was drinking, drinking the life of the dead ox from the meat. And this was the body spiritual communing with the sacrificed body of natural life: like a tiger glowing at evening and lapping blood. And when he rode after the sheep through the bush, and the horse between his knees went quick and delicate, it was the Lord tossing him in his spiritual body down the maze of living (196–7).

To accept this interpretation one must believe in original innocence, or at least in Jack's innocence; and considerable skill is deployed in the early chapters to establish it.

The slaughter of Easu is so powerfully described and prepared for that we can hardly question its rightness. It is Easu who stands for brutality, as well as for all the instinctive hatred of the mass for the life-adventurer:

I thought they would know the Lord was with me, and a certain new thing with me on the face of the earth. But if they know the Lord is with me, it is only so that they can intensify and concentrate their poison, to drive Him out again. And if they guess a new thing in me, on the face of the earth, it only makes them churn their bile and secrete their malice into a poison that would corrode the face of the Lord (379).

Jack's pioneering into the uncharted bush is an allegory of a human quest for life, ever more life and consciousness of life, and for a greater God than any known God—a 'more deeply-fulfilling God stirring subtly in the uncontaminated air about one':

As if life still held great wells of reserve vitality, strange unknown wells of secret life-source, dusky, of a strange, dim, aromatic sap which had never stirred in the veins of man, to consciousness and effect (255).

The 'life of real courage' is always the controlling theme of the book. Mollie Skinner's manuscript no doubt enabled Lawrence to recapture bearings he was not to recover in his own work for some years:

The life-long happiness lies in being used by life, hurt by life, driven and goaded by life, replenished and overjoyed with life, fighting for life's sake (102).

Jack's wisdom and courage and faith are, for the most part, convincingly realised:

If a man loves life, and feels the sacredness and mystery of life, then he knows that life is full of strange and subtle and even conflicting imperatives. And a wise man learns to recognize the imperatives as they arise—or nearly so— and to obey. But most men bruise themselves to death trying to fight and overcome their own new, life-born needs, life's ever-strange imperatives. The secret of all life is obedience: obedience to the urge that arises in the soul, the urge that is life itself, urging us to new gestures, new embraces, new emotions, new combinations, new creations.

But it is difficult to see how two or three wives are essential to the quest, and we may share some of Aunt Matilda's misgiving when we hear Jack's rather glib self-justification:

'Do you know what I am faithful to?' he said, still to the two young women, but letting the elders hear. 'I am faithful to my own inside, when something stirs in me. Gran Ellis said that was God in me. I know there's a God outside of me. But he tells me to go my own way, and never be frightened of people and the world, only be frightened of him. And if I felt I really wanted two wives, for example, I would have them and keep them both. If I really wanted them, it would mean it was the God outside me bidding me, and it would be up to me to obey, world or no world.'
'You describe exactly the devil driving you', said Aunt Matilda (357).

It is not surprising that Mollie Skinner wept over the ending, which is entirely Lawrence's.

The deep friendship and trust between Jack and Tom and Lennie, which the book so convincingly and centrally establishes through the middle chapters, is suddenly repudiated by Jack, who, with some misanthropy, seems to insist on being more isolated than he need be.

It seems likely that the stress on Jack as a Lord of Death is also Lawrence's. It follows, perhaps, as Murry suggests, that if Lawrence believed that the inertia and cowardice and life-hatred of his fellow-men made impossible his triumph in life, then he must imagine a triumph in death for consolation.

Jack lacks altogether Somers's sense of obligation towards the world of men and civilised effort. His relationships with men are to be restricted to moments of amiability followed by a recoil in anger and revulsion. His relationships with women are to be on a basis of pure submission on their part:

He demanded this submission as if it were a submission to his mysterious Lord...And yield before the immense Lord she must. Through him.

It seems a little facile to define evil as 'resistance to the life principle' and then to define the life principle as Jack Grant. Jack's achievements do not quite coincide with Lawrence's needs, which can be read, as it were, between the lines:

Jack wanted to make a place on earth for a few aristocrats-to-the-bone. He wanted to conquer the world (345).

The failure of the story to provide any such conquest is reflected in the compensating post-mortal triumph:

A little world of my own! As if I could make it with the people that are on earth today! No, no, I can do nothing but stand alone. And, then, when I die, I shall not drop like carrion on the earth's earth. I shall be a lord of death, and sway the destinies of the life to come (380).

CHAPTER 8

CHRONOLOGY

In August 1922 the Lawrences left Australia for New Mexico,
via the South Sea Islands.

INDIANS AND AN ENGLISHMAN (*Dial*, February 1923; *Phoenix*).
Describes experiences of 14–19 September 1922.

LIFE OF MABEL LUHAN.
Almost immediately Lawrence began to plan a novel based on the life of
Mabel Dodge Luhan, his hostess (*CL* 724, Luhan 59). The project was
quickly abandoned.

TAOS (*Dial*, March 1923; *Phoenix*).
Describes experiences of 29–30 September 1922.

FIRE AND OTHER POEMS (Grabhorn Press, San Francisco, 1940).
Probably late 1922.

BIRDS, BEASTS AND FLOWERS.
Eagle in New Mexico, The Red Wolf, Men in New Mexico, Autumn in Taos
and *Spirits Summoned West*, October–November 1922.
The Blue Jay, Bibbles, Mountain Lion and *The American Eagle*, December
1922 and January 1923.

STUDIES IN CLASSIC AMERICAN LITERATURE (Seltzer, 1923).
The final version was written in the winter of 1922–3.

SURGERY FOR THE NOVEL—OR A BOMB (*Literary Digest International Book
Review*, April 1923; *Phoenix*).
Probably early 1923.

AU REVOIR U.S.A. (*Laughing Horse*, December 1923; *Phoenix*).
Describes experiences of late March 1923.

THE PLUMED SERPENT (Secker, 1926).
First draft written in May and June 1923. Begun again on 19 November
1924 and finished, still called *Quetzalcoatl*, by 5 February 1925 (*CL* 831).
Revised May–June 1925 (Moore 341), cf. L. D. Clark, *The Dark Night of
the Body* 33–47.

THE PROPER STUDY (*Adelphi*, December 1923; *Phoenix*).
Written before 17 September 1923 (*CL* 753).

A BRITISHER HAS A WORD WITH HARRIET MONROE (Nehls II, 268).
October or November 1923.

ON BEING RELIGIOUS (*Adelphi*, February 1924; *Phoenix*).
ON BEING A MAN (*Vanity Fair*, June 1924; *Assorted Articles*, Secker, 1930).

ON HUMAN DESTINY (*Adelphi*, March 1924; *Assorted Articles*).
ON COMING HOME (*Texas Quarterly* 1, 3, 1958).
ON TAKING THE NEXT STEP.
ON LOVE AND MARRIAGE.
October 1923–January 1924 (Tedlock 134).

BOOKS (*Phoenix*).
Early 1924 (Tedlock 161).

THE OVERTONE (*The Lovely Lady*, Secker, 1933).
JIMMY AND THE DESPERATE WOMAN (*Criterion*, October 1924; *The Woman Who Rode Away*, Secker, 1928).
THE LAST LAUGH (*The Woman Who Rode Away*).
THE BORDER LINE (*Hutchinson's Magazine*, September 1924; *The Woman Who Rode Away*).
Probably January–February 1924 (Carswell 225–6).

PARIS LETTER (*Laughing Horse*, April 1926; *Phoenix*).
Probably 27 January 1924.

LETTER FROM GERMANY (*New Statesman*, 13 October 1934; *Phoenix*).
19 February 1924.

DANCE OF THE SPROUTING CORN (*Theatre Arts Monthly*, July 1924; *Mornings in Mexico*, Secker, 1927).
INDIANS AND ENTERTAINMENT (*N.Y. Times Magazine*, 26 October 1924; *Mornings in Mexico*).
May 1924 (Luhan 186).

PAN IN AMERICA (*Southwest Review*, January 1926; *Phoenix*).
May 1924 (*CL* 788).

THE WOMAN WHO RODE AWAY (*Dial*, July–August 1925; Secker, 1928).
June 1924 (Tedlock 54, *CL* 794, Sterne 218–19).

ST MAWR (Secker, 1925).
June 1924.

THE HOPI SNAKE DANCE (*Theatre Arts Monthly*, December 1924; *Mornings in Mexico*).
Describes a ceremony of 16 August 1924. The first version (*Laughing Horse*, September 1924; AH 607) was written almost immediately, the second some weeks later (*CL* 805).

THE BAD SIDE OF BOOKS (*A Bibliography of the Writings of D. H. Lawrence*, Edward D. MacDonald, Centaur Press, 1925; *Phoenix*).
Written on 1 September 1924.

THE PRINCESS (*Calendar of Modern Letters*, March, April, May 1925; *St Mawr*, Secker, 1925).
In December 1923, taking some hints from Catherine Carswell, Lawrence sketched out a story (Carswell 211–14) which contains the seeds of *The*

Princess. The tale proper was written in September and early October 1924 (*CL* 810, Tedlock 99).

ALTITUDE (*Laughing Horse*, summer 1938; *Complete Plays*, 1965).
The first two scenes of a satirical play. Autumn 1924.

PREFACE TO 'BLACK SWANS' BY MOLLIE SKINNER.
November–December 1924 (Tedlock 243–4).

CLIMBING DOWN PISGAH (*Phoenix*).
November–December 1924.

CORASMIN (*Adelphi*, December 1925; *Mornings in Mexico*).
MARKET DAY (*Travel*, April 1926; *Mornings in Mexico*).
WALK TO HUAYAPA (*Travel*, November 1926; *Mornings in Mexico*).
THE MOZO (*Adelphi*, February 1927; *Mornings in Mexico*).
19–26 December 1924.

THE FEAST OF THE RADISHES (*Paintings*, Cory, Adams and Mackay, 1964).
The feast took place on 23 December 1924.

NONE OF THAT (*The Woman Who Rode Away*).
Probably 1924.

In February 1925 Lawrence went down with an almost fatal illness.

RESURRECTION (*Phoenix*).
SEE MEXICO AFTER (*Phoenix*).
Probably early 1925.

SUGGESTIONS FOR STORIES (Tedlock 56).
THE FLYING FISH (*Phoenix*).
March–April 1925.

ACCUMULATED MAIL (*The Borzoi*, 1925; *Phoenix*).
April 1925.

MAN IS ESSENTIALLY A SOUL (Tedlock 138).
NOAH'S FLOOD (*Phoenix*; *Complete Plays*, 1965).
April–May 1925.

DAVID (Secker, 1926; *Plays*, 1933; *Complete Plays*, 1965).
Probably early summer 1925.

ART AND MORALITY (*Calendar of Modern Letters*, November 1925; *Phoenix*).
MORALITY AND THE NOVEL (*Calendar of Modern Letters*, December 1925; *Phoenix*).
WHY THE NOVEL MATTERS (*Phoenix*).
THE NOVEL AND THE FEELINGS (*Phoenix*).
Summer 1925.

REFLECTIONS ON THE DEATH OF A PORCUPINE (Centaur Press, 1925).
All the essays in this collection, with the exception of 'The Crown' (cf. p. 40), were probably written in the summer of 1925.

8

THE LOST TRAIL
1923–1925

The Woman Who Rode Away
St Mawr
The Plumed Serpent

Anyhow, though England may lead the world again, as you say, she's got to find a way first. She's got to pick up a lost trail. And the end of the lost trail is here in Mexico. The Englishman, per se, is not enough. He has to modify himself to a distant end. He has to balance with something that is not himself (Letter to J. M. Murry, 25 October 1923; *CL* 759).

§1

As early as the autumn of 1920, Quetzalcoatl was taking shape deep in Lawrence's consciousness:

The East a dead letter, and Europe moribund...Is that so?
And those sombre, dead, feather-lustrous Aztecs, Amerindians,
In all the sinister splendour of their red blood-sacrifices,
Do they stand under the dawn, half-godly, half-demon, awaiting the cry of
    the turkey-cock? (*Turkey-cock*.)

Two years before he had ever set foot in the New World, Lawrence was advocating a programme for America which later became Don Ramon's, in *The Plumed Serpent*:

Americans must take up life where the Red Indian, the Aztec the Maya, the Incas left it off. They must pick up the life-thread where the mysterious Red race let it fall. They must catch the pulse of the life which Cortés and Columbus murdered. There lies the real continuity...A great and lovely life-form, unperfected, fell with Montezuma. The responsibility for the producing and the perfecting of this life-form devolves upon the new American...It means a departure from the old European morality, ethic. It means even a departure from the old range of emotions and sensibilities...Montezuma had other emotions, such as we have not known or admitted. We must start from Montezuma, not from St Francis or St Bernard (*Phoenix* 90–1).

Indeed, at this time Lawrence had never left Europe, never seen any primitive life-form face to face. In the spring of 1922 he went to Ceylon and wrote home:

Those natives are *back* of us—in the living sense *lower* than we are. But they're going to swarm over us and suffocate us. We are, have been for five centuries, the growing tip. Now we're going to fall. But you don't catch me going back on my whiteness and Englishness and myself. English in the teeth of the world, even in the teeth of England (*CL* 702).

On the way to America in the late summer of that year, Lawrence spent a few days in the South Sea Islands and recorded his impressions in the final version of the *Studies in Classic American Literature*:

Whatever else the South Sea Islander is, he is centuries and centuries behind us in the life-struggle, the consciousness-struggle, the struggle of the soul into fulness...

We can't go back to the savages: not a stride. We can be in sympathy with them. We can take a great curve in their direction, onwards. But we cannot turn the current of our life backwards, back towards their soft warm twilight and uncreate mud...

We can only do it when we are renegade. The renegade hates life itself. He wants the death of life. So these many 'reformers' and 'idealists' who glorify the savages in America. They are death-birds, life-haters. Renegades (129–30).

All this is perfectly consistent with Birkin's evaluation of the African statue in *Women in Love*. Birkin might easily have written *Indians and an Englishman*, Lawrence's first recorded response to the Red Indians. Their chants evoke a sickness of the soul, a nostalgia for 'the diabolical, pre-human, pine-tree fun of cutting dusky throats and letting the blood spurt out unconfined'.

It was not for me, and I knew it. Nor had I any curiosity to understand it... I have gone a long road since then. And as I look back, like memory terrible as bloodshed, the dark faces round the fire in the night, and one blood beating in me and them. But I don't want to go back to them, ah, never. I never want to deny them or break with them. But there is no going back. Always onward, still further. The great devious onward-flowing stream of conscious human blood. From them to me, and from me on (*Phoenix* 99).

Eagle in New Mexico (October 1922) repeats the same uncompromising rejection of blood-sacrifice:

I don't yield to you, big, jowl-faced eagle.
Nor you nor your blood-thirsty sun
That sucks up blood
Leaving a nervous people.

Even the sun in heaven can be curbed and chastened at last
By the life in the hearts of men.
And you, great bird, sun-starer, heavy black beak
Can be put out of office as sacrifice bringer.

Even after finishing the first draft of *The Plumed Serpent* (then
called *Quetzalcoatl*) by the end of June 1923, Lawrence felt a
strong recoil from Mexico and a need to return to Europe. In
August he got as far as New York, then dug his heels in and let
Frieda sail alone. He followed in December, felt sicker than ever
of Europe, and returned in March 1924 to settle at the Kiowa
ranch, seventeen miles from Taos, up in the mountains, the first
home the Lawrences had owned. There, before returning to
Mexico to finish *The Plumed Serpent*, Lawrence wrote three
tales—*The Woman Who Rode Away*, *St Mawr*, and *The Princess*,
apparently in that order.

§2

At the end of *Kangaroo*, Somers declared himself ready 'to turn to
the old dark gods, who had waited so long in the outer dark'. But
it is not simply a matter of turning round and going back. The
well-head to this darkness is in every man's soul, but in the white
man it is buried fathoms deep. Should he find and release it, its
destructive–creative potency might well drown him. Men return
from these unknown regions either blessed or crazed. Literature
is full of myths which enact the journey of the soul in search of
god. The search is not only through the universe for the manifold
presences, but also into the recesses and lowest layers of the unconscious where that particular presence which is manhood or
womanhood, the divine spark, is to be found, for it is this which
puts a man in touch with all other presences. Now that Lawrence
wishes to write directly about religious and racial experiences,
about quests and conflicts in consciousness, he finds he must
invent his own myths.

The Woman Who Rode Away is the first of these, a myth of
picking up a lost trail. At the beginning of the story the woman
is dying of ennui. Her life has never revealed anything to her as
magical. The cosmos itself seems a great void. Yet, romantically,
she secretly yearns for something wonderful. When visitors come
and the conversation turns to the wild tribes of Indians in the
mountains she instinctively attaches her yearnings to them:

But surely they have old, old religions and mysteries—it *must* be wonderful, surely it must (549).

The desperate hope is as much Lawrence's as the clear-eyed scepticism which contradicts it:

Savages are savages, and all savages behave more or less alike: rather low-down and dirty, insanitary, with a few cunning tricks, and struggling to get enough to eat (549).

The woman, drawn by an inner destiny, finds the lost trail and the primitive tribe. Her initial resistance is soon beaten down. She submits entirely to their rhythms and rituals. Their drugs transform her consciousness, giving her an

exquisite sense of bleeding out into the higher beauty and harmony of things. Then she could actually hear the great stars in heaven, which she saw through her door, speaking from their motion and brightness, saying things perfectly to the cosmos, as they trod in perfect ripples, like bells on the floor of heaven, passing one another and grouping in the timeless dance, with the spaces of dark between...

   More and more her ordinary personal consciousness had left her, she had gone into that other state of passional cosmic consciousness, like one who is drugged. The Indians, with their heavy religious natures, had made her succumb to their vision (572).

She submits even to the rite which follows, when, in a ceremony surviving from Aztec times, her dripping heart is to be offered to the sun:

Only the eyes of the oldest man were not anxious. Black, and fixed, and as if sightless, they watched the sun, seeing beyond the sun. And in their black, empty concentration there was power, power intensely abstract and remote, but deep, deep to the heart of the earth, and the heart of the sun. In absolute motionlessness he watched till the red sun should send his ray through the column of ice. Then the old man would strike, and strike home, accomplish the sacrifice and achieve the power. The mastery that man must hold, and that passes from race to race (581).

   Is this, then, a myth of resurrection, the woman finding the trail, enduring the symbolic death, to be reborn into contact with the cosmos? I can see no hope of this. She is to be cast into the melting-pot like Peer Gynt, a button without a loop. The power her blood will win from the sun is not for her or her race, but for the dark races, now preparing to take over as the white race immolates itself.

   Is it the story of a renegade, a negative fable like *The Man Who Loved Islands*? In February 1924 Lawrence had written to Mabel

Luhan: 'All this poking and prying into the Indians is a form of indecency' (*CL* 780). Mabel herself had gone so far as to marry an Indian, Tony Luhan. Lawrence used her as his model for *The Woman Who Rode Away*, and Mabel refers to it as 'that story where Lorenzo thought he finished me up' (*Lorenzo in Taos* 219). Yet the woman is not as negative as Cathcart in *The Man Who Loved Islands*. Unlike him, she does seek the mystery, find it, and submit to it. How different from this is what Kate is to do in *The Plumed Serpent*?

Within the terms of the tale, the woman clearly found the right trail, that leading to the oldest Indian consciousness, and to their gods. Theirs, as Lawrence recorded in *New Mexico*, he recognised as a real and profound religion:

The whole life-effort of man was to get his life into contact with the elemental life of the cosmos, mountain-life, cloud-life, thunder-life, air-life, earth-life, sun-life. To come into immediate felt contact, and so derive energy, power, and a dark sort of joy (*Phoenix* 147).

The white man must rediscover this source of potency if his civilisation is to survive. But how? Simply to suspend one's white consciousness and submit to the consciousness of an alien race, or of the dim past, is deadly:

The life of the Indian, his stream of conscious being, is just death to the white man. And we can understand the consciousness of the Indian only in terms of the death of our consciousness (*Mornings in Mexico* 46).

The woman follows her trail too far, too literally, yields her entire being to the Indian vision. She has no selfhood to balance with it, no distant end distinct from and superior to theirs to which she must be modified.

Only the 'strange inward sun of life' (*Mornings in Mexico* 67) can save us from ennui and disintegration. How then to regain it? The potency of the sun and the cosmos is both benevolent and malevolent, and man's relationship with it must be simultaneously a submission and a conquest. How to conquer? The Indians in *The Woman Who Rode Away* achieve their penetration to the heart of the earth and the heart of the sun by sacrificing the human heart. This is one way, and the tale refuses to present it in any but its own terms, for Lawrence finds it preferable to the living death of the woman. The pure myth does not often contain within it a message or overt moral judgement. It offers, rather, an image of human experience in crisis or extremity from which numerous, sometimes apparently contradictory meanings may be drawn. *The Woman Who Rode Away* comes near to having this kind of purity, and its weakest points are, perhaps, the points at which the author intrudes with his own interpretation:

The sharpness and the quivering nervous consciousness of the highly-bred white woman was to be destroyed again, womanhood was to be cast once more into the great stream of impersonal sex and impersonal passion (569)

or in the ambivalent closing sentence, where Lawrence seems to approve the imminent Indian victory.

But in *Mornings in Mexico*, he gives his objective assessment unequivocally:

You can perform the mental trick, and fool yourself and others into believing that the befeathered and bedaubed darling is nearer to the true ideal gods than we are. This last is just bunk, and a lie (45).

And in *The Mozo* we have the story's ending rendered in very different terms. The Aztec goddess of love ('a goddess of dirt and prostitution, a dirt-eater, a horror, without a touch of tenderness') conceives and brings forth a stone knife:

It is the sacrificial knife with which the priest makes a gash in his victim's breast, before he tears out the heart, to hold it smoking to the sun. And the Sun, the Sun behind the sun, is supposed to suck the smoking heart greedily with insatiable appetite. This, then, is a pretty Christmas Eve (24).

White 'civilisation', on the other hand, should seek to take the power of the sun into the heart and transform it there into creativeness and love in terms of a vision which focuses on respect for individual life and growth and wholeness. It is much the harder vision to sustain, and the white man has failed to sustain it. He has lost touch with the sun altogether, which has led him into 'a new sort of sordidness, more vast and more stupendous than the old savage sort' (*St Mawr* 142). *St Mawr* enacts this revitalisation which the white race can win from the great, the splendid, but the essentially sub-human powers of nature—the heart of the sun and the heart of the earth—the eagle and the snake.

§3

The prose of *St Mawr* is more flexible than any Lawrence had
written since the war. It moves subtly from an apparent flippancy
in the description of Rico and his relationship with Lou ('a
charming married couple') to an earnestness and stature appropriate to the new dimension which St Mawr brings into the novel
and into Lou's life. The two styles meet and deliberately clash in
such passages as this:

> She could not bear the triviality and superficiality of her human relation-
> ships. Looming like some god out of the darkness was the head of that horse,
> with the wide, terrible, questioning eyes. And she felt that it forbade her to
> be her ordinary, commonplace self. It forbade her to be just Rico's wife,
> young Lady Carrington, and all that (14).

Her life with Rico has been purely attitude. She had not known
that relationships could be based on anything other than attitude.
The prose associated with St Mawr is, like him, the opposite of
attitude and triviality. The light, sardonic touch of the opening is
appropriate only to the world of attitudes:

> But now she realised that, with men and women, everything is an attitude
> only when something else is lacking. Something is lacking and they are
> thrown back on their own devices. That black fiery flow in the eyes of the
> horse was not 'attitude'. It was something much more terrifying, and real,
> the only thing that was real. Gushing from the darkness in menace and
> question, and blazing out in the splendid body of the horse (15).

The question St Mawr asks Lou is 'Are you alive?'. He
testifies to a mode, a dimension of living which is unquestionably
real, if dangerous, and challenges her to enter it. To Rico,
St Mawr is merely another pose:

> 'He'd be marvellous in a Composition. That colour' (16).

The choice she is offered is 'between two worlds'. She must
'meet him half-way':

> But half-way across from our human world to that terrific equine twilight
> was not a small step. It was a step, she knew, that Rico could never take.
> She knew it. But she was prepared to sacrifice Rico (18).

The other world is again associated with the world from which
the snake was a messenger:

> She realised that St Mawr drew his hot breaths in another world from Rico's,
> from our world. Perhaps the old Greek horses had lived in St Mawr's
> world. And the old Greek heroes, even Hippolytus, had known it.

With their strangely naked equine heads, and something of a snake in their way of looking round, and lifting their sensitive, dangerous muzzles, they moved in a prehistoric twilight where all things loomed phantasmagoric, all on one plane, sudden presences suddenly jutting out of the matrix. It was another world, an older, heavily potent world. And in this world the horse was swift and fierce and supreme, undominated and unsurpassed (18).

Phoenix, the groom, half-Indian, has also known the reality of that world in Arizona. Against it London is an unreal city, 'a mirage in whose actuality he never believed for a moment':

He was watching the pale deserts of Arizona shimmer with moving light, the long mirage of a shallow lake ripple, the great pallid concave of earth and sky expanding with interchanged light. And a horse-shape loom large and portentous in the mirage, like some prehistoric beast (19).

Lewis, the Welsh groom, had known that world too, as a child in Wales. Lewis, unlike Phoenix, cannot be dismissed as a mere animal. He has the integrity we associate with St Mawr. Mrs Witt has assumed that he wore his beard 'for show' and is startled when he says: 'It's part of me, Mam' (21).

The first clause of the law of life which Lawrence formulates in *Reflections on the Death of a Porcupine* is this:

Any creature that attains to its own fullness of being, its own *living* self, becomes unique, a nonpareil. It has its place in the fourth dimension, the heaven of existence, and there it is perfect, it is beyond comparison.

So little fullness of being has Lou at the beginning of *St Mawr* that she is almost unsure of her own reality or that of the people she knew—'entirely contained within their cardboard let's-be-happy world':

The talk, the eating and drinking, the flirtation, the endless dancing: it all seemed far more bodiless and in a strange way, wraith-like, than any fairy story. She seemed to be eating Barmecide food, that had been conjured up out of thin air, by the power of words. She seemed to be talking to handsome, young, bare-faced unrealities, not men at all: as she slid about with them, in the perpetual dance, they too seemed to have been conjured up out of air, merely for this soaring, slithering dance business. And she could not believe that, when the lights went out, they wouldn't melt back into thin air again and complete nonentity (26).

Against all this 'seeming' is a new vision, whose authenticity St Mawr attests, produces, indeed, by his catalytic presence.

Coleridge said of the symbol that it 'always partakes of the reality which it renders intelligible, and while it enunciates the whole, abides itself as a living part in that unity of which it is the living representative'. The unity of which St Mawr is the living representative, the matrix out of which he looms, is the divine circuit in which all living things are charged with God, or with the gods, as Lawrence at this stage phrases it.

St Mawr, like a Hopkins creature, is charged with God, his body glowing red with power, 'looming like a bonfire in the dark'. To Lou he is a visitation, he rings and tells of God:

When he reared his head and neighed from his deep chest, like deep wind-bells resounding, she seemed to hear the echoes of another darker, more spacious, more dangerous, more splendid world than ours, that was beyond her (25).

When Lawrence names his god in *St Mawr* it is Pan—'the god that is hidden in everything...the hidden mystery, the hidden cause...what you see when you see in full' (51). In a letter to Willard Johnson, editor of *The Laughing Horse*, from London on 9 January 1924, Lawrence developed the identification of the horse with Pan:

And over here the Horse is dead: he'll kick his heels no more. I don't know whether it's the pale Galilean who has triumphed, or a paleness paler than the pallor even of Jesus...When Jesus was born, the spirits wailed round the Mediterranean: Pan is dead. Great Pan is dead...It would be a terrible thing if the horse in us died for ever, as he seems to have died in Europe (*CL* 768–9).

Pan is also, as the snake was, identified with the Christian devil:

The old god Pan became the Christian devil, with the cloven hoofs and the horns, the tail, and the laugh of derision. Old Nick, the Old Gentleman who is responsible for all our wickednesses, but especially our sensual excesses—this is all that is left of the Great God Pan (*Phoenix* 23).

St Mawr is part of Lawrence's campaign to reinstate Pan-Lucifer in his original potency and brightness. In the letter to Johnson he goes on to gloss the symbol of the centaur. It stands, first, for Horse-sense:

And then, a laugh, a loud, sensible Horse Laugh. After that, these same passions, glossy and dangerous in the flanks. And after these again, hoofs, irresistible, slintering hoofs, that can kick the walls of the world down (*CL* 769).

'Wouldn't a man be wonderful in whom Pan hadn't fallen!' cries Mrs Witt, her hard-boiled, sardonic exterior beginning to break up under St Mawr's influence. 'Did you ever see Pan in the man you loved?' she asks Lou.

'As I see Pan in St Mawr?—no mother!' Her lips began to tremble and the tears came to her eyes (52).

It is in this way that St Mawr is made to serve as a standard for man:

He seems a far greater mystery to me than a clever man. He's a horse. Why can't one say in the same way of a man: 'He's a man?' But there's a terrible mystery in St Mawr...He stands where one can't get at him. And he burns with life. And where does his life come from, to him? That's the mystery. That great burning life in him, which never is dead. Most men have a deadness in them, that frightens me so, because of my own deadness. Why can't men get their life straight, like St Mawr, and then think?...A pure animal man would be as lovely as a deer or a leopard, burning like a flame fed straight from underneath. And he'd be part of the unseen, like a mouse is, even. And he'd never cease to wonder, he'd breathe silence and unseen wonder, as the partridges do, running in the stubble. He'd be all the animals in turn, instead of one, fixed, automatic thing, which he is now, grinding on the nerves.— Ah, no, mother, I want the wonder back again, or I shall die (45–7).

The need to serve a man worthy of service which both mother and daughter so strongly feel is contrasted with Flora Manby's emancipation:

I think this is the best age there ever was for a girl to have a good time in. I read all through H. G. Wells's History, and I shut it up and thanked my stars I live in nineteen-twenty odd, not in some other beastly date when a woman had to cringe before mouldy, domineering men (60).

Lou and Mrs Witt are by now no longer inhabiting the same world as these people, or speaking the same language, and the social stresses which result are presented with high comedy which is at the same time both poignant and menacing. The catastrophe comes at a significant moment:

'That's an awfully attractive tune', Rico called.
    'Do whistle it again, Fred, I should like to memorise it.'
    Fred began to whistle it again.
    At that moment St Mawr exploded again, shied sideways as if a bomb had gone off, and kept backing through the heather.
    'Fool!' cried Rico, thoroughly unnerved (62).

Who the fools are has been well-established in the preceding scene. Triviality in the face of life is what distinguishes them, the

154

old effort at serious living given up—believe in nothing, care about nothing. Rico pulls St Mawr back on top of him. 'Thrown backwards and working its hoofs in the air' St Mawr becomes 'reversed and purely evil' (65). But the grooms and the two women know where the blame lies. Phoenix tells Rico:

'That horse don't want to fall back on you, if you don't make him. If you know how to ride him. That horse wants his own way some time. If you don't let him, you got to fight him. Then look out!' (71–2).

Mrs Witt, explaining the accident to Dean Vyner, makes the same point with comedy of deadly seriousness:

I saw with my own eyes my son-in-law pull that stallion over backwards, and hold him down with the reins as tight as he could hold them; pull St Mawr's head backwards on to the ground, till the groom had to crawl up and force the reins out of my son-in-law's hands. Don't you think that was mischievous on Sir Henry's part? (77).

What Rico does to St Mawr is clearly what he also does to himself ('He had composed this tableau vivant with great effort. He didn't want to erupt like some suddenly wicked horse' (9)) and to everyone:

Never, by any chance, injure your fellow man openly. But always injure him secretly. Make a fool of him, and undermine his nature. Break him up by undermining him, if you can. It's good sport (65).

St Mawr had in fact reared at an adder that had been killed that morning with stones. In thwarting him, Rico has thwarted the deepest impulses. In this context St Mawr's destructiveness is healthy. We cheer his kick in the face of the young man. He is fighting to protect himself, destroying as he goes:

The individual can but depart from the mass, and try to cleanse himself. Try to hold fast to the living thing, which destroys as it goes, but remains sweet. And in his soul fight, fight, fight to preserve that which is life in him from the ghastly kisses and poison-bites of the myriad evil ones. Retreat to the desert, and fight. But in his soul adhere to that which is life itself, creatively destroying as it goes: destroying the stiff old thing to let the new bud come through. The one passionate principle of creative being, which recognises the natural good, and has a sword for the swarms of evil. Fights, fights, fights to protect itself. But with itself, is strong and at peace (67).

As Lou begins to make this kind of application to her own life of the bearings St Mawr gives her, his own presence in the story becomes less central. He has, of course, to be saved, first from slaughter, then from gelding. Dean Vyner exposes himself to Mrs Witt by such sentiments as:

One hates to have to destroy a fine-looking animal. But I would sacrifice a dozen rather than have our Rico limping (75).

Like Rico,

he was one of mankind's myriad conspirators, who conspire to live in absolute physical safety, whilst willing the minor disintegration of all positive living (68).

What positive living is to mean in concrete terms for Lou and Mrs Witt now comes to the forefront. St Mawr lapses into his actual as opposed to his representative life:

She could see St Mawr himself, alone as usual, standing with his head up, looking across the fences. He was streaked dark with rain. Beautiful, with his poised head and massive neck and his supple hind-quarters. He was neighing to Poppy. Clear on the wet wind came the sound of his bell-like, stallion's calling, that Mrs Vyner called cruel. It was a strange noise, with a splendour that belonged to another world age. The mean cruelty of Mrs Vyner's humanitarianism, the barren cruelty of Flora Manby, the eunuch cruelty of Rico. Our whole eunuch civilisation, nasty-minded as eunuchs are, with their kind of sneaking, sterilising cruelty (84).

Mrs Witt is terrified of dying without having ever really lived:

I want death to be real to me...If it hurts me enough, I shall know I was alive (80).

She struggles to relax her Amazonian will, crying 'Conquer me, oh God, before I die' (90). She wants to drift down the stream of life without fighting it. And her approaches to Lewis are the first actions she has ever taken without willing them. They are, in a sense, against her will, which is to spurn him. For the first time she lets the reins of her life go slack. But there is no easy resolution that way for either of the women. Lou tells her mother:

'It seems to me men and women have really hurt one another so much nowadays that they had better stay apart till they have learned to be gentle with one another again. Not all this forced passion and destructive philandering. Men and women should stay apart till their hearts grow gentle towards one another again. Now, it's only each one fighting for his own—or her own—underneath the cover of tenderness' (111).

After St Mawr's departure, Lou's aspirations can be translated into more specifically human terms, into a form of consciousness, a religion:

Love can't really come into me from the outside, and I can never, never mate
with any man, since the mystic new man will never come to me. No, no, let
me know myself and my role. I am one of the eternal Virgins, serving the
eternal fire. My dealings with men have only broken my stillness and messed
up my doorways. It has been my own fault. I ought to stay virgin, and still,
very, very still, and serve the most perfect service. I want my temple and my
Apollo mystery of the inner fire (129).

She resolves to serve only 'the other, unseen presences':

Because, after all, it seemed to her that the hidden fire was alive and burning
in this sky, over the desert, in the mountains. She felt a certain latent holiness
in the very atmosphere, a young, spring-fire of latent holiness, such as she
had never felt in Europe or in the East (129).

This fire is the same fire which had blazed from the eyes of
St Mawr. But in what sense, in this context of mountain and
desert, can it be called holy and worthy of service? What form
would this service take?

Lou and her mother buy a run-down ranch high in the Rockies,
and as the prose becomes rooted once more in the particular and
concrete, the history of the ranch, the word which emerges to
replace Lou's 'holiness' is 'malevolence':

Always some mysterious malevolence fighting, fighting against the will of
man. A strange invisible influence coming out of the livid rock fastnesses in
the bowels of those uncreated Rocky Mountains, preying upon the will of
man, and slowly wearing down his resistance, his onward-pushing spirit...
A curious disintegration working all the time, a sort of malevolent breath, like
a stupefying, irritant gas coming out of the unfathomed mountains (133).

Viewed at a distance, the landscape is beautiful and great and
splendid:

The landscape lived, and lived as the world of the gods, unsullied and un-
concerned. The great circling landscape lived its own life, sumptuous and
uncaring. Man did not exist for it. And if it had been a question simply of
living through the eyes, into the *distance*, then this would have been Paradise
(137).

But, in its details, the landscape is primitive and subhuman:

The world where each creature was crudely limited to its own ego, crude
and bristling and cold, and then crowding in packs like pine trees and wolves
(135).

So, as the woman from New England had found, a paradox, the

157

highest and the lowest, the holy and the diabolical, here indistinguishable:

> While she revelled in the beauty of the luminous world that wheeled around and below her, the grey, rat-like spirit of the inner mountains was attacking her from behind (137).

> The roses of the desert are the cactus flowers, crystal of translucent yellow or of rose-colour. But set among spines the devil himself must have conceived in a moment of sheer ecstasy (139).

The place had killed in the New England woman her conception of a merciful God:

> There is no Almighty loving God. The God there is shaggy as the pine trees, and horrible as the lightning...What nonsense about Jesus and a God of Love, in a place like this! This is more awful and more splendid. I like it better (138).

She must recognise other gods, who were 'grim and invidious and relentless, huger than man, and lower than man' (141). They are gods of tremendous energy, potency, either for creation or destruction; but they are gods without consciousness and therefore without purpose, so that the energy manifested in that place is almost sordid in its raging profusion:

> There was life, intense, bristling life, full of energy, but also, with an undertone of savage sordidness. The black ants in her cupboard, the pack-rats bouncing on her ceiling like hippopotami in the night, the two sick goats: there was a peculiar undercurrent of squalor, flowing under the curious *tussle* of wild life. That was it. The wild life, even the life of the trees and flowers seemed one bristling, hair-raising tussle (138).

> The seething cauldron of lower life, seething on the very tissue of the higher life, seething the soul away, seething at the marrow. The vast and unrelenting will of the swarming lower life, working forever against man's attempt at a higher life, a further created being (141).

'Man's attempt at a higher life' Lawrence calls, unequivocally, civilisation. The brave man is he who carries the flag into deeper and darker places. Indeed 'man is only himself when he is fighting on and on, to overcome the sordidness', which includes all savagery:

> All the time, man has to rouse himself afresh to...win from the crude, wild nature the victory and the power to make another start (142).

Our civilisation has lost its 'inward vision and its cleaner energy' and must be purified by this strife, must pass through this fire. It is not suggested that the fight against black ants and pack-rats is representative of the highest potentialities of civilisation; it is a cleansing and renewal prior to a further effort in the world of men.

Life on the ranch indeed saves Lou from cheapness, keeps bright before her the meaning and the mystery she had first seen in the eyes of St Mawr. But her claim that the spirit of the place loves her and wants her cannot be sustained against the experiences of the New England woman so vividly recounted in the preceding pages. She is projecting into the landscape her own further need, for a 'mystic new man' to embody in distinctively human, conscious, civilised form the vitality of horse and landscape. No future heroine is to be denied her hero.

§4

The Plumed Serpent has been mauled by the critics from Frieda, who called it 'desiccated swelled head', onwards. Any critic might be expected to have reservations about this novel, but the whole-sale condemnation it has received is indicative, it seems to me, of far deeper failings in the critics than in the book; a failure in imaginative range and flexibility; a failure to meet the basic critical challenge, the challenge to enter wholly, if only tem-porarily, into the fictional world. Critics have kept the book at arms' length, with an almost hysterical defensiveness, as if it were not art but propaganda. Indeed, this very charge has been often made. I do not wish for a moment to argue that Lawrence does not expect his readers to take Don Ramon's programme perfectly seriously: 'I do mean what Ramon means—for all of us', only that this programme has been grossly misrepresented and is, in any case, fully embodied as art within a larger complex structure, a structure controlled not by Ramon but by Kate.

The novel has been fortunate in its more recent critics. Jascha Kessler, John B. Vickery and, particularly, L. D. Clark, have testified most persuasively to its coherence as art, stressing Kate's mythic quest for a source of renewal. She undergoes a spiritual death, receives and responds to a call, finds herself in strange territory with horrors, but also glimpses of a deeper reality (in visions and visitations), struggles in the death-throes of the old way, the old consciousness, the strings which bind to the old life, does not, like the great mythic heroes, then return to the world renewed and bringing renewal (as the man who died is to do), but is left at the end still standing outside her own mythic role, testing and testing it against her conscience and the realities of her experience, testing these in turn against the new life. For Lawrence is not preaching, he is using the novel to explore the possibilities of experience. Is Don Ramon's trail the right one: for him? for Mexico? for Kate?

This structure differs from that of *The Woman Who Rode Away* in that Ramon and Cipriano are by no means primitive Indians (and it is to them rather than to their cult that she gives her allegiance, though she respects and is sympathetic towards what they are trying to do), and in that Kate does not passively submit, but fights her own transformation every step of the way.

Kate does not really know why she has come to Mexico, except that

over in England, in Ireland, in Europe, she had heard the *consummatum est* of her own spirit. It was finished, in a kind of death agony (45).

She had lived, until recently, through her love for her husband, Joachim, who had died, broken in his efforts to do something for Ireland. Joachim is clearly Lawrence, who had almost broken himself trying to do something for England, but had now decided to turn away from Europe altogether to seek the old gods. When she quotes Joachim she is quoting Lawrence himself:

Joachim said that evil was the lapsing back to old life-modes that have been surpassed in us (133).

But her instinct to believe drives her to defend Don Ramon against Joachim:

No! It's not a helpless, panic reversal. It is conscious, carefully chosen. We must go back to pick up old threads. We must take up the old, broken impulse that will connect us with the mystery of the cosmos again, now we are at the end of our own tether (134).

Mexico itself certainly offers no hope to Kate or anyone else. The shedding of blood, however inhuman, had been a meaningful act for the Aztecs; but the spilling of blood and bowels in the Mexico bull-ring is obscenely gratuitous, an expression of the corruption and cowardice of those who performed and those who

applauded. The first chapter closes with one of the book's central
images:

She felt again, as she felt before, that Mexico lay in her destiny almost as a
doom. Something so heavy, so oppressive, like the folds of some huge
serpent that seemed as if it could hardly raise itself (18).

People and place alike seem characterised by ugliness, squalid
evil, brutality, jeering malevolence:

There was a ponderous, down-pressing weight upon the spirit: the great
folds of the dragon of the Aztecs, the dragon of the Toltecs winding around
one and weighing down the soul (44).

Perhaps something came out of the earth, the dragon of the earth, some
effluence, some vibration which militated against the very composition of the
blood and nerves in human beings (49).

How can this serpent, this 'dragon of degenerate or of incomplete
existence' (54) be transformed into the living Quetzalcoatl of
Don Ramon's pantheon? Apparently the Aztecs themselves began
the degeneration when they 'raised their deity to heights of
horror and vindictiveness' (53). And underneath the Catholicism
of modern Mexico is a 'profound unbelief' which has made the
dragon still more malevolent, still more of a burden, a con-
stricting inertia, strangling life. If Don Ramon can restore belief
by resurrecting Quetzalcoatl as a young and shining god, the
dragon will raise himself and resume his good aspect.

Ruskin described the snake as 'a divine hieroglyph of the
demoniac power of the earth—of the entire earthly Nature'. It is
exactly in this sense that Lawrence's snake functions in its mythic
status, a status which he later enlarged upon in *Etruscan Places*:

In the old world the centre of all power was at the depths of the earth, and at
the depths of the sea, while the sun was only a moving subsidiary body:
and...the serpent represented the vivid powers of the inner earth, not only
such powers as volcanic and earthquake, but the quick powers that run up
the roots of plants and establish the great body of the tree, the tree of life,
and run up the feet and legs of man, to establish the heart (107).

In *Apocalypse* Lawrence goes on to discuss the 'half-divine half-
demonish nature' of the potency for which the snake stands:

It is this which surges in us to make us move, to make us act, to make us
bring forth something: to make us spring up and live. Modern philosophers
may call it Libido or *Elan Vital*, but the words are thin, they carry none of
the wild suggestion of the dragon (162).

His coils within the sun make the sun glad, till the sun dances in radiance. For in his good aspect, the dragon is the great vivifier, the great enhancer of the whole universe (164).

The plumed serpent is compounded of snake and eagle. It is the eagle who is held to demand blood-sacrifice to the sun whence he comes:

The eagle flies nearest to the sun, no other bird flies so near. So he brings down the life of the sun, and the power of the sun, in his wings, and men who see him wheeling are filled with the elation of the sun. But all creatures of the sun must dip their mouths in blood, the sun is for ever thirsty, thirsting for the brightest exhalation of blood (*Phoenix* 67).

Quetzalcoatl is a phoenix, for he threw himself into a volcano when Christ came to Mexico, and so ascended as smoke to the place behind the sun where the gods live, there to sleep the great sleep of regeneration until his cycle should come round.

It is not, however, as a plumed serpent that Quetzalcoatl manifests himself, but as a man of great stature, dark and bearded, his body shining like gold, who rises naked from the Lake of Sayula. It is the newspaper article reporting this supposed event which acts as Kate's call:

Strangely, a different light than the common light seemed to gleam out of the words of even this newspaper paragraph...Quetzalcoatl was, she vaguely remembered, a sort of fair-faced bearded god; the wind, the breath of life, the eyes that see and are unseen, like the stars by day (53).

The experience of reading this paragraph affects Kate much as the cell under the microscope or the final rainbow had affected Ursula:

Amid all the bitterness that Mexico produced in her spirit, there was still a strange beam of wonder and mystery, almost like hope. A strange darkly-iridescent beam of wonder, of magic...

Gods should be iridescent, like the rainbow in the storm...Gods die with men who have conceived them. But the god-stuff roars eternally, like the sea, with too vast a sound to be heard (53).

The rainbow signified the arc of the covenant between man and God, the guarantee of continuing creative intercourse, primarily between heaven and earth, by rain and sunshine. The Quetzal-coatl symbol, a snake with his tail in his mouth, the markings on his back forming the rays of a sun within which an eagle spreads his wings, signifies also this covenant and this intercourse, so that the rituals centre on the coming of the rains, and the men of

Quetzalcoatl call themselves Lords of the Two Ways, of heaven
and earth, fire and water, day and night. Quetzalcoatl is also
Lord of the Morning Star, because he stands between the day
and the night, in the creative twilight, time of rebirth. His return
is the return of Pan, or Lucifer in all his pristine brightness:

Lucifer is brighter now than tarnished Michael or shabby Gabriel. All
things fall in their turn, now Michael goes down, and whispering Gabriel,
and the Son of the Morning will laugh at them all. Yes, I am all for Lucifer,
who is really the Morning Star (Frieda, *Not I But the Wind* 252).

The Morning Star is also the Soul-star, the spark, 'the Quick
of all beings and existence, which he called the Morning Star,
since men must give all things names' (249). And it is the
meeting-ground, the sacrament, in all creative human relationships. It is Don Ramon's self-appointed task to transform the
fanged serpent of the horror of Mexico into this new and ancient
god, who is but a manifestation of the godhead within all living
things:

Quetzalcoatl is to me only the symbol of the best a man may be, in the next
days. The universe is a nest of dragons, with a perfectly unfathomable life-
mystery at the centre of it. If I call the mystery the Morning Star, surely it
doesn't matter! A man's blood can't beat in the abstract (270).

Don Ramon comes very close to those modern Christians who
call their God not the Morning Star, but 'the infinite and inexhaustible depth and ground of all being' (Tillich). John
Robinson, in *Honest to God*, quotes Bonhoeffer's definition of
God as 'the "beyond" in the midst of our life...not on the
borders of life, but at its centre'. He also quotes Don Ramon:

And then—when you find your own manhood—your womanhood...then
you know it is not your own, to do as you like with. You don't have it of your
own will. It comes from—from the middle—from the God. Beyond me, at
the middle, is the God (70).

Tillich virtually paraphrases this:

The most intimate motions within the depths of our souls are not completely
our own. For they belong also to our friends, to mankind, to the universe,
and to the Ground of all being, the aim of our life.

Don Ramon later tells his son:

I believe that the hearts of living men are the very middle of the sky. And
there God is; and Paradise; inside the hearts of living men and women (353).

When Kate, through the words of the newspaper, hears 'the soundless call, across all the hideous choking' (54) she knows why she has come to Mexico:

To be alone with the unfolding flower of her own soul, in the delicate, chiming silence that is at the midst of things (55).

She recognises in Don Ramon and Cipriano 'men face to face not with death and self-sacrifice, but with the life-issue' (62). She is drawn to the magic Lake of Sayula, and finds there that the horror and heaviness of the atmosphere of Mexico for the first time relaxes. Another spirit emanates from the 'sperm-like' waters of the lake. The lake is sacred to the oldest gods and offerings were thrown into it by the ancients. The lake is the centre of the new world, the bath of life, the mixing-bowl. A man emerges from the water to demand tribute to Quetzalcoatl. In his face, and that of the crippled boatman, her Charon, she sees

a look of extraordinary, arresting beauty, the silent, vulnerable centre of all life's quivering, like the nucleus gleaming in tranquil suspense, within a cell (88).

As they part, the boatman gives her a token, an ollita, a little earthenware pot from the time of the old gods, which he fishes from the bed of the lake. This is the beginning of Kate's initiation.

Only a miracle could save Mexico, Don Ramon had told Kate, but 'the miracle is always there...for the man who can pass his hand through to it, to take it'. Kate touches it when she says 'Come then!' to 'the silent life-breath which hung unrevealed in the atmosphere, waiting' (103). What she submits to here is not the horror, but what she takes to be its opposite, the promise of fulfilment, a power which will help her to build her self, to win her soul out of the chaos:

In her soul she was thinking of the communion of grace. With the black-eyed man it was the same. He was humbler. But as he peeled his orange and dropped the yellow peel on the water, she could see the stillness, the humility, and the pathos of grace in him; something very beautiful and truly male, and very hard to find in a civilised white man. It was not of the spirit. It was of the dark, strong, unbroken blood, the flowering of the soul (103).

The Morning Star is 'the gleaming clue to the two opposites', but not the opposites of blood-knowledge and mental consciousness, soul and spirit:

But down on it all, like a weight of obsidian, comes the passive negation of the Indian. He understands soul, which is of the blood. But spirit, which is superior, and is the quality of our civilisation, this, in the mass, he darkly and barbarically repudiates (112).

Kate was attracted and repelled. She was attracted, almost fascinated by the strange nuclear power of the men in the circle. It was like a darkly glowing, vivid nucleus of new life. Repellant the strange heaviness, the sinking of the spirit into the earth, like dark water. Repellant the silent, dense opposition to the pale-faced spiritual direction. Yet here and here alone, it seemed to her, life burned with a deep new fire...Surely this was a new kindling of mankind! (118).

Or is it merely a new kindling of old lusts?

It was not that their eyes were exactly fierce. But their blackness was inchoate, with a dagger of white light in it. And in the inchoate blackness the blood-lust might arise, out of the sediment of the uncreated past...They are caught in the toils of old lusts and old activities as in the folds of a black serpent that strangles the heart...So, these men, unable to overcome the elements, men held down by the serpent tangle of sun and electricity and volcanic emission, they are subject to an ever-recurring, fathomless lust of resentment, a demonish hatred of life itself. Then, the instriking thud of a heavy knife, stabbing into a living body, this is the best. No lust of woman can equal that lust. The clutching throb of gratification as the knife strikes in and the blood spurts out! (130-1).

In his efforts to transform this 'black serpent that strangles the heart' into a fine new god who can redeem a murderous people, Don Ramon can hardly change the elements of Mexico. He cannot push Mexico towards Europe. He must come to terms with the old lusts and old activities, with a race which will never come forth from its own darkness into 'the upper world of daylight and fresh air', never be 'frank' and 'open', never see that other creatures have lives of their own, to be respected, as one's own life is to be respected. He knows that blood-lust itself must be satisfied by offering up the blood of defeated enemies to the sun. In fact the men Don Ramon executes would have been executed by normal processes of law in most countries today (as L. D. Clark has pointed out). It is rather in the power and licence he gives to Cipriano that Don Ramon compromises with the horror:

If it seemed to him a knave, a treacherous cur, he stabbed him to the heart, saying: 'I am the red Huitzilopochtli, of the knife' (364).

Cipriano openly embraces the horror:

Why not? Horror is real...The bit of horror is like the sesame seed in the nougat, it gives the sharp wild flavour. It is good to have it there (232).

What Don Ramon offers Kate is a dream of innocence regained:

When great plains stretched away to the oceans, like Atlantis and the lost continents of Polynesia, so that seas were only great lakes, and the soft, dark-eyed people of that world could walk around the globe. Then there was a mysterious, hot-blooded, soft-footed humanity with a strange civilisation of its own (413).

The 'mental-spiritual life of white people' is quickly withering and will soon die. But Kate, drawing on the mysticism and potency of the aboriginal Celtic people at the bottom of her soul, can then help to bring about

a new germ, a new conception of human life, that will arise from the fusion of the old blood-and-vertebrate consciousness with the white man's present mental-spiritual consciousness. The sinking of both beings into a new being (413).

She sees her marriage in these terms: 'the marriage which is the only step to the new world of man' (414). But she is here affirming a position very different from Don Ramon's. He will have no truck with the mental-piritual consciousness. His rituals are entirely devoted to the blood-and-vertebrate consciousness to the exclusion of mind. He marries a woman who, unlike Kate, will totally submit to him; and he calls Kate renegade when she proposes to return to Europe.

Kate's own standards of balance, 'fusion', demand that she should retain some independence, not submit wholly. Yet Cipriano, in his role as Pan, as demon lover, enforces such a submission to his 'great pliant column', his 'huge erection':

Submission absolute, like the earth under the sky. Beneath an overarching absolute (308).

This terrible, complete marriage offers her passivity and abandon, the abandoning of everything, including her own selfhood:

Her world could end in many ways, and this was one of them. Back to the twilight of the ancient Pan world, where the soul of the woman was dumb, to be forever unspoken (309).

Is this not, by her own standards and Lawrence's, truly renegade? Is it not a reversal of Ursula's painful struggle towards selfhood and articulation, back to the uncreated surcharged consciousness of the early Brangwens? Is not the denial that one alone can have a soul—'It takes a man and a woman together to make a soul'

(387)—a denial of the star-polarity Birkin and Ursula found in marriage? This is the terrible price Kate has to pay for her abandon:

What do I care if he kills people? His flame is young and clean. He is Huitzilopochtli, and I am Malintzi. What do I care, what Cipriano Viedma does or doesn't do? Or even what Kate Leslie does or doesn't do! (392).

Her marriage to Cipriano is clearly seen by the novel as equivalent to the death of the woman who rode away: 'Was this the knife to which she must be sheath?' (388).

What holds Kate in Mexico at the end is not her belief in Don Ramon's 'high-flown bunk', not her own belief in the fusion of the two types of consciousness, not even her own submergence in the older consciousness she occasionally experiences, but the man, Cipriano, who must take her to give her life, at forty, some meaning, and prevent her deterioration into another Mrs Witt.

Ramon and Cipriano no doubt were right for themselves, for their people and country. But for herself, ultimately, ultimately she belonged elsewhere (385).

In the last chapter Mexico softens for her. The peons loading a spangled bull into a ship's hold are the opposite of the obscene bullfighters of the opening chapter. The peon with the baby donkey is the opposite of the urchin who tortured the water-fowl:

In the shadow of a great tree a mother-ass was tethered, and her foal lay in the shadow, a little thing black as ink, curled up, with fluffy head erect and great black ears spreading up, like some jet-black hare full of witchcraft.
'How many days?' called Kate to the peon, who had come out of the straw hut.
He gave her the flash of his dark eyes, in a sort of deference. And she felt her breast surge with living pride.
'Last night, Patrona!' he smiled in answer.
'So new! So new! He doesn't get up, can't he?' The peon went round, put his arm under the foal and lifted it to its feet. There it straddled on high, in amaze, upon its black legs like bent hair-pins.
'How nice it is!' cried Kate in delight, and the peon laughed at her with a soft, grateful flame, touched with reverence.
The ink-black ass-foal did not understand standing up. It rocked on its four loose legs and wondered. Then it hobbled a few steps, to smell at some green, growing maize. It smelled and smelled and smelled, as if all the dark aeons were stirring awake in its nostrils.
Then it turned, and looked with its bushy-velvet face straight at Kate, and put out a pink tongue at her. She laughed aloud. It stood wondering, dazed.

Then it put out its tongue again. She laughed at it. It gave an awkward little skip, which surprised its own self very much. Then it ventured forward again, and all unexpectedly even to itself, exploded into another little skip.

'Already it dances!' cried Kate. 'And it came into the world only last night!'...

Glancing up, Kate met again the peon's eyes, with their black, full flame of life heavy with knowledge and with a curious reassurance. The black foal, the mother, the drinking, the new life, the mystery of the shadowy battlefield of creation; and the adoration of the full-breasted, glorious woman beyond him: all this seemed in the primitive black eyes of the man.

'Adios!' said Kate to him, lingeringly.

'Adios, Patrona!' he replied, suddenly lifting his hand high, in the Quetzalcoatl salute (433–4).

But the Quetzalcoatl salute cannot fully explain the miraculous transformation. In the earlier part of this passage it is hard to credit that we are still in Mexico. The language here is not the language of the earlier part of the novel. It is invested with a quite new freshness and gentleness. It is like an incident from another novel; like Mellors showing Connie the newly-hatched pheasant chicks. It seems that, at the end, Lawrence himself has had too much of a good thing with Quetzalcoatl and all that, and is ready to leave the dark gods to the Mexicans, turning to seek for the clue in human relationships, in love, in togetherness:

Yet Kate herself had convinced herself of one thing, finally: that the clue to all living lay in the vivid blood-relation between man and woman. A man and a woman in this togetherness were the clue to all present living and future possibility. Out of this clue of togetherness between a man and a woman, the whole of the new life arose. It was the quick of the whole (397).

After his almost fatal illness of February 1925 Lawrence turned against Mexico:

Altogether I think of Mexico with a sort of nausea:...really I feel I never want to see an Indian or an 'aboriginee' or anything in the savage line again (Moore 341).

His next novel was to be called *Tenderness*.

CHAPTER 9

CHRONOLOGY

In September 1925 the Lawrences returned to Europe for good.

REVIEW OF 'HADRIAN VII' BY BARON CORVO (*Adelphi*, December 1925; *Phoenix*).
REVIEW OF 'SAID THE FISHERMAN' BY MARMADUKE PICKTHALL (*Adelphi*, January 1927; *Phoenix*).
    October 1925 (*CL* 860).

REVIEW OF 'THE ORIGINS OF PROHIBITION' BY J. A. KROUT (*N.Y. Times Books*, 31 January 1926; *Phoenix*).
    October–November 1925 (Tedlock 255).

A LITTLE MOONSHINE WITH LEMON (*Laughing Horse*, April 1926; *Mornings in Mexico*).
    25 November 1925 (St Catherine's Day).

SUN (*New Coterie*, Autumn 1926; *Archer*, London, 1926; *The Woman Who Rode Away*, 1928; Unexpurgated Edition, Black Sun Press, Paris, 1928).
    November/December 1925 (*CL* 870).

SMILE (*Nation and Athenaeum*, 19 June 1926; *The Woman Who Rode Away*).
    Probably late 1925 (Moore 350).

GLAD GHOSTS (*Dial*, July–August 1926; *The Woman Who Rode Away*).
    December 1925 (*CL* 870–73).

EUROPE *v.* AMERICA (*Laughing Horse*, April 1926; *Phoenix*).
    Late 1925 or early 1926.

THE VIRGIN AND THE GYPSY (Orioli, Florence, 1930).
    Probably January 1926 (AH 650).

BEYOND THE ROCKIES (*The Laughing Horse*, April 1926; *Complete Poems*, 1964).
MEDITERRANEAN IN JANUARY (*ibid*).
    January 1926.

THE ROCKING HORSE WINNER (*The Ghost Book*, Hutchinson, 1926; *The Lovely Lady*, Secker, 1933).
    By March 1926 (Nehls III, 43).

TWO BLUE BIRDS (*Dial*, April 1927; *The Woman Who Rode Away*).
By 13 May 1926 (AH 658).

IN LOVE (*Dial*, November 1927; *The Woman Who Rode Away*).
RAWDON'S ROOF (Elkin Mathews and Marrot, 1928; *The Lovely Lady*).
Both of uncertain date. Possibly 1926.

REVIEW OF 'HEAT' BY ISA GLENN (*Phoenix*).
Probably April 1926 (Tedlock 256).

GERMANS AND LATINS (*La Cultura*, November 1934; *Phoenix*).
30 April 1926 ('Tomorrow is the first of May').

INTRODUCTION TO 'MAX HAVELAAR' BY W. SIEBENHAAR (Knopf, 1927; *Phoenix*).
Early May 1926 (AH 658).

THE NIGHTINGALE (*Forum*, September 1927; *Phoenix*).
23 June 1926 (unpublished diary of Wilkinson family).

FIREWORKS (*Nation and Athenaeum*, 16 April 1927; *Phoenix*).
25 June 1926 (Tedlock 193).

ETRUSCAN EMBROIDERY (AH 344).
25 June 1926 (Wilkinson diary).

MERCURY (*Atlantic Monthly*, February 1927; *Phoenix*).
July 1926 (Tedlock 193).

MAN IS A HUNTER (*Phoenix*).
Probably 1926 (Tedlock 192).

THE MAN WHO LOVED ISLANDS (*Dial*, July 1927; *The Woman Who Rode Away*, American Edition; *The Lovely Lady*).
Probably Autumn 1926 (*CL* 918).

In August 1926 Lawrence made his last visit to England.

REVIEW OF 'THE WORLD OF WILLIAM CLISSOLD' BY H. G. WELLS (*Calendar*, October 1926; *Phoenix*).
Autumn 1926.

REVIEW OF 'GIFTS OF FORTUNE' BY H. M. TOMLINSON (*T.P.'s and Cassell's Weekly*, 1 January 1927; *Phoenix*).
Probably October 1926 (Tedlock 257).

THE DUC DE LAUZUN (*Phoenix*).
THE GOOD MAN (*Phoenix*).
Probably October 1926.

LADY CHATTERLEY'S LOVER (Orioli, Florence, 1928).
First version begun mid-October 1926 (Tedlock 20) and finished probably in late November or early December (*CL* 948). The letters make it clear that Lawrence did not touch the novel in the spring and summer of 1927, as Tedlock suggests.
The second version must therefore have followed the first almost immediately, probably beginning in December 1926. This version was completed by the end of February 1927 (*CL* 969).
The third version was probably begun on 3 December 1927 (Tedlock 25) and was finished on 8 January 1928 (*CL* 1032).

REVIEW OF 'PEDRO DE VALDIVIA' BY R. B. CUNNINGHAM GRAHAM (*Calendar*, January 1927; *Phoenix*).
Probably late 1926 (Tedlock 257).

THE HOLY FAMILY (Paintings, Mandrake Press, 1929).
First week in November 1926 (*CL* 945).

BOCCACCIO STORY (Paintings).
Early December 1926 (Nehls III, 121).

FIGHT WITH AN AMAZON (Paintings).
Late December 1926 (*CL* 955).

RED WILLOW TREES (Paintings).
Probably 9–10 January 1927 (AH 678).

THE INDIVIDUAL CONSCIOUSNESS *v*. THE SOCIAL CONSCIOUSNESS (*Phoenix*).
Probably January/February 1927 (Tedlock 169).

RETURN TO PARADISE (Paintings).
6–9 February 1927 (*CL* 964, 965).

JOHN GALSWORTHY (*Scrutinies*, Wishart, 1928; *Phoenix*).
February 1927 (*CL* 968).

THE LOVELY LADY (*The Black Cap*, Hutchinson, 1927; Secker, 1933)
Early 1927 (Nehls III, 129).

THE MAN WHO WAS THROUGH WITH THE WORLD (*Essays in Criticism*, July 1959, 213).
27 February–8 March 1927. Possibly a fragment of a novel of 25,000–30,000 words (AH 792, 813).

REVIEW OF 'NIGGER HEAVEN' BY CARL VAN VECHTEN, 'FLIGHT' BY WALTER WHITE, 'MANHATTAN TRANSFER' BY JOHN DOS PASSOS, 'IN OUR TIME' BY ERNEST HEMINGWAY (*Calendar*, April 1927; *Phoenix*).
Probably March 1927. *Nigger Heaven* done by the 8th (*CL* 969).

RESURRECTION (Paintings).

Begun by 8 March (*CL* 969), then set aside. Finished in the second half of May (*CL* 976, 979, 981).

MEN BATHING (AH 472).

Probably done during the early months at the Villa Mirenda.

THE JEUNE FILLE WANTS TO KNOW (*Evening News*, 8 May 1928; *Assorted Articles*, Secker, 1930).

LAURA PHILIPPINE (*T.P.'s and Cassell's Weekly*, 7 July 1928; *Assorted Articles*).

Describes incidents of 18–20 March 1927 (*Poste Restante* 90).

FAUNS AND NYMPHS (Paintings).

This picture, begun towards the end of March, 'passed through many metamorphoses' (Brewster 275). It was altered on 8 November 1927 (*CL* 1017) and 'done up' on 13 April 1928 (Brewster 168).

9

THE HOLY GROUND
1926–1927

Sun
Lady Chatterley's Lover

Until a few men have an active feeling that the world, the social world, can offer little or nothing any more; and until there can be some tangible desire for a new sort of relationship between people, one is bound to beat about the bush. It is difficult not to fall into a sort of preciosity and a sort of faddism.

I think, one day, I shall take a place in the country, somewhere, where perhaps one or two other men might like to settle in the neighbourhood, and we might possibly slowly evolve a new rhythm of life: learn to make the creative pauses, and learn to dance and sing together, without stunting, and perhaps also publish some little fighting periodical, keeping fully alert and alive to the world, living a different life in the midst of it, not merely apart. You see, one cannot suddenly decapitate oneself. If barren idealism and intellectualism are a curse, it's not the head's fault. The head is really a quite sensible member, which knows what's what: or *must* know. One needs to establish a fuller relationship between oneself and the universe, and between oneself and one's fellow man and fellow woman. It doesn't mean cutting out the 'brothers-in-Christ' business simply: it means expanding it into a full relationship, where there can be also physical and passional meeting, as there used to be in the old dances and rituals. We have to know how to go out and meet one another, upon the third ground, the holy ground (Letter to Rolf Gardiner, 11 October 1926, *CL* 940).

§1

THE Italian sun of *Sun* is very different from the sun of Mexico. It is no longer thirsty for blood, but rather a great cleansing and ripening source of health and energy and wholeness. The sun is still, for Juliet, a source of vitality and power, but in a sense more therapeutic than mystical:

It was not just taking sunbaths. It was much more than that. Something deep inside her unfolded and relaxed, and she was given. By some mysterious power inside her, deeper than her known consciousness and will, she was put into connection with the sun, and the stream flowed of itself, from her womb.

She herself, her conscious self, was secondary, a secondary person, almost an onlooker. The true Juliet was this dark flow from her deep body to the sun. She had always been mistress of herself, aware of what she was doing, and held tense for her own power. Now she felt inside her quite another sort of power, something greater than herself, flowing by itself. Now she was vague, but she had a power beyond herself (535).

She is full of sap, rousing to a new way of life, outside the 'vast cold apparatus of civilisation'. The child, too, thrives in the sun, becoming self-sufficient, because 'she took the strain of her anxiety and her will from off him' (532). Though, when real harm threatens 'she was quick as a serpent, leaping to him'. They are no longer shut outside the natural paradise—'the snake was part of the place, along with her and the child'. The husband, Maurice, is very much an outsider, like Lawrence in his pyjamas at the water trough. He is out of his depth in the presence of the Greater Day:

Maurice was standing grey-faced, in his grey felt hat and his dark grey suit, at a loss among the vine terraces. He looked pathetically out of place, in that resplendent sunshine and the grace of the old Greek world; like a blot of ink on the pale, sun-glowing slope (538).

He dare hardly look at her:

Sometimes he glanced at her, furtively, from under his black lashes. He had the gold-grey eyes of an animal that has been caught young, and reared completely in captivity...There was a little soft white core of fear, like a snail in a shell, where the soul of the man cowered in fear of death, and in fear of the natural blaze of life (542, 533).

Juliet recognises in one of the peasants, 'the violent generosity of his blood':

He would have been a procreative sun-bath to her, and she wanted it.

But she does not want him as a permanent connection. In any case they are both married, and desire flickers in her husband with a little courage.

We are aware from the beginning that the sun is, in part, a substitute for a risen man and in part a symbol of the phallus:

She was thinking inside herself, of the sun in his splendour, and her mating with him (532).

She goes to the lemon groves already naked under her wrapper, so that she is ready for the sun in an instant. Lady Chatterley is to leave off her underthings for Mellors in the same ritual spirit.

Juliet has a conviction, 'that the sun knew her, in the cosmic carnal sense of the word' (533). When Maurice finds her naked, she asks, 'What are you going to do about it?' as though she has been discovered in the arms of a lover.

The unexpurgated version of *Sun* (Black Sun Press, 1928) is quite different and takes much further the relationship between Juliet and the peasant. The triangular relationship between husband, wife and peasant links the story much more closely with *Lady Chatterley's Lover*; but, as in *The Virgin and the Gypsy*, the vitalising relationship with the potent outsider is not consummated. As this version is inaccessible (and incorrectly quoted by H. T. Moore, *The Life and Works of D. H. Lawrence*, p. 257), I quote the concluding sections at some length:

The sea was blue, very blue and soft and still-looking, and her womb inside her was wide open, wide open like a lotus-flower, or a cactus flower, in a radiant sort of eagerness. She could feel it, and it dominated her consciousness. And a biting chagrin burned in her breast, against the child, against the complication of frustration...

But now the strange challenge of his eyes had held her, blue and overwhelming like the sun's heart. And she had seen the fierce stirring of the phallus under his thin trousers: for her. And with his red face, and with his broad body, he was like the sun to her, the sun in its broad heat...

And Juliet thought: Why shouldn't I go to him! Why shouldn't I bear his child? It would be like bearing a child to the unconscious sun and the unconscious earth, a child like a fruit.—And the flower of her womb radiated. It did not care about sentiment or possession. It wanted man-dew only, utterly improvident.

We see here how central is the phallus in Lawrence's regenerating vision of the potentialities of human relationships. The mystery, the hidden fire, once symbolised by the rainbow and arched in the blood of men, is now identified with the phallus, though not in the branded little city man, Juliet's husband:

And the little etiolated body of her husband, city-branded, would possess her, and his little frantic penis would beget another child in her. She could not help it. She was bound to the vast, fixed wheel of circumstance, and there was no Perseus in the universe to cut the bonds.

§2

In *Lady Chatterley's Lover* Lawrence is determined, for once, to face the problem of creating a resurrection story which is literally phallic, with a real man as the phallus-bearer. What sort of man could this be? It has to be a freed man, a man who has successfully thrown off the fatal chain and separated himself from the mob. Lawrence returns to his early archetype of non-conformity, the gamekeeper, a kind of hermit, preserving his garden of Eden. But the hermit figure is not wholly acceptable. The hermit might be escaping to or from life.

The negative implications are worked out in *The Man Who Loved Islands*, where Cathcart gradually reduces the world until he can fill it with his own personality. His personality being sterile and null, the result is that death comes to cover the abominable void with its snow-shroud. The hermit life is a denial of relationship. In this case it is also the willed reduction of the varied colours of human experience to a flat white. Cathcart would annihilate the living universe to the single point of the self, a point which then collapses upon itself. He cannot at last deny relationship with the elements. The last remaining inescapable contact is fatal:

As he looked, the sky mysteriously darkened and chilled. From far off came the mutter of the unsatisfied thunder, and he knew it was the signal of the snow rolling over the sea. He turned, and felt its breath on him (746).

The ambiguities of the hermit's position are faced in an interesting fragment, which John R. Elliott Jr. has called *The Man Who Was Through with the World* (Essays in Criticism, IX, 3), written immediately after the first draft of *Lady Chatterley's Lover*.

Henry the Hermit is very much a misanthropist, and the ironic tone suggests that the tale is not to be read as sanctioning his attitudes. On the other hand, the prose does not seek to undercut his position completely, like the prose of *The Man Who Loved Islands*.

The failure is here not so much a soft centre in Henry as a hard-headed refusal to be taken in by, as it were, the mystique of being a hermit:

If you're a hermit, you've got to concentrate. You've got to sit in the door of your hut in the sunshine, and concentrate on something holy. This hermit would sit in the door of his hut in the sunshine right enough, but he couldn't find anything holy enough really to keep him concentrated. If he tried some nice Eastern mode of meditation, and sat cross-legged with a faint lotus-like smile on his face, some dog-in-the-manger inside him growled: Oh, cut it out, Henry, Nirvana's a cold egg for the likes of you (218).

Holiness evades him; but he achieves a healthy self-sufficiency when he can escape the pressure to be holy:

For long hours he sat near his hut in the sun, not meditating, not even musing, just being stubborn, and getting browned to a beautiful gold-brown colour. He did not mind so much, while the sun shone, and he could stroll nude through the trees, or sit out in the glow or in the shade. Then he didn't mind not being able to meditate nor to concentrate, and not having any holiness to bless himself with. The sun on his body seemed to do all the meditating and concentrating he needed. His limbs were thin, and golden brown, and his thin body was as brown as his face. He was, like the savage in the story, 'face all over'.

'I am face all over', he thought to himself, with a smile (219).

He is a pleasant enough fellow, unpretentious and honest. What he misses in the hermit life is a purpose—'some sort of salvation'. Going naked in the sun is purpose enough, but, as the fragment ends, winter and the snow-winds sweep the mountains, and it is going to be more and more difficult to keep himself clean of 'the pollution of people'.

It is not possible to tell whether Henry is going to lose his grip on life as the winter advances and die for lack of human warmth and contact, or whether the following spring was to see him enter the world again to be resurrected like the man who died emerging from the isolation of *noli me tangere*. Either way we have a rejection of the hermit state as a permanent way of life or as an end in itself.

The rejection of the world may be a prelude to renewal:

I think one must for the moment withdraw from the world, away towards the inner realities that ARE real: and return, maybe, to the world later, when one is quiet and sure (*CL* 687)

or to suicide. At worst, the hermit life is a means of nursing and nourishing a jaundiced misanthropy until the hatred extends to the hermit's own life.

§3

In the autumn of 1925 Lawrence's own withdrawal from Europe ended. New Mexico had given him the renewal he had sought:

In the magnificent fierce morning of New Mexico one sprang awake, a new part of the soul woke up suddenly and the old world gave way to a new (*Phoenix* 142).

But now, it seems, he felt Quetzalcoatl to have been something of a stunt, and pronounced himself 'very glad to abandon my rather meaningless isolation' (*CL* 928). His last visit to England, the following summer, brought him, despite the industrial deadlock, a glimpse of hope:

Curiously, I like England again, now I am up in my own regions. It braces me up: and there seems a queer odd sort of potentiality in the people, especially the common people. One feels in them some odd, unaccustomed sort of plasm twinkling and nascent. They are not finished. And they have a funny sort of purity and gentleness, and at the same time, unbreakableness, that attracts one (*CL* 933).

Lawrence is now beginning to place his American experience in a way which became articulate in 1929 in the Introduction to *Bottom Dogs*, where even that superb ending of *St Mawr* is strongly qualified:

The spirit and the will survived: but something in the soul perished: the softness, the floweriness, the natural tenderness. How could it survive the sheer brutality of the fight with that American wilderness, which is so big, vast, and obdurate!...The flow from the heart, the warmth of fellow-feeling which has animated Europe and been the best of her humanity, individual, spontaneous, flowing in thousands of little passionate currents often conflicting, this seems unable to persist on the American soil.

Lawrence is now emerging from his misanthropy, recovering the bearings of *The Rainbow*.

I tell you, we'd better buck up and do something for the England to come, for they've pushed the spear through the side of my England (*CL* 952),

he wrote to Rolf Gardiner. But doing something for the England to come no longer presented itself, as it had during the war, as a challenge to social or political activity. He saw that there must be a change in the individual consciousness before such action would be possible:

...there was nothing to be 'done' in Murry's sense. There is still nothing to be 'done'. Probably not for many, many years will men start to 'do' something. And even then, only after they have changed gradually, and deeply...

It is no use trying to merely modify present forms. The whole great form of our era will have to go. And nothing will really send it down but the new shoots of life springing up and slowly bursting the foundations. And one can do nothing, but fight tooth and nail to defend the new shoots of life from being crushed out, and let them grow. We can't make life. We can but fight for the life that grows in us (Introductory Note to 'The Crown', 1925).

English folk were now to be his concern, not half-sordid savages;
and he wanted 'some sort of tenderness, sensitive, between men
and men, and men and women' (*CL* 1045), on which could be
built a real, clean, vital civilisation.

The renewal of faith in men brings with it a renewed faith in his
art:

It is the way our sympathy flows and recoils that really determines our lives.
And here lies the vast importance of the novel, properly handled. It can inform and lead into new places the flow of our sympathetic consciousness, and
it can lead our sympathy away in recoil from things gone dead. Therefore, the
novel, properly handled, can reveal the most secret places of life: for it is in
the *passional* secret places of life, above all, that the tide of sensitive awareness
needs to ebb and flow, cleansing and freshening (*Lady Chatterley's Lover*,
Penguin, 104).

§4

Ours is essentially a tragic age, so we refuse to take it tragically.

Thus the novel opens—with a stiff upper lip, mouthing the post-
war platitudes:

...there is now no smooth road into the future...we've got to live, no matter
how many skies have fallen...one must live and learn (5).

The cataclysm to which Connie had adjusted so easily was the
paralysing from the waist down of her husband with whom she
had known only a month's honeymoon. The marriage, the honeymoon, the embarkation, the wounding, the return, are all given in
a brief paragraph of three sentences in a tone which is resigned to
the point of flippancy—a tone of not being, and never having
been, really implicated:

Then he went back to Flanders: to be shipped over to England again six
months later, more or less in bits (5).

Our normal sympathy is deliberately inhibited. Why doesn't
Clifford's body matter, even to Connie? 'His hold on life was
marvellous', we are told; 'he was pronounced a cure, and could
return to life again' (5). To what sort of 'life' could Clifford
return 'cured', 'with the lower half of his body from the hips
down, paralysed forever'? A 'small motor attachment' seems to
replace the damaged parts quite adequately.

Having got Clifford crippled for life and having reduced
Connie's world to ruins with apparently needless economy, the

pace slows, just a little, for a flash-back to the girlhood of Constance and her sister Hilda in Germany before the war. Nameless young Germans became their lovers.

However, came the war...before Christmas of 1914 both the German young men were dead: whereupon the sisters wept, and loved the young men passionately, but underneath forgot them. They didn't exist any more (9).

Again the tone arrests our responses. But the irony no longer seems gratuitous for it follows an account, at some length, of the sexual relationships these men had established with the sisters. Their attraction had been intellectual; the real thing had been passionate talk. 'The sex thing' involved no giving, no submission, for that would have been a threat to the girl's freedom. It was exploited for a thrill, indulged in as a 'sort of primitive reversion'. Consequently, it was reductive: 'one was less in love with the boy afterwards, and a little inclined to hate him'. And the boy, afterwards, 'looked as if he had lost a shilling and found sixpence'. There was no interchange, only a loss on both sides, of privacy for the woman and of manhood for the man. They failed to exist for the girls in the last analysis, failed to impinge on their womanhood.

Clifford offers Connie an intimacy which is 'beyond sex'—

the sex part did not mean much to him...one of the curious obsolete, organic processes which persisted in its own clumsiness, but was not really necessary (13).

It is not out of manhood, strength, purpose, that Clifford seeks to share his life with Connie, but out of weakness, dependence—

A man needed support and comfort. A man needed to have an anchor in the safe world. A man needed a wife (12).

He needed someone to believe in him before he could know he existed, for all he had instead of a belief in anything was 'a wincing sense of the ridiculousness of everything, and the paramount ridiculousness of his own position' (12). He is defined by his baronetcy, by Wragby. Despite 'all the defence of privilege', he is 'in some paralysing way, conscious of his own defencelessness'. We begin to realise that the man who is shipped home smashed and paralysed from the war, was spiritually paralysed before he went.

The reality on which Wragby depends is Tevershall,

a village which began almost at the park gates, and trailed in utter hopeless ugliness for a long and gruesome mile: houses, rows of wretched, small, begrimed, brick houses, with black slate roofs for lids, sharp angles, and wilful, blank dreariness (13–14).

The prose toughens to convey the hellishness of the whole show, soulless and ugly, and insidiously destructive of freshness and beauty as if possessed by an evil, obscene will. The people are like souls in purgatory; Connie feels she is living underground. But there is nothing else she can take as real.

Connie's relationship with Clifford offers only mental intimacy —a mutual absorption in Clifford and his work, composition. But the stories have no substance, 'only this endless spinning of webs of yarn, of the minutiae of consciousness' (19). At least they pretend to be real, which is more than can be said of the physical relationship, for 'bodily they were non-existent to one another'. Connie feels that there is 'no substance to her or anything'; the whole fabric of her life seems to be disintegrating:

All the great words, it seemed to Connie, were cancelled for her generation: love, joy, happiness, home, father, mother, husband, all these great dynamic words were half dead now, and dying from day to day. Home was a place you lived in, love was a thing you didn't fool yourself about, joy was a word you applied to a good Charleston, happiness was a term of hypocrisy used to bluff other people, a father was an individual who enjoyed his own existence, a husband was a man you lived with and kept going in spirits. As for sex, the last of the great words, it was just a cocktail term for an excitement that bucked you up for a while, then left you more raggy than ever. Frayed! It was as if the very material you were made of was cheap stuff, and was fraying out to nothing (64).

The last straw is Clifford's unfeeling suggestion that she should have a child by another man; it involves, after all, only a little occasional connection, irrelevant in a marriage of true minds.

Connie looks in the mirror at her own body, and finds it opaque, slack, meaningless:

She was old, old at twenty-seven, with no gleam and sparkle in the flesh. Old through neglect and denial, yes, denial (72).

Clifford has defrauded her of her own body, for there is in him 'no healthy human sensuality, that warms the blood and freshens the whole being' (73).

Tommie Dukes amuses Connie with his forthright declarations:

Intellectually I believe in having a good heart, a chirpy penis, a lively intelligence, and the courage to say 'shit' in front of a lady (41).

It is perhaps significant that this is not the four-letter word Mellors has the courage to say in front of Connie. The word 'intellectually' also gives him away. It is all 'in the head'. He is honest enough not to claim these qualities himself. 'The mental life' has killed off his manhood. 'Real knowledge' has given way to spite and a desire to 'strip the rotten old show'. He serves, however, to introduce our first positive standards—with his notions of 'real men and women', a 'democracy of touch', the resurrection of the body, and the phallus as the only bridge across the bottomless pit of civilised nullity. He introduces also the imagery of the fall which is to carry so much of the structure of the novel:

While you live your life, you are in some way an organic whole with all life. But once you start the mental life you pluck the apple. You've severed the connection between the apple and the tree: the organic connection. And if you've nothing in your life but the mental life, then you yourself are a plucked apple...you've fallen off the tree. And then it is a logical necessity to be spiteful, just as it's a natural necessity for a plucked apple to go bad (39).

Connie does not take him seriously; but the novel does. From this point it follows a formal ritual pattern:

'Ye must be born again! I believe in the resurrection of the body! Except a grain of wheat fall into the earth and die, it shall by no means bring forth. When the crocus cometh forth I too will emerge and see the sun!' In the wind of March endless phrases swept through her consciousness (87).

Dukes' theories and Connie's desires find their embodiment in the keeper and his world. After Wragby, the very cottage seems alive, organic,

the green-stained stone cottage, looking almost rosy, like the flesh underneath a mushroom, its stone warmed in a burst of sun. And there was a sparkle of yellow jasmine at the door (88).

Behind it the keeper, naked to the hips, washes himself 'utterly unaware...subtle as a weasel playing with water, and utterly alone'. Connie accidentally invades his privacy, and is struck as by a visionary experience:

It had hit her in the middle of the body. She saw the clumsy breeches slipping down over the pure, delicate, white loins, the bones showing a little, and the sense of aloneness, of a creature purely alone, overwhelmed her. Perfect, white, solitary nudity of a creature that lives alone, and inwardly alone. And beyond that, a certain beauty of a pure creature. Not the stuff of beauty, not even the body of beauty, but a lambency, the warm, white flame of a single life, revealing itself in contours that one might touch: a body!

Connie had received the shock of vision in her womb, and she knew it; it lay inside her (68–9).

Here is something which does not throw out the old question— what's the point of it all?—something which, like St Mawr, cannot be mistaken for show, façade, nothingness.

There is no facile throwing together of Connie and the keeper. At first he is hostile, jealous of his privacy and freedom. The wood is his refuge from the outer world in which he had suffered much, especially at the hands of women. The hut in the secret clearing is his sanctuary, now invaded by another woman, the wife of his master. He recoils from human contact. He has settled for a half-life, a muted interchange with woods, birds, his dog. As a human being, consequently, he too awaits resurrection. He retreats into heavy dialect and insolence.

Connie also uses the wood as a retreat to a world of health and sanity. She is Persephone, fleeing across the park 'like one who fears to be called back'. Her sterility is set against the life-symbol of a newly-hatched chick:

Then, one day, a lovely sunny day with great tufts of primroses under the hazels, and many violets dotting the paths, she came in the afternoon to the coops and there was one tiny, tiny perky chicken tinily prancing round in front of a coop, and the mother hen clucking in terror. The slim little chick was greyish brown with dark markings, and it was the most alive little spark of a creature in seven kingdoms at that moment. Connie crouched to watch in a sort of ecstasy. Life, life! Pure, sparky, fearless new life! New life! So tiny and so utterly without fear. Even when it scampered a little, scrambling into the coop again, and disappeared under the hen's feathers in answer to the mother hen's wild alarm-cries, it was not really frightened, it took it as a game, the game of living. For in a moment a tiny sharp head was poking through the gold-brown feathers of the hen, and eyeing the Cosmos.

Connie was fascinated. And at the same time, never had she felt so acutely the agony of her own female forlornness. It was becoming unbearable (117–18).

The keeper 'with sure, gentle fingers' draws out a chick for her from under the mother bird. The incident leads directly, with the utmost tact and rightness, to the first love-making:

'There!' he said, holding out his hand to her. She took the little drab thing between her hands, and there it stood, on its impossible little stalks of legs, its atom of balancing life trembling through its almost weightless feet into Connie's hands. But it lifted its handsome, clean-shaped little head boldly, and looked sharply round, and gave a little 'peep'. 'So adorable! so cheeky!' she said softly.

The keeper, squatting beside her, was also watching with an amused face the bold little bird in her hands. Suddenly he saw a tear fall on to her wrist (119).

His desire and his compassion are one:

He turned again to look at her. She was kneeling and holding her two hands slowly forward, blindly, so that the chicken should run in to the mother-hen again. And there was something so mute and forlorn in her, compassion flamed in his bowels for her.

Without knowing, he came quickly towards her and crouched beside her again, taking the chick from her hands, because she was afraid of the hen, and putting it back in the coop. At the back of his loins the fire suddenly darted stronger.

He glanced apprehensively at her. Her face was averted, and she was crying blindly, in all the anguish of her generation's forlornness. His heart melted suddenly, like a drop of fire, and he put out his hand and laid his fingers on her knee.

'You shouldn't cry', he said softly. But then she put her hands over her face and felt that really her heart was broken and nothing mattered any more.

He laid his hand on her shoulder, and softly, gently, it began to travel down the curve of her crouching loins. And there his hand softly, softly, stroked the curve of her flank, in the blind instinctive caress.

She had found her scrap of handkerchief and was blindly trying to dry her face.

'Shall you come to the hut?' he said, in a quiet neutral voice (120).

He approaches her 'without knowing', he touches her with a 'blind instinctive caress'. When he puts his hand out to a woman in need of love, he is exposing himself once more to betrayal. But the instinct to give without reservation, to offer one's body with all its emotions and faculties instead of some formula of words, is stronger than the instinct of self-preservation, of distrust. His brief life as a hermit is brought to an end. He is forced to recognise the illusory nature of his seclusion. Acceptance of the human connection with Connie connects him also, inevitably, with 'the rest of things...Sir Clifford, other folk, complications'. The industrial noises too, the sharp lights from Tevershall pit, can no longer be shut out or ignored. Mellors must face up to life once again, with reluctance and a certain bitterness:

'I thought I'd done with it all. Now I've begun again.'
'Begun what?'

'Life.'

'Life!' she re-echoed, with a queer thrill.

'It's life', he said. 'There's no keeping clear. And if you do keep clear you might almost as well die. So if I've got to be broken open again, I have' (122).

Life includes not only the peace on Connie's breast in the heart of the wood:

He thought with infinite tenderness of the woman. Poor forlorn thing, she was nicer than she knew, and oh! so much too nice for the tough lot she was in contact with. Poor thing, she too had some of the vulnerability of the wild hyacinths, she wasn't at all tough rubber goods and platinum, like the modern girl. And they would do her in! As sure as life, they would do her in, as they do in all natural tender life. Tender! Somewhere she was tender, tender with a tenderness of the growing hyacinths, something that has gone out of the celluloid women of today. But he would protect her with his heart for a little while. For a little while, before the insentient iron world and the Mammon of mechanized greed did them both in, her as well as him (124).

His commitment to Connie in tenderness involves the renewal of the fight against Mammon, a fight which should bring him shoulder to shoulder with the best men of his class and generation. He begins immediately to contemplate social and political forms of activity. He wants to use the strength and hope which he derives from Connie to apply to more broadly human purposes and endeavours.

Clifford's energies, on the other hand, are poured into the void which is at the centre of him, where his maleness and human warmth should be. His will has effectively harnessed his emotions and instincts. He reassures himself of his own existence and importance by becoming a high-priest of Mammon by day and by sinking his head on Mrs Bolton's comforting motherly breast at night, where he could 'forget himself'. The wood is preserved only so that more life can be created for him and his friends to destroy.

Clifford's sterility is, of course, germane to his class. Nothing creative is to be expected from his class. The 'seed' in Clifford's paralysed body is as life-bearing as the cradle in the dry-rotten lumber-room at Wragby. 'A Tevershall baby in the Wragby cradle' is viewed by Mrs Bolton as a blood-transfusion for a decadent aristocracy. Meanwhile Clifford's cronies hope he might produce an heir himself 'to keep up the level of the race'.

Wragby implies Tevershall:

The gentry was departing to pleasanter places, where they could spend their money without having to see how it was made (162).

But the reader is made to see, in the streets of Tevershall

the utter negation of natural beauty, the utter negation of the gladness of life, the utter absence of the instinct for shapely beauty which every bird and beast has, the utter death of the human intuitive faculty (158).

The dirt and squalor combine with human philistinism, vulgarity and commercial exploitation to kill off the 'living intuitive faculty' in men, women and children. In work and leisure, school and play, there is the same pervasive ugliness. The cinema offers *A Woman's Love* as an escape from the reality from which human warmth and giving have been excluded:

Ah God, what has man done to man? What have the leaders of men been doing to their fellow men? They have reduced them to less than humanness; and now there can be no fellowship any more! (159).

A life without beauty has produced a generation without life:

She...saw the colliers trailing from the pits, grey-black, distorted, one shoulder higher than the other, slurring their heavy ironshod boots. Underground grey faces, whites of eyes rolling, necks cringing from the pit roof, shoulders out of shape. Men! Men! Alas, in some ways patient and good men. In other ways, non-existent. Something that men should have was bred and killed out of them (166).

Yet Mellors has come out of this world. The same background had, after all, produced Lawrence himself. And there are those like Mrs Bolton's Ted—living men with a certain blitheness but without a sufficiently developed consciousness to survive for long. But they keep the spark alive.

The descriptions of the woods are also related to wider themes. Connie's expectancy, her half-fearful eagerness as she rushes through the wood hoping to meet her lover again, is conveyed not in romantic, personal terms, but in the richly suggestive description of the wood 'everywhere the bud-knots and the leap of life!':

She went to the wood next day. It was a grey, still afternoon, with the dark-green dogs'-mercury spreading under the hazel copse, and all the trees making a silent effort to open their buds. Today she could almost feel it in her own body, the huge heave of the sap in the massive trees, upwards, up, up to the bud-tips, there to push into little flamey oak-leaves, bronze as blood. It was like a tide running turgid upward, and spreading on the sky...

The wood was silent, still and secret in the evening drizzle of rain, full of the mystery of eggs and half-open buds, half unsheathed flowers. In the dimness of it all trees glistened naked and dark as if they had unclothed themselves, and the green things on earth seemed to hum with greenness (126-7).

The same force and mystery drives Connie to her consummation, which is described throughout in imagery of blossoming.

After her first orgasm, Connie feels 'filled with new life', as if she has conceived:

'If I had a child!' she thought to herself; 'if I had him inside me as a child!'— and her limbs turned molten at the thought, and she realised the immense difference between having a child to oneself, and having a child to a man whom one's bowels yearned towards. The former seemed in a sense ordinary: but to have a child to a man whom one adored in one's bowels and one's womb, it made her feel she was very different from her old self, and as if she was sinking deep, deep to the centre of all womanhood and the sleep of creation (140-1).

Her womanhood had hitherto been erased by her social identity as Lady Chatterley and by her personality, the face she showed to others, even to Clifford, or perhaps most of all to Clifford. Mellors responds to her primarily as a woman and restores her to life at this level of her being. He connects her to the freshness and fertility of the woods. Her run-down body is recharged with life. She vibrates to herself with a sense of creativeness:

She was gone in her own soft rapture, like a forest soughing with the dim, glad moan of spring, moving into bud. She could feel in the same world with her the man, the nameless man, moving on beautiful feet, beautiful in the phallic mystery. And in herself, in all her veins, she felt him and his child. His child was in all her veins, like a twilight.
'For hands she hath none, nor eyes, nor feet, nor golden Treasure of hair...'
She was like a forest, like the dark interlacing of the oak wood, humming inaudibly with myriad unfolding buds. Meanwhile the birds of desire were asleep in the vast interlaced intricacy of her body (143).

Spring here carries the same connotations for Lawrence that it carries for Hopkins in the poem of that name:

What is all this juice and all this joy?
A strain of earth's sweet being in the beginning,
In Eden garden.

The sense of his flesh touching her, his very stickiness upon her, was dear to her, and in a sense holy (142).

In submitting to it she enters the rhythm, the flux of creation. Great courage is required to give oneself to the purifying flood, to let go the reservations and false prudery, to relax the grip of the will. It is an act of faith in life and human kindness:

And oh, if he were not tender to her now, how cruel, for she was all open to him and helpless!

Religious terminology is appropriate here for the reward is a kind of grace:

But it came with a strange slow thrust of peace, the dark thrust of peace and a ponderous, primordial tenderness, such as made the world in the beginning. And her terror subsided in her breast, her breast dared to be gone in peace, she held nothing. She dared to let go everything, all herself, and be gone in the flood (181).

Also a kind of rebirth, a resurrection in the flesh:

She was gone, she was not, and she was born: a woman (181).

Godhead is incarnate in the human body 'alive and potent in the flesh', beautiful. It plays not only in eyes and faces and limbs, but in buttocks and balls—'root of all that is lovely, the primeval root of all full beauty'.

And now she touched him, and it was the sons of god with the daughters of men. How beautiful he felt, how pure in tissue! How lovely, how lovely, strong, and yet pure and delicate, such stillness of the sensitive body! Such utter stillness of potency and delicate flesh. How beautiful! How beautiful! Her hands came timorously down his back, to the soft smallish globes of the buttocks. Beauty! What beauty! A sudden little flame of new awareness went through her. How was it possible, this beauty here where she had previously only been repelled? The unspeakable beauty to the touch of the warm, living buttocks! The life within life, the sheer warm, potent loveliness (182).

The halting rhythm of the prose conveys Connie's wonder as at a revelation of 'life within life'. Each punctuation is an intake of breath:

The sky was dark blue, with crystalline, turquoise rim. He went out, to shut up the hens, speaking softly to his dog. And she lay and wondered at the wonder of life, and of being...As she ran home in the twilight the world seemed a dream; the trees in the park seemed bulging and surging at anchor on a tide, and the heave of the slope to the house was alive (184-5).

At points the natural descriptions carry so much weight that one is reduced to calling them symbolic, though they are never arbitrary or in any way tampered with to fit a formula. The most striking example is the scene where Clifford sallies out into the wood in his motorised wheel-chair:

'I ride upon the achievements of the mind of man', he says, 'and that beats a horse' (186).

He sets himself up as the representative of an intellectualised, industrialised, mechanised civilisation as against the natural world of Mellors which he here enters, very much as an alien. In accordance with his maxim that 'the industry comes before the individual', Clifford expounds his Tory view of the strike situation; yet he disclaims any responsibility for depriving the people of their natural life and manhood: 'Every beetle must live its own life' (189). Clifford will not acknowledge a common humanity, not give 'one heart-beat of real sympathy'. The 'cottony young cowslips standing up still bleared with their down' seem to Connie to refute Clifford utterly, just as the unicellular organism under Ursula's microscope had seemed to her to refute the biology teacher's claim that life was merely a conjunction of physical and chemical mechanisms. They assert a fullness of being which is clearly an end in itself. Meanwhile the chair puffs slowly on, 'surging into the forget-me-nots'. Connie, walking behind,

watched the wheels jolt over the wood-ruff and the bugle, and squash the little yellow cups of the creeping-jenny (191).

The woods have come forth with a profusion of blossom and buds and soft young leaves while Clifford complacently steers his 'weird wheeled ship' of 'civilisation' through these 'last wild waters', leaving a wake of destruction. This rather grotesque contraption is Clifford's substitute for his body and for everything we have seen to be associated with the body. Consequently it is sterile. It struggles and falters 'like a sick thing' and has to be pushed by someone else. The nervous energy and pressure of will with which Clifford tries to keep it going is ineffectual. The impotence of the man is seen in his yellow anger at the necessity of having to put himself into the hands of another man when his machine fails him. At first his anger is merely comic:

They waited, among the mashed flowers, under a sky softly curdling with cloud. In the silence a wood-pigeon began to coo roo-hoo hoo! roo-hoo hoo! Clifford shut her up with a blast on the horn (195).

But later it takes him to the brink of hysteria. His composure masks an incipient insanity. Moreover, it is necessary for Mellors, who has not fully recovered from a bout of pneumonia, to lift both Clifford and chair. Master and machine, as always, take a toll in human terms. 'I must get a different sort of motor' is Clifford's solution, because he sees the fault as purely functional. He might eliminate breakdowns and obstacles, but other faults will appear as the machine grows in size and power; more dangerous, explosive, mechanical faults and human breakdowns: so that the whole process is seen as ultimately suicidal. The Cliffords of the world, Mellors prophesies, will destroy it in an *auto da fé*:

And if we go on in this way, with everybody, intellectuals, artists, government, industrialists and workers all frantically killing off the last human feeling, the last bit of their intuition, the last healthy instinct; if it goes on in algebraical progression, as it is going on; then ta-tah! to the human species! Goodbye! darling! the serpent swallows itself and leaves a void, considerably messed up, but not hopeless. Very nice! When savage wild dogs bark in Wragby, and savage wild pit-ponies stamp on Te22shall pit-bank! *te deum laudamus!* (227).

Like Birkin, Mellors takes a perverse satisfaction in contemplating the end of the world, and having a child seems to him 'a ghastly treachery to the unborn creature' (228). Connie begs him to want a child as a gesture of hope, and gradually draws from him a declaration of his ideals. To make a world fit for themselves and their children to live in, men must be shown what to live for other than money:

'I stand for the touch of bodily awareness between human beings', he said to himself, 'and the touch of tenderness. And she is my mate. And it is a battle against the money, and the machine, and the insentient ideal monkeyishness of the world. And she will stand behind me there. Thank God I've got a woman! Thank God I've got a woman who is with me, and tender and aware of me. Thank God she's not a bully, nor a fool. Thank God she's a tender aware woman.' And as his seed sprang in her, his soul sprang towards her too, in the creative act that is far more than procreative (292).

His relationship with the woman is the core of his life. It gives him the courage of his convictions. He wants to make people pause from earning money to look at themselves and see what this toil has done to them, to make them aware of beauty, to 'pull down Tevershall and build a few beautiful buildings'.

They ought to learn to be naked and handsome, and to sing in a mass and dance the old group dances, and carve the stools they sit on, and embroider their own emblems. Then they wouldn't need money. And that's the only way to solve the industrial problem: train the people to be able to live and live in handsomeness, without needing to spend (315).

But Mellors has no illusions about ever seeing such a life. He knows that there is little or nothing he or anyone else can do single-handed. And this was not, and still is not, the programme of any political party or the creed of any church. Civilisation has become the very evil it should seek to destroy, in whose destruction it should, for the present, take its very purpose. Mellors's vision is frankly Utopian. His real expectations are far from sanguine:

There's a bad time coming, boys, there's a bad time coming! If things go on as they are, there's nothing lies in the future but death and destruction, for these industrial masses. I feel my inside turn to water sometimes, and there you are, going to have a child by me. But never mind. All the bad times that ever have been, haven't been able to blow the crocus out: not even the love of women. So they won't be able to blow out my wanting you, nor the little glow there is between you and me (315-16).

It is enough that he and Connie should shelter the glow and believe in it: for that glow is not just a 'romance'. It is

love in all its manifestations, from genuine desire to tender love, love of our fellow men, and love of God.

It is

love, joy, delight, hope, true indignant anger, passionate sense of justice and injustice, truth and untruth, honour and dishonour, and real belief in anything (SLC 233).

It is the only hope for a dying civilisation. And it is phallic.

§5

The 'twinkling plasm', guaranteeing 'new shoots of life', is transformed, in the last works, into the new symbols of the phoenix ('I rise up') and the phallus or lingam:

The phallus is a great sacred image; it represents a deep, deep life which has been denied in us, and still is denied (CL 967).

The phallus takes over many of the associations of the earlier rainbow symbol, particularly that of pure naked contact between people at the deepest level of their being, and, through this, a sense of relatedness to the greater purposes of creation:

It will be a phallic rather than a sexual regeneration. For the phallus is only the great old symbol of godly vitality in a man, and of immediate contact. It will also be a renewal of marriage: the true phallic marriage. And, still further, it will be marriage set again in relationship to the rhythmic cosmos (*SLC* 258).

From it all things human spring, children and beauty and well made things; all the true creations of humanity. And all we know of the will of God is that He wishes this, this oneness, to take place, fulfilled over a lifetime, this oneness within the great dual blood-stream of humanity (*ibid.* 253).

From the phallus issues

the physical effluence of life which has its own peace, of passion which identifies itself with life, faith in life itself, in the soft splendour of the flesh, in the bigness of destiny, which is so much beyond the carping of human knowledge (*The Second Lady Chatterley*, quoted by Tedlock 308).

Lady Chatterley's Lover, Lawrence insisted, is a phallic, not a sexual, novel:

You will understand what I'm trying to do: the full natural *rapprochement* of a man and a woman; and the re-entry into life of a bit of the old phallic awareness and the old phallic insouciance (*CL* 1063).

The insistence on tenderness, purity, gentleness, beauty, is clearly a rejection of the power-principle which had dominated *The Plumed Serpent*. Another letter of 1928 states:

I sincerely believe in restoring the other, the phallic consciousness, into our lives: because it is the source of all real beauty, and all real gentleness. And those are the two things, tenderness and beauty, which will save us from horrors (*CL* 1046).

The word 'horrors', despite the savage indictments of modern life, is one that we associate with Mexico, with the cult of Quetzalcoatl, which had been hailed at the time as the supreme manifestation of phallic potency. To be in touch with the source of life is now seen as a matter not of blood-knowledge only, but of a total awareness. The word 'physical' is retained as a protest against the idea that consciousness can ever be independent of the body, which is the only vehicle for life, and the only incarnation for the soul. He rejects the 'immutable, eternal spirit' conceived of as independent of the flesh. The conception had led to nullity and inertia, a 'tragic excursus' from life and, therefore, from God.

As I say, it's a novel of the phallic Consciousness: or the phallic Consciousness versus the mental-spiritual Consciousness: and of course you know which side I take. The *versus* is not my fault: there should be no *versus*. The two things must be reconciled in us. But now they're daggers drawn (Brewster 166).

This awareness, 'the naïve or physical or sexual mode of consciousness', 'the honest state before the apple' (*CL* 994), is set against the mental cognitive mode with its mechanical idealism and self-consciousness.

The two modes in the novel are realised not only in Mellors and Clifford Chatterley, but also in the setting of the action. The surrounding colliery towns persist with a self-generating hellish energy:

the frictional, seething, resistant, explosive, blind sort, like that of steam engines and motor cars and electricity, and of such people as Clifford and Bill Tewson and modern insistent women, and these queer vacuous miners: then there was the other, forest energy, that was still and softly powerful, with tender frail bud-tips and gentle finger-ends full of awareness (*The Second Lady Chatterley*, quoted by Tedlock 308).

The wood in which Mellors and Connie seek refuge is the last bit of Eden suburbia has not yet spread over. And the phallic consciousness is the only remnant of the old pre-cognitive state not yet completely beaten down. Here, if anywhere, one can make a start. Two people meeting and mating on this holy ground can restore into life a little of the natural flow of common sympathy without which life putrifies. They are not escaping into a dream world. They are stepping aside from the stifling accumulations of refuse, refreshing themselves in the living stream of desire:

Desire itself is a pure thing, like sunshine, or fire, or rain. It is desire that makes the whole world living to me, keeps me in the flow connected. It is my flow of desire that makes me move as the birds and animals move through the sunshine and the night, in a kind of accomplished innocence, not shut outside of the natural paradise (*SLC* 99).

In thus running together the Christian myth of prelapsarian innocence and a pagan phallicism, Lawrence draws heavily on Whitman's *Children of Adam* poem-cycle:

From what I am determined to make illustrious, even if I stand sole among men,
From my own voice resonant, singing the phallus.

193

Whitman celebrates the 'act divine', and prophesies a resurrection of the world to the garden. The resurrection is through love—'life that is only life after love'. The physical processes of sex are indistinguishable, in Whitman's imagery, from the natural intercourse of the woods, and the forces working through the climbing sap and the body of the earth:

Love-thoughts, love-juice, love-odor, love-yielding, love-climbers, and the
    climbing sap,
Arms and hands of love, lips of love, phallic thumb of love, breasts of love,
    bellies press'd and glued together with love,
Earth of chaste love, life that is only life after love,
The body of my love, the body of the woman I love, the body of the man, the
    body of the earth,
Soft forenoon airs that blow from the south-west,
The hairy wild-bee that murmurs and hankers up and down, that gripes the
    full-grown lady-flower, curves upon her with amorous firm legs, takes
    his will of her, and holds himself tremulous and tight till he is satisfied;
The wet of woods through the early hours,
Two sleepers at night lying close together as they sleep, one with an arm
    slanting down across and below the waist of the other. (*Spontaneous Me*)

It is by a closely similar merging and parallelism of sexual and natural imagery that Lawrence seeks to fashion his myth of paradise regained, a myth he had cherished since *Look! We Have Come Through!*, where he tells of 'beautiful, candid lovers...sure in sinless being':

> But we storm the angel-guarded
> Gates of the long-discarded
> Garden...as victors we travel
> To Eden home.   (*Paradise Re-entered*)

In *Sons and Lovers* Lawrence had interpreted sexual experience more conventionally, as a loss of innocence and paradise, but a challenge to creative activity in the outer world:

They felt small, half afraid, childish, and wondering, like Adam and Eve when they lost their innocence and realised the magnificence of the power which drove them out of Paradise and across the great night and the great day of humanity (353–4).

In *Lady Chatterley's Lover*, the lovers flee from the little, unreal, life-denying day of humanity (as in the painting *Return to Paradise*) in a rather forlorn attempt to regain the innocence, wonder and faith which sexual experience is now seen to generate, and without which any further effort in the civilised world is doomed to sterility:

> If only our civilisation had taught us how to let sex appeal flow properly and subtly, how to keep the fire of sex clear and alive, flickering or glowing or blazing in all its varying degrees of strength and communication, we might, all of us, have lived all our lives in love, which means we should be kindled and full of zest in all kinds of ways and for all kinds of things...(*Assorted Articles* 29).

§6

Yet, for all this, *Lady Chatterley's Lover* is far from giving us a complete return to the creative wholeness of *The Rainbow*.

The use of dialect seems to me unsuccessful, despite Yeats's admiration: 'The coarse language of the one, accepted by both, becomes a forlorn poetry uniting their solitudes, something ancient, humble and terrible.' It offers to guarantee the unequivocal sincerity and integrity of what is being said. It is a language which springs out of direct experience, not one to manipulate experience with, analysing and hedging. When Tommy Dukes uses the four-letter words, he tries to fit them into Clifford's language, a language which serves only the intellect and enables Clifford to evade and ultimately to annihilate the promptings of his senses. In this context, the words are merely swear-words, tokens of Dukes's emancipation. In the context of the dialect, they are meant to appear, after the first shock, natural, spontaneous, really the only honest, unselfconscious words available. Perhaps in Parkin's mouth they would; but Mellors uses them just as deliberately and self-consciously as Tommy Dukes. He hammers the bewildered Connie with them until she becomes almost insensible. The language matches the element of bullying which, despite the emphasis on tenderness, and the numerous episodes of real tenderness, characterises Mellors's treatment of Connie. Neither her readiness at the beginning of love-making, nor her satisfaction at the end seem to interest him. He enters her with almost brutal haste and absence of preliminary love-play. He seldom kisses her, or shows any interest in parts of her body other than her genitals; still less in her non-physical attributes. Copulation looms out of all proportion to other activities in a fully human relationship. The symbolism of the phallus is hardly realised in the novel, so that it does not need a particularly insensitive reader to translate 'the bearer and keeper of the bright phallus' into 'my Lady's fucker' and to accept Mellors's own valuation of Connie as a 'bit o' cunt'.

The relationship is artificially protected from any impingement of the outside world or of other people, so that it compares badly with the Ursula–Birkin relationship in *Women in Love*.

Perhaps the most glaring failure is the treatment of Clifford. I do not see this, however, as a failure of compassion in Lawrence. Clifford earns Lawrence's hatred and the reader's for what he does to others. He is the pure egoist:

The egoist, he who has no more spontaneous feelings, and can be made to suffer humanly no more. He who derives all his life henceforth at second-hand, and is animated by self-will and some sort of secret ambition to *impose* himself, either on the world or another individual (*Phoenix* 200).

It is Clifford who is directly responsible for the suffering of the miners, for the sterility not only of Connie's life, but, for example, of the lives of the children of Tevershall, as we glimpse them having the awareness of life educated out of them in order to fit them for the hellish system. Clifford is the presiding devil, Mammon, instigating this fall from grace, encroaching on Eden with his destructive machinery, running the whole show. We need feel no more compassion for him than we do for the devil in a harrowing of hell. We can nevertheless admit that Lawrence hounds Clifford unnecessarily, exposing what is already naked and lashing what is already mutilated. And Clifford is hardly realised in his human, as opposed to mythic character; he does not transcend the mere machinery of the novel. He is too important to dismiss as economically as Rico in *St Mawr*. And the exigencies of a full-length, overtly realistic novel preclude the highly stylised treatment which Cathcart receives in *The Man Who Loved Islands*. We expect more of the weight and density of a Gerald Crich and do not get it.

The conclusion I am driven to is that *Lady Chatterley's Lover* should have been a short novel like *The Virgin and the Gypsy* or *The Man Who Died*, where the pressure to provide a realistic setting and fully drawn characters would not have sunk the myth of innocence regained.

Lady Chatterley's Lover takes its place in the long-term development of Lawrence's fiction from realism towards myth. That part of it which takes place in the wood is as far removed from the real world as *The Man Who Died*. But the effort to achieve a kind of tragic depth by setting this forlorn idyll within the real England of 1926 just fails to come off.

Lawrence said that he wrote every book three times:

By that I don't mean copying and revising as I go along, but literally. After I finish the first draft I put it aside and write another. Then I put the second aside and write a third. The first draft is generally somewhat like *Sons and Lovers* (Nehls II, 106).

I take this to mean that his first version is normally realistic. This certainly applies to the first version of *Lady Chatterley's Lover*. In the second version the symbolism is much more obtrusive. Mark Schorer (*A Propos* . . . , Penguin, 150) quotes this passage:

To Connie, the wood where she had known Parkin in the spring had become the image of another world.

The third version attempts to fuse the symbolism with the naturalism, and loses a good deal of it in the process. 'They were together in a world of their own', for example, sounds more like women's magazine fiction than a major novel. Mark Schorer (*op. cit.* 145-6) describes the more successful aspects of the process:

The progress from the first through the third version of Lady Chatterley is the history of the effort to make the events at once maximumly plausible in realistic terms and maximumly meaningful in psychic terms. The result in the third version is a novel in a solid and sustained social context, with a clear and happily developed plot, in which the characters function fully and the author allows them to speak for themselves; at the same time it is a novel in which everything is symbolic, in which 'every bush burns', and which in itself finally forms one great symbol, so that one can easily remember it as one remembers a picture. In the background of this picture black machinery looms cruelly against a darkening sky; in the foreground, hemmed in and yet separate, stands a green wood; in the wood, two naked human beings dance.

But the method is not here so wholly successful as this implies. The phallus is asked to stand for life itself. But the naturalistic texture and framework of the third version almost forces us to read it as a sexual rather than a phallic novel. You cannot have a real man and a real woman in a real wood copulating with symbolic genitals. The fusion of the naturalism of the first draft with the stylisation of the second has not been achieved. It is too easy to dismiss the vestigial symbolism merely as overwriting—purple passages. The residue is an insistent, obsessive sexuality.

The clues are elsewhere—in the letters and in *A Propos of Lady Chatterley's Lover* particularly. There the phallus stands for 'the holiness of the heart's affections', even for 'the basic consciousness, and the thing we mean, in the best sense, by common sense' (*CL* 1049). But instead of this, the phallus in the novel almost abrogates the consciousness and becomes a homunculus. Lawrence has failed to marry the finely civilised and civilising consciousness with the deeper awareness of the natural man which is 'the root of poetry, lived or sung' (*CL* 1047).

Making Love to Music deals at some length with the part played by the phallus in the Etruscan consciousness:

> There was a phallic symbol everywhere, so everybody was used to it, and they no doubt all offered it small offerings, as the source of inspiration. Being part of the everyday life, there was no need to get it on the brain, as we tend to do.

> There it is, the delightful quality of the Etruscan dance. They are neither making love to music, to avoid copulation, nor are they bouncing towards copulation with a brass band accompaniment. They are just dancing a dance with the elixir of life. And if they have made a little offering to the stone phallus at the door, it is because when one is full of life one is full of possibilities, and the phallus gives life.

> To the music one should dance, and dancing, dance. The Etruscan young woman is going gaily at it, after two-thousand five-hundred years. She is not making love to music, nor is the dark-limbed youth, her partner. She is just dancing her very soul into existence, having made an offering on one hand to the lively phallus of man, on the other hand, to the shut womb-symbol of woman, and put herself on real good terms with both of them. So she is quite serene, and dancing herself as a very fountain of motion and of life, the young man opposite her dancing himself the same, in contrast and balance, with just the double flute to whistle round their naked heels (*Phoenix* 165–6).

Lady Chatterley's Lover quite lacks this serenity. The Etruscans had it because they externalised the phallus symbol, leaving themselves free for the dance of life, with the delicate brushing of fingertips as the only physical contact. Mellors and Connie make their offerings to the real phallus and pudenda, and have little time for anything else. The full orchestral accompaniment of Lawrence's prose cannot quite reconcile us to the persistent indulgence in copulation. Lawrence has not quite succeeded here in creating a modern embodiment of the Etruscan or prelapsarian innocence.

CHAPTER 10

CHRONOLOGY

THE ESCAPED COCK, PART I (*Forum*, February 1928; Black Sun Press, Paris, 1929).

10–28 April 1927 (*CL* 975, 982).

MAKING LOVE TO MUSIC (*Phoenix*).

26 April 1927 (Tedlock 210).

FLOWERY TUSCANY (*New Criterion*, October–November 1927; *Phoenix*). April/May 1927.

REVIEW OF 'THE PEEP SHOW' BY WALTER WILKINSON AND 'SOLITARIA' BY V. V. ROZANOV (*Calendar*, July 1927; *Phoenix*).

May/June 1927 (Tedlock 259).

ETRUSCAN PLACES (*Travel*, November–December 1927, January–February 1928; Secker, 1932).

Describes experiences of 6–10 April 1927, but not begun until 28 May. 'Cerveteri' and 'Tarquinia' finished by 9 June (*CL* 984), 'Volterra' by 25 June (*CL* 986). The remaining sections were completed by October. A second set of Etruscan essays was planned, but never executed.

THE FINDING OF MOSES (Paintings).

Begun early in June 1927 (Nehls III, 144), then set aside until mid-April 1928 (AH 723, 728).

REVIEW OF 'THE SOCIAL BASIS OF CONSCIOUSNESS' BY TRIGANT BURROW (*Bookman*, N.Y., November 1927; *Phoenix*).

August 1927 (Tedlock 260).

'CAVALLERIA RUSTICANA' BY VERGA (Cape, 1928).

By 13 August 1927 (*CL* 997) Lawrence had begun to translate five more stories to add to the four translated in 1922–3: *Rosso Malpelo*, *Gramigna's Lover*, *War of the Saints*, *Brothpot* and *The How, When, and Wherefore*. These were finished by 25 September, and the introduction added shortly afterwards (*CL* 1004).

THROWING BACK THE APPLE (Paintings).

Probably late October 1927 (*CL* 1013).

NEWTHORPE IN 2927 (my title for the misleading 'Autobiographical Fragment' of *Phoenix*).

Late October 1927 (*CL* 1015).

THE JAGUAR (Paintings, 1964).
6 November 1927 (Nehls III, 166–7).

COLLECTED POEMS (Secker, 1928).
Lawrence was busy throughout November 1927 and January 1928 collecting and revising his poems (Nehls III, 167, 177).

LADY CHATTERLEY'S LOVER (Orioli, Florence, 1928).
Third version 3 December 1927 to 8 January 1928 (*CL* 1032).

THE MANGO TREE (Paintings).
By the end of February 1928 (*CL* 1052).

FIRE DANCE (Paintings).
8–10 March 1928 (*CL* 1044).

YAWNING (Paintings).
LIZARD (Paintings).
8–16 March 1928 (Nehls III, 190; *CL* 1052).

PHOENIX (Design for the cover of *Lady Chatterley's Lover*).
Probably March 1928 (AH 713).

UNDER THE HAYSTACK (Paintings).
DANDELIONS (a painting).
Late March 1928 (*CL* 1052).

RAPE OF THE SABINE WOMEN (Paintings).
2 April 1928 (*CL* 1052).

FAMILY ON A VERANDAH (Paintings).
25 April 1928 (AH 728).

CHAOS IN POETRY (*Exchanges*, December 1929; *Chariot of the Sun*, by Harry Crosby, Black Sun Press, 1931; *Phoenix*).
Late April 1928 (Tedlock 247).

FOREWORD TO 'COLLECTED POEMS' (Secker, 1928).
12 May 1928 (Tedlock 103).

AUTOBIOGRAPHICAL SKETCH (*Assorted Articles*).
Before 10 June 1928.

THE KISS (Paintings).
CONTADINI (Paintings).
PIERO PINI LEADING HIS OXEN TO WORK (a painting).
ITALIAN LANDSCAPE (Paintings, 1964).
BEHIND THE VILLA MIRENDA (Paintings, 1964).
By 10 June when the Lawrences left the Villa Mirenda and Italy for the last time.

THE ESCAPED COCK (Black Sun Press, Paris, 1929) (later *The Man Who Died*).

Part 2. Probably begun in the last month at the Villa Mirenda. 'Worked over' during the third week in June 1928 (*Frieda* 197). Finished by 27 August 1928 (*CL* 1065).

INSOUCIANCE (*Evening News*, 12 July 1928 as *Over-Earnest Ladies*; *Assorted Articles*).

17 June–6 July 1928.

REVIEWS OF 'THE STATION' BY ROBERT BYRON, 'ENGLAND AND THE OCTOPUS' BY CLOUGH WILLIAMS-ELLIS, 'COMFORTLESS MEMORY' BY MAURICE BARING, AND 'ASHENDEN OR THE BRITISH AGENT' BY SOMERSET MAUGHAM (*Vogue*, 20 July 1928; *Phoenix*).

Probably late June or early July 1928.

MASTER IN HIS OWN HOUSE (*Evening News*, 2 August 1928; *Assorted Articles*).

June/July 1928.

DULL LONDON (*Evening News*, 3 September 1928; *Assorted Articles*).
COCKSURE WOMEN AND HENSURE MEN (*Forum*, January 1929; *Assorted Articles*).
WOMEN ARE SO COCKSURE (*Phoenix*).
MATRIARCHY (*Evening News*, 5 October 1928 as *If Women Were Supreme*; *Assorted Articles*).
GIVE HER A PATTERN (*Daily Express*, 19 June 1929 as *The Real Trouble About Women*; *Assorted Articles*).

All probably August 1928.

ACCIDENT IN A MINE (Paintings).
THE MILK WHITE LADY (a painting).

August 1928 (Nehls III, 227).

THINGS (*Bookman*, N.Y., August 1928; *The Lovely Lady*, Secker, 1933).
THE BLUE MOCCASINS (*Plain Talk*, February 1929; *The Lovely Lady*).

August 1928 (Nehls III, 228; Tedlock 72).

NORTH SEA (Paintings).

Late August 1928 (*CL* 1085).

HYMNS IN A MAN'S LIFE (*Evening News*, 13 October 1928; *Assorted Articles*).

29 August 1928 (Nehls III, 229).

RED TROUSERS (*Evening News*, 27 September 1928 as *Oh! For A New Crusade*; *Assorted Articles*).

Early September 1928 (Tedlock 229).

SEX VERSUS LOVELINESS (*Sunday Dispatch*, 25 November 1928 as *Sex Locked Out*; *Assorted Articles*).

IS ENGLAND STILL A MAN'S COUNTRY? (*Daily Express*, 29 November 1928; *Assorted Articles*).

THINKING ABOUT ONESELF (*Sunday Dispatch*, 17 February 1929 as *Myself Revealed*; *Phoenix*).

ALL THERE (*Phoenix*).

> All probably autumn 1928.

PANSIES (Secker, 1929).

> It seems likely that all the poems in this volume were written between leaving Italy in June and taking up residence in Bandol in November 1928.

'THE STORY OF DOCTOR MANENTE' BY IL LASCA (Orioli, Florence, 1929).

> Begun by 21 October 1928 (Moore 391). Still working on it in late November (AH 762). The Introduction was added the following July.

OWNERSHIP (*Assorted Articles*).
THE STATE OF FUNK (*Assorted Articles*).

> Probably late 1928.

NEW MEXICO (*Survey Graphic*, 1 May 1931; *Phoenix*).

> December 1928 (Nehls III, 281).

INTRODUCTION TO 'PANSIES' (Secker, 1929).

> The three versions are dated 'Christmas 1928', 'January 1929' and 'March 1929' (Tedlock 103).

LEDA (Paintings).
RENASCENCE OF MEN (Paintings).

> By 5 January 1929 (Nehls III, 289).

ELECTRIC NUDES (my title; black and white drawing reproduced in *The Paintings*).

INTRODUCTION TO THESE PAINTINGS (Mandrake Press, 1929; *Phoenix*).

> By 11 January 1929 (*CL* 1118).

SPRING (Paintings).
SUMMER DAWN (Paintings).

> Late January 1929 (Nehls III, 408; *CL* 1121).

DANCE SKETCH (Paintings).

> Probably also January 1929.

MOTHER AND DAUGHTER (*New Criterion*, April 1929; *The Lovely Lady*).

> Probably January 1929 (*CL* 1126).

MORE PANSIES (*Last Poems*, Orioli, Florence, 1932).

> The MS is dated 23 November 1928, but the earliest poems appear to date from January/February 1929—i.e. *Ultimate Reality* refers to the visit

of Brewster Ghislin in January, *To A Certain Friend*, *The Emotional Friend* and *Correspondence in After Years* to the letter from Murry received in February.

WE NEED ONE ANOTHER (*Scribner's Magazine*, May 1930; *Equinox*, N.Y., 1933; *Phoenix*).
THE REAL THING (*Scribner's Magazine*, June 1930; *Phoenix*).
NOBODY LOVES ME (*Life and Letters*, July 1930; *Phoenix*).
DO WOMEN CHANGE? (*Sunday Dispatch*, 28 April 1929 as *Women Don't Change*; *Assorted Articles*).

Probably early 1929.

INTRODUCTION TO 'BOTTOM DOGS' BY EDWARD DAHLBERG (Putnam, 1929).

Probably February 1929 (*CL* 1120, 1138).

SINGING OF SWANS (Painting).

25 February 1929 (AH 788).

MY SKIRMISH WITH JOLLY ROGER (popular ed. of *Lady Chatterley's Lover*, Paris, 1929; N.Y. Random House, 1929).

By 3 April 1929 (*CL* 1139). Later extended into *A Propos of Lady Chatterley's Lover*.

MAKING PICTURES (*Creative Art*, July 1929; *Assorted Articles*).

Barcelona, 15/16 April 1929 (*Assorted Articles* 169).

MORE PANSIES (*Last Poems*, Orioli, Florence, 1932).

From *Andraitx-Pomegranate Flowers* to *The Spanish Wife*, June 1929, before the 18th. From *The Painter's Wife* to *The Triumph of the Machine*, June 1929, before the 22nd. *Forte Dei Marmi* to *City Life*, 22 June–7 July 1929. *Thirteen Pictures* to *Lonely, Lonesome, Loney-O!*, 9–17 July 1929. *Trees in the Garden* to *Dearly Beloved Mr Squire*, 17 July–26 August 1929.

NOTTINGHAM AND THE MINING COUNTRY (*New Adelphi*, June 1930; *Phoenix*).

Summer 1929.

THE RISEN LORD (*Everyman*, 3 October 1929; *Assorted Articles*).

Late July 1929 (Tedlock 236).

NETTLES (Faber, 1930).

July–August 1929 (Nehls III, 379; Brewster 208).

COLOUR DECORATIONS FOR 'THE ESCAPED COCK' (Black Sun Press, Paris, 1929).

Mid-August 1929 (*CL* 1180).

PORNOGRAPHY AND OBSCENITY (*This Quarter*, July–September 1929; Faber, 1929; *Phoenix*).

Rottach, between 26 August and 18 September 1929.

ENSLAVED BY CIVILISATION (*Vanity Fair*, September 1929 as *The Manufacture of Good Little Boys*; *Assorted Articles*).

MEN MUST WORK AND WOMEN AS WELL (*Star Review*, November 1929 as *Men and Women*; *Assorted Articles*).

Before October 1929 (Tedlock 237).

VENUS IN THE KITCHEN (Frontispiece to *Venus in the Kitchen* by Norman Douglas, Heinemann, 1952).

Uncertain. Probably 1927–9.

10

A DREAM OF LIFE
1927–1929

The Flying Fish
Etruscan Places
Newthorpe in 2927
The Man Who Died

The Resurrection is to life, not to death. Shall I not see those who have risen again walk here among men perfect in body and spirit, whole and glad in the flesh, loving in the flesh, begetting children in the flesh, arrived at last to wholeness, perfect without scar or blemish, healthy without fear of ill-health? Is this not the period of manhood and of joy and fulfilment, after the Resurrection? Who shall be shadowed by Death and the Cross, being risen, and who shall fear the mystic, perfect flesh that belongs to heaven? Can I not, then, walk this earth in gladness, being risen from sorrow? Can I not eat with my brother happily, and with joy kiss my beloved, after my resurrection, celebrate my marriage in the flesh with feastings, go about my business eagerly, in the joy of my fellows? Is heaven impatient for me, and bitter against this earth, that I should hurry off, or that I should linger pale and untouched? Is the flesh which was crucified become as poison to the crowds in the street, or is it as a strong gladness and hope to them, as the first flower blossoming out of the earth's humus? (*The Rainbow* 280).

§1

RESURRECTION had been a primary theme of Lawrence's ever since *The Rainbow*. But it became even more central after his almost fatal illness in February 1925, when the doctor in Oaxaca forbade him to return to Europe and sent him back to Del Monte. There, in the spring and summer, he made a splendid recovery, was himself resurrected:

How thrilling it was to feel the inrush of new vitality in him; it was like a living miracle. A wonder before one's eyes. How grateful he was inside him! 'I can do things again. I can live and do as I like, no longer held down by the devouring illness.'

How he loved every minute of life at the ranch. The morning, the squirrels, every flower that came in its turn, the big trees, chopping wood, the chickens, making bread, all our hard work, and the people and all assumed the radiance of new life (*Frieda*, 'Not I But the Wind', 144).

The essay *Resurrection* was written at this time:

The Cross was only the first step into achievement. The second step was into the tomb. And the third step, whither? (*Phoenix* 737).

This question was to dominate Lawrence's work for the rest of his life, and the 'radiance of new life' was to shine from his prose, from *The Flying Fish* onwards.

The Flying Fish was written in March or April 1925 when Lawrence was still so weak that he dictated the first pages to Frieda. The hero, Gethin Day, has almost died of malaria in Mexico, and is returning home to England. Gethin Day's homecoming to Daybrook, his ancestral home in Derbyshire, takes on a mythic significance from the *Book of Days*, a mystical work by an Elizabethan ancestor, Sir Gilbert Day, which Gethin almost knows by heart, and which comes back to him insistently during his illness.

> No Day in Daybrook;
> For the Vale a bad outlook

is the family motto.

At present his sister Lydia is there, but she is dying. Lydia has always taunted him with the futility of his wanderings:

You would find far more room for yourself in Daybrook than in these foreign parts, if you knew how to come into your own (*Phoenix* 781).

She expects something of him that he has not yet achieved. What is the nature of 'his own', his inheritance, his birthright? He left because he felt England to be tight and little and overcrowded and full of furniture; he had felt stifled by the atmosphere of Daybrook, the weight of family tradition, the authority the house seemed to have over him. But now common day seemed not to matter to him any more, for he had, in his sickness, entered the Greater Day of which Sir Gilbert had written. This was now his kingdom. The ordinary day had lost its reality to him:

It had cracked like some great bubble, and to his uneasiness and terror, he had seemed to see through the fissures the deeper blue of that other Greater Day where moved the other sun shaking its dark blue wings. Perhaps it was the malaria; perhaps it was his own inevitable development; perhaps it was the presence of those handsome, dangerous, wide-eyed men left over from the ages before the flood in Mexico, which caused his old connexions and his accustomed world to break for him. He was ill, and he felt as if at the very middle of him, beneath his navel, some membrane were torn, some membrane which had connected him with the world and its day (*Phoenix* 782).

For most people, the Greater Day is permanently hemmed in by the lesser, and the life effort is to assert the self against time and death by acquisition, conquest, display, licentiousness, spirituality, gluttony and so forth. The flying fish are likened to the tall men who will re-enter the Greater Day:

Even as the flying fish, when he leaves the air and recovereth his element in the depth, plunges and invisibly rejoices. So will tall men rejoice, after their flight of fear, through the thin air, pursued by death. For it is on wings of fear, sped from the mouth of death, that the flying fish riseth twinkling in the air, and rustles in astonishment silvery through the thin small day. But he dives again into the great peace of the deeper day, and under the belly of death, and passes into his own (*Phoenix* 785–6).

In the essay *Life* in 1917, Lawrence had written:

When he comes into his own, man has being beyond life and beyond death; he is perfect of both. There he comprehends the singing of birds and the silence of the snake (*Phoenix* 695).

Death is part of the creative unknown. Life is the consummation of the two unknowns, that of the beginning and that of the end:

Do I fear the strange approach of the creative unknown to my door? I fear it only with pain and with unspeakable joy. And do I fear the invisible dark hand of death plucking me into the darkness, gathering me blossom by blossom from the stem of my life into the unknown of my afterwards? I fear it only in reverence and with strange satisfaction. For this is my final satisfaction, to be gathered blossom by blossom, all my life long, into the finality of the unknown which is my end (*Phoenix* 698).

This theme is returned to in the last poems.

Daybrook has a flying fish as a weather vane. Lawrence's notes tell us that Gethin Day was to marry on his return and that his wife's thoughts turning on herself ('she is cold about everything, but her will sparkles') the zodiac which revolves beneath the fish, is reversed, and the fish turns its belly upwards. This fish cannot dive under the belly of death: death is in its own belly. All nature is thrown into chaos: 'the world is widdershins'. The woman, in trying to reverse the vane again, is killed by lightning. She had tried to shut out the Greater Day. But you cannot make life dance to your will. Gethin Day knows that if he is to enter the Greater Day (and enter it he must, for the little day is crumbling away) he must wrap himself in patience, 'be still, as an apple on its core, as a nightingale in winter, as a long-waiting mountain upon its fire':

Thou art a fish of the timeless Ocean, and must needs fall back. Take heed lest thou break thyself in the fall! For death is not in dying, but in the fear. Cease then the struggle of thy flight, and fall back into the deep element where death is and is not, and life is not a fleeing away. It is a beauteous thing to live and to be alive. Live then in the Greater Day, and let the waters carry thee, and the flood bear thee along, and live, only live, no more of this hurrying away (*Phoenix* 788).

Caring too much, caring on principle, is also deadly:

Take no care, for what thou knowest is ever less than what thou art. The full fire even of thine own sun in thine own body, thou canst never know. So how shouldst thou load care upon thy sun? Take heed, take thought, take pleasure, take pain, take all things as thy sun stirs. Only fasten not thyself in care about anything, for care is impiety, it spits upon the sun (*Phoenix* 789).

It is in a school of porpoises that Gethin Day sees how the creatures of the Greater Day live; and Lawrence records their movements in limpid, delicate, sensitive prose:

It was a spectacle of the purest and most perfected joy in life that Gethin Day ever saw. The porpoises were ten or a dozen, round-bodied torpedo fish, and they stayed there as if they were not moving, always there, with no motion apparent, under the purely pellucid water, yet speeding on at just the speed of the ship, without the faintest show of movement, yet speeding on in the most miraculous precision of speed (*Phoenix* 794).

Time and again the sentence seems to exhaust itself, only to recover with a new surge, each new clause suddenly appearing from nowhere to take up the meaning, to sustain the even onrush and gliding:

It seemed as if the tail-flukes of the last fish exactly touched the ship's bows, under-water, with the frailest, yet precise and permanent touch. It seemed as if nothing moved, yet fish and ship swept on through the tropical ocean. And the fish moved, they changed places all the time. They moved in a little cloud, and with the most wonderful sport they were above, they were below, they were to the fore, yet all the time the same one speed, the same one speed, and the last fish just touching with his tail-flukes the iron cut-water of the ship. Some would be down in the blue, shadowy, but horizontally motionless in the same speed. Then with a strange revolution, these would be up in pale green water, and others would be down. Even the toucher, who touched the ship, would in a twinkling be changed.

The shorter sentence here, with its distinctive, expectant rhythm, focuses attention on to the last monosyllable. The abrupt halt leaves us gaping. The toucher, so fixed by the earlier clauses, vanishes under our eyes.

And ever, ever the same pure horizontal speed, sometimes a dark back skimming the water's surface light, from beneath, but never the surface broken. And ever the last fish touching the ship, and ever the others speeding in motionless, effortless speed, and intertwining with strange silkiness as they sped, intertwining among one another, fading down to the dark blue shadow, and strangely emerging again among the silent, swift others in pale green water. All the time so swift, they seemed to be laughing. Gethin Day watched spell-bound, minute after minute, an hour, two hours, and still it was the same, the ship speeding, cutting the water, and the strong-bodied fish heading in perfect balance of speed underneath, mingling among themselves in some strange single laughter of multiple consciousness, giving off the joy of life, sheer joy of life, togetherness in pure complete motion, many lusty-bodied fish enjoying one laugh of life, sheer togetherness, perfect as passion. They gave off into the water their marvellous joy of life, such as the man had never met before. And it left him wonderstruck. 'But they know joy, they know pure joy!' he said to himself in amazement. 'This is the most laughing joy I have ever seen, pure and unmixed. I always thought flowers had brought themselves to the most beautiful perfection in nature. But these fish, these fleshy, warm-bodied fish achieve more than flowers, heading along. This is the purest achievement of joy I have seen in all my life: these strong, careless fish. Men have not got in them that secret to be alive together and make one like a single laugh, yet each fish going his own gait. This is sheer joy—and men have lost it, or never accomplished it. The cleverest sportsmen in the world are owls beside these fish. And the togetherness of love is nothing to the spinning unison of dolphins playing under-sea. It would be wonderful to know joy as these fish know it. The life of the deep waters is ahead of us, it contains sheer togetherness and sheer joy. We have never got there.' There as he leaned over the bowsprit he was mesmerized by one thing only, by joy, by joy of life, fish speeding in water with playful joy. No wonder Ocean was still mysterious, when such red hearts beat in it! No wonder man, with his tragedy, was a pale and sickly thing in comparison! What civilisation will bring us to such a pitch of swift laughing togetherness, as these fish have reached? (*Phoenix* 794–5).

The warm-bodied porpoises combine in perfect balance the instinctive life of the fish and the consciousness of the higher intelligence, the coldness of isolated pride and power—'each fish going his own gait'—and the warmth of contact, love, laughter, interchange. Lawrence is seeking now some equivalent poise, harmony, first in an individual man, later in a society, a civilisation. Gethin Day was to have been such a man, perhaps with others:

The last part will be regenerate man, a real life in this Garden of Eden (Brewster 288).

But Lawrence never finished the story:

It was written so near the borderline of death, that I never have been able to carry it through, in the cold light of day (Brewster 288).

The regenerate man reappears in *The Man Who Died*, where Lawrence recaptures something of the incredible beauty and serenity of *The Flying Fish*.

§2

In New Mexico Lawrence had found religion, Pan alive and dancing. But the rhythm was not one the European races could dance to. The joy was 'dark' in a sense which would exclude the European whose joy demands 'the upper world of daylight and fresh air'.

In the tombs of Etruria in the spring of 1927, Lawrence discovered 'a living, fresh, jolly people' (Nehls III, 137). As he peered at the flaked and faded frescoes with the aid of a pocket torch in dark underground caverns, he imaginatively recreated the life of these people:

You cannot think of art, but only of life itself, as if this were the very life of the Etruscans, dancing in their coloured wraps with massive yet exuberant naked limbs, ruddy from the air and the sea-light, dancing and fluting along through the little olive trees, out in the fresh day (*Etruscan Places* 39).

The word 'jolly' reminds us of the standards of normality formulated in *Sons and Lovers*, but dropped for many years when Lawrence saw life with a more jaundiced eye. The descent into the Etruscan tombs was a descent into light and air, freedom and normality:

The tombs seem so easy and friendly, cut out of rock underground. One does not feel oppressed, descending into them. It must be partly owing to the peculiar charm of natural proportion which is in all Etruscan things of the unspoilt, unromanticised centuries. There is a simplicity, combined with a most peculiar, free-breasted naturalness and spontaneity, in the shapes and movements of the underworld walls and spaces, that at once reassures the spirit. The Greeks sought to make an impression, and Gothic still more seeks to impress the mind. The Etruscans, no. The things they did, in their easy centuries, are as natural and as easy as breathing. They leave the breast breathing freely and pleasantly, with a certain fullness of life. Even the tombs. And that is the true Etruscan quality: ease, naturalness, and an abundance of life, no need to force the mind or the soul in any direction (12).

Even death, which had so dominated the Mexican consciousness, is here defeated of its horrors, incorporated into life:

And death, to the Etruscan, was a pleasant continuance of life, with jewels and wine and flutes playing for the dance. It was neither an ecstasy of bliss, a heaven, nor a purgatory of torment. It was just a natural continuance of the fullness of life. Everything was in terms of life, of living (12).

The sexual symbols of the lingam and the ark dominated the Etruscan consciousness, but with a blitheness and naturalness which contrasts forcibly with the obsessive insistence of Mellors. But the Etruscan world was annihilated by the Romans. It proved too vulnerable. Such joy in life was interpreted by the Romans as viciousness:

They hated the phallus and the ark, because they wanted empire and dominion and, above all, riches: social gain. You cannot dance gaily to the double flute and at the same time conquer nations or rake in large sums of money (14).

Historically, this contrast is unsound, exaggerated, for the Etruscans were primarily a trading people and were not above a little colonisation on their own account. But Lawrence's imaginative reconstruction, for the most part, rings true enough.

'One cannot think of art, but only of life itself.' For Etruscan art does not try to hold life down with heavy monuments, but keeps it fluid and changing, like song and dance. Their temples were wooden—

small, dainty, fragile, and evanescent as flowers...and alive with freely modelled painted figures in relief, gay dancing creatures, rows of ducks, round faces like the sun, and faces grinning and putting out a tongue, all vivid and fresh and unimposing. The whole thing small and dainty in proportion, and fresh, somehow charming instead of impressive. There seems to have been in the Etruscan instinct a real desire to preserve the natural humour of life (26).

These 'amusing, free, bold designs' remind us of the gargoyles in Lincoln Cathedral which Anna clung to when the jewelled vault threatened to imprison her spirit. We think too of Picasso and the way in which his art has broken down elegant conventions in the name of life:

It is there nearly always in Etruscan things, the naturalness verging on the commonplace, but usually missing it, and often achieving an originality so free and bold, and so fresh, that we, who love convention and things 'reduced to a norm', call it a bastard art, and commonplace (32).

When the creative act is 'an act of pure attention' to the object, when it achieves complete awareness and sees into the life of things, it becomes a kind of divination, a religious insight:

All it depends on is the amount of true, sincere, religious concentration you can bring to bear on your object. An act of pure attention, if you are capable of it, will bring its own answer. And you choose that object to concentrate upon which will best focus your consciousness. Every real discovery made, every serious and significant decision ever reached, was reached and made by divination. The soul stirs, and makes an act of pure attention, and that is a discovery (55).

Conventional art cannot communicate this vision:

A painter like Sargent, for example, is so clever. But in the end he is utterly uninteresting, a bore. He never has an inkling of his own triviality and silliness. One Etruscan leopard, even one little quail, is worth all the miles of him (57–8).

From the dancing figures it is an easy step to the religious sense of the Etruscans:

The curves of their limbs show pure pleasure in life, a pleasure that goes deeper still in the limbs of the dancers, in the big, long hands thrown out and dancing to the very ends of the fingers, a dance that surges from within, like a current in the sea. It is as if the current of some strong different life swept through them, different from our shallow current today: as if they drew their vitality from different depths that we are denied (48).

Behind all the dancing was a vision, and even a science of life, a conception of the universe and man's place in the universe which made men live to the depth of their capacity. To the Etruscan all was alive; the whole universe lived; and the business of man was himself to live amid it all. He had to draw life into himself, out of the wandering huge vitalities of the world (49).

This religion is not superseded. The gods can still be known by the act of attention and awareness which is also joy:

As the pagan old writer says: 'For no part of us nor of our bodies shall be, which doth not feel religion: and let there be no lack of singing for the soul, no lack of leaping and of dancing for the knees and heart; for all these know the gods.'

Which is very evident in the Etruscan dancers. They know the gods in their very finger-tips. The wonderful fragments of limbs and bodies that dance on in a field of obliteration still know the gods, and make it evident to us (47).

The Etruscans really knew what a man might be:

The active religious idea was that man, by vivid attention and subtlety and exerting all his strength, could draw more life into himself, more life, more and more glistening vitality, till he became shining like the morning, blazing like a god (50).

But 'we have lost the art of living' (59). Lawrence had sought it for many years. It had started with his own community Rananim:

If only it will all end up happily, like a song or poem, and we live blithely by a big river, where there are fish, and in the forest behind wild turkeys and quails: there we make songs and poems and stories and dramas, in a vale of Avalon, in the Hesperides, among the Loves! (CL 389).

A pipe-dream.

He had found no prelapsarian community in existence which could answer. Not even the Indians. In 1925 Gethin Day had found the embodiment of his dream in a school of porpoises. Lawrence knew that dolphins had leaped for centuries in the Etruscan tombs; but not that science would confirm his estimate of their highly developed intelligence and social sense. Dolphins 'have the rainbow within them' (53). They are creatures of the two elements, air and water, equally at home in life and death, carrying life down to the womb of all things:

The dolphin leaps in and out of it suddenly, as a creature that suddenly exists, out of nowhere. He was not: and lo! there he is! The dolphin which gives up the sea's rainbows only when he dies. Out he leaps; then, with a head-dive, back again he plunges into the sea. He is so much alive, he is like the phallus carrying the fiery spark of procreation down into the wet darkness of the womb (53).

Balance is his secret, the perfect balance of soul and body, blood and consciousness, carelessness and responsibility, love and power. The rainbow which is arched in his blood makes for a relationship which is both singleness and togetherness. Lawrence knew that a civilisation once accomplished this, not perfectly, but 'more than now', and therefore might again.

§3

The nearest Lawrence comes to such a society is in the unfinished fantasy published in *Phoenix* as 'Autobiographical Fragment'. The author as a boy enters a little crevice of Blue John spar in the hills near Matlock and falls asleep there. He dreams that he wakes a thousand years later and is given hospitality by the natives. They combine the qualities of Etruscan civilisation with those of the mining communities of the Midlands which are described in 'Nottingham and the Mining Country'—the 'physical awareness and intimate togetherness', the 'remote sort of contemplation which shows a real awareness of the presence of beauty', the 'instinct of community' before the men had been beaten down and betrayed. The naked girls are

as comely as berries on a bush. That was the quality of all the people: an inner stillness and ease, like plants that come to flower and fruit (*Phoenix* 830).

It is clear in the description of the dance that Lawrence has Gethin Day's porpoises in mind:

The dance swept into swifter and swifter rhythm, with the most extraordinary incalculable unison. I do not believe there was any outside control of the dance. The thing happened by instinct, like the wheeling and flashing of a shoal of fish or of a flock of birds dipping and spreading in the sky. Suddenly, in one amazing wing-movement, the arms of all the men would flash up into the air, naked and glowing, and with the soft, rushing sound of pigeons alighting the men ebbed in a spiral, grey and sparkled with scarlet, bright arms slowly leaning, upon the women, who rustled all crocus-blue, rustled like an aspen, then in one movement scattered like sparks, in every direction, from under the enclosing, sinking arms of the men, and suddenly formed slender rays of lilac branching out from red and grey knot of the men.

All the time the sun was slowly sinking, shadow was falling, and the dance was moving slower, the women wheeling blue around the obliterated sun. They were dancing the sun down, and dancing as birds wheel and dance, and fishes in shoals, controlled by some strange unanimous instinct. It was at once terrifying and magnificent. I wanted to die, so as not to see it, and I wanted to rush down, to be one of them. To be a drop in that wave of life (832).

As the Etruscans had placed lingams in every tomb, Lawrence put them in his paintings, and he puts one at the centre of his imaginary civilisation:

We came out on top into a circular space, it must have been where our Congregational Chapel stood, and in the centre of the circle rose a tower shaped tapering rather like a lighthouse, and rosy-coloured in the lamplight. Away in the sky, at the club-shaped tip of the tower, glowed one big ball of light (834).

Lawrence calls this fantasy 'a dream of life':

There was an instinctive cleanliness and decency everywhere, in every movement, in every act. It was as if the deepest instinct had been cultivated in the people, to be comely. The soft quiet comeliness was like a dream, a dream of life at last come true (834).

It was the Etruscan experience which freed Lawrence from the 'world of care', which restored to him the ability to stand aside from the rush towards death, from clocks and calendars, trains and motor-cars, self-sacrifice and salvation; to give up his 'savage pilgrimage', his exhaustive and exhausting quest. He has not found a living embodiment of his desire. Yet what could be more living than the hunters, fishers and divers, dancers and musicians, wrestlers and horsemen of Tarquinia?

It is all small and gay and quick with life, spontaneous as only young life can be (*Etruscan Places* 35).

As New Mexico had liberated him from our era of civilisation, Etruria liberated him from the death-mode of Mexico. He emerges at last, in the spring of 1927, from the tomb he had entered during the war. He throws off the burden he had assumed, the responsibility for the single-handed salvation of Western Civilisation. Now, like the man who died, he finds he ends in his own finger-tips, and is content, for with them he can touch 'the quick ripple of life' around him. He learns 'insouciance' from the Etruscans; not ceasing to care, but caring freely, without the dead weight of responsibility for other lives, not inhibited from living the single life out of the shadow.

The Man Who Died is autobiographical to this extent. And the face of the resurrected Christ in Lawrence's painting is appropriately his own.

§4

Gradually, through the turkey cock, Quetzalcoatl and the phoenix, the snake has acquired plumage, the colours of resplendent assertive life and potency, and has lost the reptilian coldness, the earth-bound secrecy and darkness of his origins. Gradually he

THE ART OF D. H. LAWRENCE

has ceased to be the malignant demon-king of the underworld and has come into his own, his kingdom on earth.

In *The Virgin and the Gypsy*, the cock, like the original snake, is still denied:

> She felt rather like Peter when the cock crew, as she denied him. Or rather, she did not deny the gypsy; she didn't care about his part in the show, anyhow. It was some hidden part of herself which she denied: that part which mysteriously and unconfessedly responded to him. And it was a strange, lustrous black cock which crew in mockery of her (56).

The genesis of *The Escaped Cock* was closely bound up with Lawrence's visit, together with Earl Brewster, to the Etruscan tombs in April 1927. The later title, *The Man Who Died*, derives from the Etruscan symbol of the egg, which Lawrence interprets thus:

> It seems as if they too are saluting the mysterious egg held up by the man at the end; who is, no doubt, the man who has died, and whose feast is being celebrated...He holds up the egg of resurrection, within which the germ sleeps as the soul sleeps in the tomb, before it breaks the shell and emerges again (*Etruscan Places* 40, 45).

On the last day of that expedition, in Volterra, Brewster tells us:

> We passed a little shop, in the window of which was a toy rooster escaping from an egg. I remarked that it suggested the title—'The Escaped Cock—a story of the Resurrection'. Lawrence replied that he had been thinking about writing a story of the Resurrection (Brewster 123–4).

The cock in Lawrence's story escapes not from a shell, but from the cord which ties him by the leg, and condemns him to live in the little day of the barnyard. He is the creative urge—'resplendent with arched and orange neck by the time the fig trees were letting out leaves from their end-tips'—denied its full expression, repressed and confined, 'in a dirty little yard with three patchy hens'. Even the peasants admit that 'he is good for twenty hens' while the cockerel tips his head, 'listening to the challenge of far-off unseen cocks, in the unknown world'. 'He answered with a ringing defiance, never to be daunted.' He is crowing for his kingdom, a world in which his life can blossom and assert itself, with many hens to favour and many cocks to defy and master. He cries out for his kingdom, his power and his glory, which is his birthright, as the human body cries out for its life in the flesh. The cord thwarts him, but he refuses to conform:

His voice, above all, had lost the full gold of its clangour. He was tied by the leg, and he knew it. Body, soul and spirit were tied by that string. Underneath, however, the life in him was grimly unbroken. It was the cord that should break (4).

The young cock's break is an assertion of dauntless life and maleness. His triumphant crow wakes the peasant, and also the man who had died:

He was roused by the shrill, wild crowing of a cock just near him, a sound which made him shiver as if electricity had touched him...Leaping out of greenness, came the black and orange cock with the red comb, his tail-feathers streaming lustrous (7).

It is as if the man who died is recharged with life, the vivid life of the escaping cock. In him desire has failed. But in the cock is 'the necessity to live, and even to cry out the triumph of life' (10):

The man who had died saw not the bird alone, but the short, sharp wave of life of which the bird was the crest. He watched the queer, beaky motion of the creature as it gobbled into itself the scraps of food; its glancing of the eye of life, ever alert and watchful, over-weening and cautious, and the voice of its life, crowing triumph and assertion, yet strangled by a cord of circumstance (10-11).

The cock crows from the world Christ had denied, as he had denied 'the greater life of the body':

The world, the same as ever the natural world, thronging with greenness, a nightingale singing winsomely, wistfully, coaxingly calling from the bushes beside a runnel of water, in the world, the natural world of morning and evening, forever undying, from which he had died (6).

It is the bird which has risen to the Father. The man who died is not yet in touch with the world of life. His earlier denial of it he now sees to have been an evasion of the life issue, leading to the crucifixion as inevitably as Cathcart's loathing 'with profound revulsion the whole of the animal creation' had led to his physical and spiritual dissolution. Lawrence summarised the story to Earl Brewster in these words:

I wrote a story of the Resurrection, where Jesus gets up and feels very sick about everything, and can't stand the old crowd any more—so cuts out—and as he heals up, he begins to find what an astonishing place the phenomenal world is, far more marvellous than any salvation or heaven—and thanks his stars he needn't have a 'mission' any more (CL 975).

The Etruscans had impressed Lawrence as a people who 'lived their own lives without wanting to dominate the lives of others' (Nehls III, 137). Both conquering and saving are now seen as forms of domination, of interference; and self-sacrifice as the ultimate life-denial, blasphemy:

No more crucifixions, no more martyrdoms, no more autos da fe, as long as time lasts, if I can prevent it. Every crucifixion starts a most deadly chain of karma, every martyr is a Laocoon snake to tangle up the human family. Away with such things (*CL* 1164).

The man who died does not see his crucifixion as a triumph:

My triumph is that I am not dead, I have outlived my mission and know no more of it. It is my triumph. I have survived the day and the death of my interference, and am still a man. I am young still, Madeleine, not even come to middle age. I am glad all that is over. It had to be. But now I am glad it is over, and the day of my interference is done. The teacher and the saviour are dead in me; now I can go about my business, into my own single life...
Now I can live without striving to sway others any more. For my reach ends in my finger-tips, and my stride is no longer than the ends of my toes. Yet I would embrace multitudes, I who have never truly embraced even one (13).

Salvation is seen as the opposite of destiny. To be saved in that sense is to be cut off from life. 'From what, and to what, could this infinite whirl be saved?' In giving more than he took he had falsified the true balance and mutuality and spontaneity of love and turned it into a sort of prostitution, and bullying:

> And whoever forces himself to love anybody
> begets a murderer in his own body.   (*Retort to Jesus*)

Compulsion is a string around the leg, keeping a man from his life in the world, his kingdom in the greater day:

Whatever came of touch between himself and the race of men, henceforth, should come without trespass or compulsion. For he said to himself: 'I tried to compel them to live, so they compelled me to die. It is always so with compulsion.'...So he healed of his wounds, and enjoyed his immortality of being alive without fret. For in the tomb he had slipped that noose which we call care. For in the tomb he had left his striving self, which cares and asserts itself (18-19).

This is the first kingdom of the risen Lord, the single life voyaging alone in the phenomenal world, which is the body of God.

When he is ready to return to the world of men, he decides that he will go as a physician, and he takes the cock under his arm. The cock is clearly related to the healing power:

'I am a healer, and the bird hath virtue.'
'You are not a believer?'
'Yes! I believe that the bird is full of life and virtue' (21).

The healing mission is to involve the freeing of men not only from physical infirmities, but also from their ties and limitations. At an inn the escaped cock fights and kills the common cock of the yard, and wins his hens, a goodly number. The man who had died leaves him there:

Thou at least hast found thy kingdom, and the females to thy body. Thy aloneness can take on splendour, polished by the lure of thy hens (22).

For he had bought the bird in order to toss him 'into the seethe of phenomena, for he must ride his wave' (20). The man who had died moves on, avoiding the Romans and the press of cities, to seek a woman who can lure his risen body, and, perhaps, restore his desire for human contact.

The second part of *The Man Who Died* was not written until the spring and early summer of 1928. The impact of the Etruscan tomb paintings is evident from the opening description of the little wooden temple of Isis, which stood 'pink and white, like a flower in the little clearing', facing south and west towards Egypt and the winter sun. The symbol of the virgin priestess is the lotus, an Etruscan sexual symbol. But her lotus-bud has not been stirred by the 'golden brief day sun' of Antony, nor by Caesar's 'hard winter sun of power'. She waits for the rising of the reborn invisible sun, for a man who has died to the lesser day in which the slaves copulate and the mother manages the affairs of the estate and Antony displays himself and Caesar rules, and has risen to the other life of the Greater Day. She has waited, like Lou, for the 'mystic new man' who will not break her stillness and mess up her doorways, not tear open the bud of the lotus, but meet her on holy ground, on ground made holy by the meeting, touch her 'with the flame-tip of life'.

The man who died is similarly virgin. He finds in the priestess of Isis 'a tender flame of healing'. The meeting of the two flames is tenderness 'more terrible and lovely than the death I died—':

I have never before stretched my limbs in such sunshine, as her desire for me. The greatest of all gods granted me this... If I am naked enough for this contact, I have not died in vain (38).

219

Thus the man who had died remains on the periphery of life until he is anointed back into the life of the flesh. 'A power of living warmth' enters his wounds from the hands of the priestess, and he responds by desiring her. It draws him into a state of grace. For the first time in his life he is alive in the flesh, and the phallic thrust is literally a rising to the Father:

'I am risen!'

Magnificent, blazing indomitable in the depths of his loins, his own sun dawned, and sent its fire running along his limbs, so that his face shone unconsciously. He untied the string on the linen tunic and slipped the garment down, till he saw the white glow of her white-gold breasts. And he touched them, and he felt his life go molten. 'Father!' he said, 'why did you hide this from me?' And he touched her with the poignancy of wonder, and the marvellous piercing transcendence of desire. 'Lo!' he said, 'this is beyond prayer' (43).

Immediately he becomes aware that he is 'part of the living, incarnate cosmos' (*Apocalypse* 223):

But the man looked at the vivid stars before dawn, as they rained down to the sea, and the dog-star green towards the sea's rim. And he thought: How plastic it is, how full of curves and folds like an invisible rose of dark-petalled openness that shows where the dew touches its darkness! How full it is, and great beyond all gods. How it leans around me, and I am part of it, the great rose of Space. I am like a grain of its perfume, and the woman is a grain of its beauty. Now the world is one flower of many-petalled darknesses, and I am in its perfume as in a touch.

So, in the absolute stillness and fullness of touch, he slept in his cave while the dawn came. And after the dawn, the wind rose and brought a storm, with cold rain. So he stayed in his cave in the peace and the delight of being in touch, delighting to hear the sea, and the rain on the earth, and to see one white-and-gold narcissus bowing wet and still wet. And he said: This is the great atonement, the being in touch. The grey sea and the rain, the wet narcissus and the woman I wait for, the invisible Isis and the unseen sun are all in touch, and at one (44).

Imperceptibly Christ has become Osiris. The corpse of Christianity has been resurrected as a young fertility god.

The seasonal pattern of the tale is clear, yet moves subtly from one cycle to another. The first resurrection, the emergence from the tomb, takes place in spring. Through the first summer, he regains his health in the sunshine and learns to be alone. It is January when he reaches the shores of Sidon and meets the priestess of Isis in search of the torn Osiris. It is as if Lawrence in search of regenerate man has moved from paganism to the very frontier of Christendom, and lured Christ to meet him with the sun and the woman of his choice. The second resurrection, a resurrection of the flesh, carries over the Christian terms and overtones, but is really enacted in the form of a fertility ritual. The rain on the earth accompanies the woman's conceiving.

Plum blossom blew from the trees, the time of the narcissus was past, anemones lit up the ground and were gone, the perfume of bean-field was in the air. All changed, the blossom of the universe changed its petals and swung round to look another way. The spring was fulfilled, a contact was established; the man and the woman were fulfilled of one another, and departure was in the air (44).

But the reborn man promises to perpetuate the fertility cycle:

And when the nightingale calls again from your valley-bed, I shall come again, sure as spring...The suns come back in their seasons: and I shall come again (46).

At last, like the escaped cock, he is free of 'the little life of jealousy and property', and rides his wave:

The man who had died rowed slowly on, with the current, and laughed to himself: I have sowed the seed of my life and my resurrection, and put my touch forever upon the choice woman of this day, and I carry her perfume in my flesh like essence of roses. She is dear to me in the middle of my being. But the gold and flowing serpent is coiling up again, to sleep at the root of my tree.

So let the boat carry me. Tomorrow is another day (47).

It is not expertise or discipline which gives the man who died his control, rather a submission to that within himself which is holy and which puts him in touch with the universe, in harmony with its currents. The assurance is gained by letting the boat carry him, not manipulating life with sail and oar. But the stronger image here is that of the serpent. In so far as the serpent is a phallic symbol, the passage implies what Lawrence writes to Lady Ottoline Morrell in December 1928:

There is a brief time for sex, and a long time when sex is out of place. But when it is out of place as an activity there should still be the large and quiet space in the consciousness where it lives quiescent (*CL* 1111).

According to the Hindus, there is a green dragon which 'coils quiescent at the base of the spine of a man' (*Apocalypse* 165). The man in whom the great divine dragon coils is a hero. The dragon also has its red aspect, demonic and destructive. But now

Lawrence is more interested in creation than destruction. Green is the colour of creation:

The dawn of all creation took place in greenish pellucid gleam that was the shine of the very presence of the Creator (*Apocalypse* 168).

So that when the gleaming green dragon leans down from among the stars 'to vivify us and make us great', it is the Creator breathing the Holy Ghost into us.

The Man Who Died, like *Lady Chatterley's Lover*, leaves us doubtful about what, specifically, the hero is going to do in the world. Yet again Lawrence leaves his hero poised on the brink of the world of men, held back by a resurgence of the old nausea.

The purpose Lawrence set himself in *Fantasia of the Unconscious* is still to be achieved:

We've got to rip the old veil of a vision across and find what the heart really believes in, after all: and what the heart really wants for the next future.

The essay *The Risen Lord*, written in July 1929, is almost a third part to the story. The Risen Lord has retained several of Christ's qualities—the determination not to let that which is God's fall into Caesar's hands, nor the moneylenders desecrate the temple. This, apart from his healing, is the purposive activity in the world of men which the man who died rose to do: 'My wits against theirs' (45). The ending of this essay must be quoted in full:

If Jesus rose a full man in the flesh, He rose to continue His fight with the hard-boiled conventionalists like Roman judges and Jewish priests and money-makers of every sort. But this time, it would no longer be the fight of self-sacrifice that would end in crucifixion. This time it would be a freed man fighting to shelter the rose of life from being trampled on by the pigs. This time, if Satan attempted temptation in the wilderness, the Risen Lord would answer: Satan, your silly temptations no longer tempt me. Luckily, I have died to that sort of self-importance and self-conceit. But let me tell you something, old man! Your name's Satan, isn't it? And your name is Mammon? You are the selfish hog that's got hold of all the world, aren't you? Well, look here, my boy, I'm going to take it all from you, so don't worry. The world and the power and the riches thereof, I'm going to take them all from you, Satan or Mammon or whatever your name is. Because you don't know how to use them. The earth is the Lord's, and the fulness thereof, and it's going to be. Men have risen from the dead and learned not to be so greedy and self-important. We left most of that behind in the late tomb. Men have risen beyond you, Mammon, they are your risen lords. And so, you hook-nosed, glisten-eyed, ugly, money-smelling anachronism, you've got to get out. Men have not died and risen again for nothing. Whom do you think the earth belongs to, you stale old rat? The earth is the Lord's and is given to the men who have died and had the power to rise again. The earth is given to the men who have risen from the dead, risen, you old grabber, and when did you ever rise? Never! So go you down to oblivion, and give your place to the risen men, and the women of the risen men. For man has been dispossessed of the full earth and the earth's fulness long enough. And the poor women, they have been shoved about manless and meaningless long enough. The earth is the Lord's and the fulness thereof, and I, the Risen Lord, am here to take possession. For now I am fully a man, and free above all from my own self-importance. I want life, and the pure contact with life. What are riches, and glory, and honour, and might, and power, to me who have died and lost my self-importance? That's why I am going to take them all from you, Mammon, because I care nothing about them. I am going to destroy all your values, Mammon; all your money values and conceit values, I am going to destroy them all.

Because only life is lovely, and you, Mammon, prevent life. I love to see a squirrel peep round a tree; and left to you, Mammon, there will soon be no squirrels to peep. I love to hear a man singing a song to himself, and if it is an old, improper song, about the fun between lads and girls, I like it all the better. But you, beastly, mealy-mouthed Mammon, you would arrest any lad that sings a gay song. I love the movement of life, and the beauty of life, O Mammon, since I am risen, I love the beauty of life intensely; columbine flowers, for example, the way they dangle, or the delicate way a young girl sits and wonders, or the rage with which a man turns and kicks a fool dog that suddenly attacks him—beautiful that, the swift fierce turn and lunge of a kick, then the quivering pause for the next attack; or even the slightly silly glow that comes over some men as they are getting tipsy—it still is a glow, beautiful; or the swift look a woman fetches me, when she would really like me to go off with her, but she is troubled; or the real compassion I saw a woman express for a man who slipped and wrenched his foot: life, the beauty, the beauty of life! But that which is anti-life, Mammon, like you, and money, and machines, and prostitution, and all that tangled mass of self-importance and greediness and self-conscious conceit which adds up to Mammon, I hate it. I hate it, Mammon, I hate you and am going to push you off the face of the earth, Mammon, you great mob-thing, fatal to men (*Assorted Articles* 114-17).

The word which seems most appropriate here is joy. The happiness of the lovers in *Lady Chatterley's Lover* had been muted, always under the shadow of encroaching evil, unsure of its own ability to survive in the world. Now the Risen Lord smiles confidently to himself as he rows into the bay. The ending of the story sees him, having outwitted the Romans in the first trial, rowing into the unknown future, a life-adventurer, to seek his adversary, secure in the first kingdom of his own body, the second kingdom of his marriage, the third kingdom of his purposive activity in the world and the fourth kingdom of the phenomenal world, the circumambient universe, the house of the God of Life:

Every step I move forward into being brings a newer, juster proportion into the world, gives me less need of storehouse and barn, allows me to leave all and to take what I want by the way, sure it will always be there; allows me in the end to fly the flag of myself, at the extreme tip of life (*Study of Thomas Hardy*).

The Lawrence of these years is usually presented to us as a tortured, embittered outcast, circling wildly round Europe and throwing things at Frieda. We need only look at the rhythms of the ending of *The Man Who Died* to see the complete falsity of this picture. As he nears death, Lawrence seems to live more fully, with an almost preternatural awareness of the quality of life in the instant moment, and with a joy, an insouciance which glows through the later prose.

Compare the tone and rhythms of the later story with this, from *The Plumed Serpent*:

As the bird of the sun, treads the earth at the dawn of the day like a brown hen under his feet, like a hen and the branches of her belly droop with the apples of birth, with the eggs of gold, with the eggs that hide the globe of the sun in the waters of heaven, in the purse of the shell of earth that is white from the fire of the blood, tread the earth, and the earth will conceive like the hen 'neath the feet of the bird of the sun; 'neath the feet of the heart, 'neath the heart's twin feet. Tread the earth, tread the earth that squats as a pullet with wings closed in—(126).

The insistence of the rhythms and the repetitions, the phrases proliferating like 'The House That Jack Built', demand that the passage be chanted as an incantation, which, indeed it is. But the incantation does not serve to simplify and make memorable the meaning; rather to make it impossible to stop long enough over the crush of images to get any coherent meaning at all. Cock and hen, earth and sun and waters, apples and eggs, purse and shell, fire and blood, all combine to make what Hopkins would have called a bloody broth. And the prose which is not part of the actual ceremonial of the new religion does not altogether escape the same tendencies.

The Escaped Cock is written in a clear, fresh prose which does not assume its own inability to convince without a drum-beat and a plethora of images. The prose is poised and self-sufficient and implies a creating imagination similarly at one with itself and its material. Even in *Lady Chatterley's Lover* the prose had sought, at times, to lay a compulsion on us. Now the preacher, the saviour, the leader, are dead in Lawrence too, as he was to admit, a year later to Witter Bynner:

> ...about *The Plumed Serpent* and 'the hero'. On the whole, I think you're right. The hero is obsolete, and the leader of men is a back number. After all, at the back of the hero is the militant ideal: and the militant ideal, or the ideal militant seems to me also a cold egg. We're sort of sick of all forms of militarism and militantism, and Miles is a name no more, for a man. On the whole I agree with you, the leader-cum-follower relationship is a bore. And the new relationship will be some sort of tenderness, sensitive, between men and men and men and women, and not the one up one down, lead on I follow, ich dien sort of business (*CL* 1045).

This tenderness and sensitivity has now entered the prose (and the poetry) and is to remain a prominent characteristic until the end. The letters abound with passages such as this of September 1927 from Bavaria:

> The woods are simply uncanny with mushrooms, all sorts and sizes and shapes and smells, in camps and circles and odd ones—the brightest red, the blackest black and the sea-weediest green—and we pick the little orange-yellow ones and eat them fried in butter.—The dark blue Autumn gentian is out—and the deer are about—little roe-buck—they fly across the paths just like a Persian picture—and then they stop fascinated by my famous little white jacket. The jays are so cheeky they almost steal the tears out of your eyes. I really like it here—but when it's dark and rainy then you sing: 'A little ship was on the sea'—for the oceans of old Time seem to sweep over you (*Review of English Literature*, October 1962, p. 71).

The essay *Insouciance*, written in June 1928, has the same quality:

> When it comes to living, we live through our instincts and our intuitions. Instinct makes me run from little over-earnest ladies; instinct makes me sniff the lime blossom and reach for the darkest cherry. But it is intuition which makes me feel the uncanny glassiness of the lake this afternoon, the sulkiness of the mountains, the vividness of near green in thunder-sun, the young man in bright blue trousers lightly tossing the grass from the scythe, the elderly man in a boater stiffly shoving his scythe-strokes, both of them sweating in the silence of the intense light (*Assorted Articles* 35-6).

'Insouciance', as Lawrence uses it, means the integrity, composure and joy of a free soul which, without ceasing to care deeply about humanity, fights from a position of strength and assurance, health and sanity, independent of praise or blame, chance or even death, sitting like a dandelion on his own stem. One is reminded of the mellowness, simplicity and serenity of Shakespeare's late plays. And of Whitman's *Outline Sketch of a Superb Calm Character*:

His emotions &. are complete in himself irrespective (indifferent) of whether his love, friendship, &. are returned or not.
He grows, blooms, like some perfect tree or flower, in Nature, whether viewed by admiring eyes, or in some wild or wood entirely unknown.
His analogy the earth complete in itself enfolding in itself all processes of growth, effusing life and power for hidden purposes.

They need to be taught the art of living almost from scratch. Lawrence's style has now matured into the purest English prose I know, open and vigorous and clean. It is, in Whitman's words, 'the free channel of himself'. Wordsworth, in 1802, had defined the purpose of the great poet in relevant terms:

He ought, to a certain degree, to rectify men's feelings, to give them new compositions of feeling, to render their feelings more sane, pure, and permanent, in short, more consonant to nature, that is, to eternal nature, and the great moving spirit of things.

Whitman believed that such writing can do the reader a profound service, can 'give him good heart as a radical possession and habit'. Lawrence believed that it can

inform and lead into new places the flow of our sympathetic consciousness, and it can lead our sympathy away in recoil from things gone dead (*Lady Chatterley's Lover*).

Things gone dead had been his subject in *Women in Love*, his *Paradise Lost*. His late works explore the new places and capture their radiance, exuding freshness. The formal difficulties are transcended, the appropriate myths create themselves, as the vision itself is purged and clarified.

Lawrence's myths combine elements of pagan and Christian mythologies, Utopias, and private patterns of symbols, some traditional, some new-minted. They are, in the late works, simple and coherent. They remain stimulating and highly relevant despite the fact that he often withdraws from the immediate struggle into a distant, serene world in which to create his men like gods. His heroes remain solitaries, Gethin Day alone with his dolphins, the man who died alone with the stars, letting the boat carry him.

And the boy in the Blue John crevice will awake alone from what was only a dream. Even the myths would not accommodate a whole society or civilisation of such men. For the myths are in no sense romantic evasions of reality: they make incarnate what is only immanent in reality, bring into sharp focus what is blurred there, penetrate behind the veil of naturalism.

The hopeful heart which Lawrence has regained after the dark years is not fed on notions of social perfectibility:

There will never be a millenium. There will never be a 'true societal flow'— all things are relative. Men were never, in the past, fully societal—and they never will be in the future. But more so, more than now (*CL* 993).

This qualified hope is expanded in the late essay *Nottingham and the Mining Country* which contains a paragraph on the ideal community—unique in Lawrence's work in that it is both industrial and urban. The result is something not unlike New Lanark:

If the company, instead of building those sordid and hideous squares, then, when they had that lovely site to play with, there on the hill-top: if they had put a tall column in the middle of the small market-place, and run three parts of a circle of arcade round the pleasant space, where people could stroll or sit, and with the handsome houses behind! If they had made big, substantial houses, in apartments of five and six rooms, and with handsome entrances. If above all, they had encouraged song and dancing—for the miners still sang and danced—and provided handsome space for these. If only they had encouraged some form of beauty in dress, some form of beauty in interior life—furniture, decoration. If they had given prizes for the handsomest chair or table, the loveliest scarf, the most charming room that the men or women could make! If only they had done this, there would never have been an industrial problem. The industrial problem arises from the base forcing of all human energy into a competition of mere acquisition (*Phoenix* 138).

Lawrence's new-found 'insouciance' was, of course, subject to changes of mood, and did not preclude caring deeply. Part of him is 'a single man' unique and separate, going his own gait. Part is a member of the race of man, an Englishman who has never gone back on his Englishness or his class:

And though the pomegranate has red flowers outside the window
and oleander is hot with perfume under the afternoon sun
and I am 'Il Signore' and they love me here,
yet I am a mill-hand in Leeds
and the death of the Black Country is upon me
and I am wrapped in the lead of a coffin-lining, the living death of my fellow
    men (*We Die Together*).

In a sense, it marks an admission of defeat, a recognition that there was nothing he could do to 'save' his fellow men. It was not for him to interfere, even if he could have done so. He had to admit that he would not live to see any vast changes. He could only cast his words on the air like frail dandelion seeds, which might take root here and there.

CHAPTER 11

CHRONOLOGY

MORE PANSIES (*Last Poems*, Orioli, Florence, 1932).
From *Let There be Light* to *Prayer*.
Probably early September 1929.

'THE LIFE OF J. MIDDLETON MURRY' BY J.C. (privately printed, 1930).
September 1929 (*CL* 1196).

THE ELEPHANTS OF DIONYSOS (*Phoenix*).
September/November 1929 (Tedlock 212).

LAST POEMS (Orioli, Florence, 1932).
From *The Greeks Are Coming* to *The Ship of Death*, late September and October 1929.
From *Difficult Death* to *Shadows*, November 1929.
Change and *Phoenix*, probably November/December 1929.

A PROPOS OF LADY CHATTERLEY'S LOVER (Mandrake Press, 1930).
Probably Autumn 1929.

PICTURES ON THE WALLS (*Vanity Fair*, December 1929 as *Dead Pictures on the Walls*; *Assorted Articles*).
November/December 1929.

APOCALYPSE (Orioli, Florence, 1931).
Conceived at the beginning of October 1929 (*CL* 1204), 'roughly finished' by 15 December (*CL* 1222).

REVIEW OF 'FALLEN LEAVES' BY V. V. ROZANOV (*Everyman*, 23 January 1930; *Phoenix*).
Late 1929 (Tedlock 262).

INTRODUCTION TO 'THE REVELATION OF ST JOHN THE DIVINE' BY FREDERICK CARTER (*London Mercury*, July 1930; *Phoenix*).
By 6 January 1930 (*CL* 1228).

MYSTICAL PREFATORY NOTE TO THE 1930 EDITION OF 'BIRDS, BEASTS AND FLOWERS' (*Phoenix*).
Probably beginning of 1930.

INTRODUCTION TO 'THE GRAND INQUISITOR' BY DOSTOEVSKY (Elkin Mathews and Marrot, 1930; *Phoenix*).
After 9 January and before 6 February 1930 (*CL* 1233, 1241).

On 6 February Lawrence entered the Ad Astra Sanatorium at Vence.

REVIEW OF 'ART NONSENSE' BY ERIC GILL (*Book Collector's Quarterly*, October–December 1933; *Phoenix*).
Late February 1930 (Tedlock 263).

THE UNDYING MAN (*Phoenix*).
I am unable to find any clue to the dating of this remarkable fragment. It is clearly a very late work.

Lawrence died at Vence on 2 March 1930 at the age of 44.

II

'NEW BLOSSOMS OF ME'

1927–1929

Pansies
The Paintings
More Pansies
Last Poems

And if, in the changing phases of man's life
I fall in sickness and in misery
my wrists seem broken and my heart seems dead
and strength is gone, and my life
is only the leavings of a life:

and still, among it all, snatches of lovely oblivion, and snatches of renewal
odd, wintry flowers upon the withered stem, yet new, strange flowers
such as my life has not brought forth before, new blossoms of me.

(*Shadows*)

§1

LAWRENCE himself never took *Pansies* as seriously as his hostile
critics, as his two introductions make clear: he called them 'rag
poems'. His theory is that a single thought, not part of an
argument, is more naturally expressed as verse than prose. The
poems themselves vary considerably in type and in quality. There
are several sorts of successes: bits of doggerel—

> I can't stand Willy wet-leg,
> can't stand him at any price.
> He's resigned, and when you hit him
> he lets you hit him twice.

—but Lawrence's wit is not really epigrammatic and his control
of rhythm and rhyme not usually precise enough to bring off his
doggerel. His best satirical poems need more room and colloquial
freedom to establish a distinctive tone of voice, which Richard
Hoggart has characterised as 'the voice of a down-to-earth, tight,

bright, witty Midlander...slangy, quick, flat and direct, lively, laconic, sceptical, nonconforming, nicely bloody-minded'. The voice is also sometimes exasperated, flippant and spiteful, as Richard Aldington has argued, but I do not find these faults in, say, *Natural Complexion*:

> But you see, said the handsome young man with the chamois gloves
> to the woman rather older than himself,
> if you don't use rouge and a lip-stick, in Paris
> they'll take you for a woman of the people.
>
> So spoke the british gentleman
> pulling on his chamois gloves
> and using his most melodious would-be-oxford voice.
>
> And the woman said: Dear me!
> how rough that would be on you, darling!
> Only, if you insist on pulling on those chamois gloves
> I swear I'll pull off my knickers, right in the Rue de la Paix.

The incident is related economically; just the right tone of voice is established; nothing else is required of the verse. Indeed several equally successful satirical poems (such as *What is He?* and *Canvassing for the Election*) are not written out as verse at all. This pungent prose easily heightens to a free-verse as accomplished as the best of *Birds, Beasts and Flowers*, but with a new assurance, buoyancy, airiness, playfulness, which is to be the form Lawrence's wit turns to in *Last Poems*:

> A lizard ran out on a rock and looked up, listening
> no doubt to the sounding of the spheres.
> And what a dandy fellow! the right toss of a chin for you
> and swirl of a tail!
>
> If men were as much men as lizards are lizards
> they'd be worth looking at.

Some of the shortest poems achieve an almost oriental simplicity:

> The gazelle calf, O my children,
> goes behind its mother across the desert,
> goes behind its mother on blithe bare foot
> requiring no shoes, O my children!

Leda creates in a few bold strokes a picture of striking sensuousness and immediacy:

> Come not with kisses
> not with caresses
> of hands and lips and murmurings;
> come with a hiss of wings
> and sea-touch tip of a beak
> and treading of wet, webbed, wave-working feet
> into the marsh-soft belly.

The most formally skilled poem in the collection is probably *Desire is Dead*:

> Desire may be dead
> and still a man can be
> a meeting place for sun and rain,
> wonder outwaiting pain
> as in a wintry tree.

This is a lovely poem, but against *Lizard* or *Leda* seems curiously distant and muted.

There are clearly too many poems in *Pansies*, and many of them are no more than notebook jottings, 'sketches for poems', as Eliot called them. The worst of them do not even have the virtues of good prose:

> Things men have made with wakened hands, and put soft life into,
> are awake through years with transferred touch, and go on glowing
> for long years.
> And for this reason, some old things are lovely
> warm still with the life of forgotten men who made them.

The same 'thought' is much better expressed in a letter to the Brewsters:

Life flows into the object—and life *flows out again* to the beholder. So that whoever makes anything with real interest, puts life into it, and makes it a little fountain of life for the next comer (Brewster 174).

Lawrence's verse comes to life when he stops generalising and begins to specify. *Whatever Man Makes* starts off as a further attempt to express the same 'thought', but the concrete images themselves generate a further delightful insight in the last two lines:

> Whatever man makes and makes it live
> lives because of the life put into it.
> A yard of India muslin is alive with Hindu life.
> And a Navajo woman, weaving her rug in the pattern of her dream
> must run the pattern out in a little break at the end
> so that her soul can come out, back to her.
>
> But in the odd pattern, like snake-marks on the sand
> it leaves its trail.

§2

Lawrence put life into his paintings as he put life into everything he touched. He painted his late pictures in the same way that he wrote his late poems—as the spontaneous outpouring, without conscious technique, of a vision which had long matured in the consciousness:

I have learnt now not to work from objects, not to have models, not to have a technique... The picture must all come out of the artist's inside, awareness of forms and figures. We can call it memory, but it is more than memory. It is the image as it lives in the consciousness, alive like a vision, but unknown (*Assorted Articles* 173).

It is a hazardous method. When it fails, there is no technique, no anatomy, for example, to fall back on. But his successful figures are independent of anatomy. They take their life from a distinctively Lawrentian 'luminosity' of the flesh. His suggestions for improvements to the proofs of the Mandrake reproductions stress this again and again:

Summer Dawn (not very good)—Again too much mere *black*, especially under the man's buttocks—Try to put the light along the man's back, to restore the modelling—The bodies of both should be lifted a little paler to differentiate them from the background. It's too much of a smudge, the different *luminous* places are lost, sunk in. It's not a question of edge, but of the local glow (*CL* 1146).

Such paintings succeed because, like the late poems and prose, they are bathed in a 'delicate awareness of life' which is a matter of vision, not realism:

Art is a form of supremely delicate awareness and atonement—meaning at-oneness, the state of being at one with the object...

One may see the divine in natural objects; I saw it today, in the frail, lovely little camellia flowers on long stems, here on the bushy and splendid flower-stalls of the Ramblas in Barcelona. They were different from the usual fat camellias, more like gardenias, poised delicately, and I saw them like a vision. So now, I could paint them. But if I had bought a handful, and started in to paint them 'from nature', then I should have lost them. By staring at them I should have lost them (*Assorted Articles* 169–70).

This was also the quality of Hopkins's vision:

> ...a glance
> Master more may than gaze, gaze out of countenance.

Lawrence called his pictures 'almost holy'.

Brewster Ghiselin visited Lawrence at Bandol early in 1929 when Lawrence was at the height of his output as a painter. Ghiselin was himself a painter, of the kind who would have bought the bunch of camellias. He has recorded Lawrence's response to one of his paintings:

Late in the sunny morning, Lawrence found me on the plage finishing a water-colour of some brilliant fingerlings I had bought in the market: one emerald; one russet-gold; one green-grey with flecks of blue and purple on belly and gills; and a purple-dark eel. He remarked on their vividness and on the full detail of the painting, for which he himself could never have found enough patience, he said...

Most of all he was concerned about the uncoloured ground of white around the figures...

The feeling for the fishes themselves was true, he said, but they were isolated in the midst of bare space in a way that deprived them of their actual relation to other things, to water, for instance. My pleasure in setting them apart like intense flames in consciousness was 'a form of spiritual will desiring power', refusing to admit and to express the relatedness, the vital interchange, between them and all other things, each in their special quality and degree...

He himself was trying to find some expression in paint for the relations of things, he told me, perhaps by means of the touching and mingling of colours flowing from different things: as the colour of the background, for example, approached any body it would diminish and take some of the colour and quality of that body (Nehls III, 295).

We can see this method in operation in *Dance Sketch*, painted at just this time. Man, woman, goat and vegetation all dance to the same rhythm, united in a 'flow of touch'.

But Lawrence had achieved this flow much earlier, without any mingling of colours. *Boccaccio Story* was only the second picture Lawrence painted after taking up really imaginative painting for the first time in 1926. It is his most accomplished painting. The same rhythm and vitality which runs down the ranks of spurting silvery olive trees and the furrows of the ploughed field also runs along the glowing limbs of the sleeping gardener, the lines all converging upon his exposed phallus. And the incandescence of his thighs seems to shine on to the face of the nearest nun, as the file of nuns, in thick lavender habits and quaint bobbing hats, is drawn almost unwillingly into the same rhythm. Two white dogs trot inquisitively towards the nuns to make up the circle.

There are many other delights—the stately biblicals (*Resurrection* and *The Finding of Moses*); the amusing mock-biblicals (*Throwing Back the Apple*); the radiant *Summer Dawn*; the finely modelled *Contadini*; the sensuous *Leda*. But my own favourite is *Renascence of Men*, where the two naked men glow as if indeed new-born, their flesh iridescent, even in the rather dim re-production:

> The flood subsides, and the body, like a worn sea-shell
> emerges strange and lovely. (*The Ship of Death*)

§3

In *More Pansies* and *Last Poems* Lawrence's thoughts become poems much more consistently than in *Pansies*. The poem *Thought* itself gives us the clue:

> Thought is a man in his wholeness wholly attending.

The poet strives to make 'a new act of attention' and then to give 'direct utterance from the instant, whole man' in language which will make us prick our innermost ear.

Life's tremendous characterisation is Lawrence's theme, 'the magnificent here and now of life in the flesh' (*Apocalypse*). What characterises man is his capacity for wonder and joy:

> we can but touch, and wonder, and ponder, and make our effort
> and dangle in a last fastidious fine delight
> as the fuschia does, dangling her reckless drop
> of purple after so much putting forth
> and slow mounting marvel of a little tree. (*Terra Incognita*)

The supremely delicate awareness with which Lawrence has here caught the fuschia finds its fullest expression in a magnificent but neglected poem, *God is Born*:

> The history of the cosmos
> is the history of the struggle of becoming.
> When the dim flux of unformed life
> struggled, convulsed back and forth upon itself,
> and broke at last into light and dark
> came into existence as light,
> came into existence as cold shadow
> then every atom of the cosmos trembled with delight.
> Behold, God is born!
> He is bright light!
> He is pitch dark and cold!
>
> And in the great struggle of intangible chaos
> when, at a certain point, a drop of water began to drip downwards
> and a breath of vapour began to wreath up

Lo again the shudder of bliss through all the atoms!
Oh, God is born!
Behold, he is born wet!
Look, He hath movement upward! He spirals!

And so, in the great aeons of accomplishment and débâcle
from time to time the wild crying of every electron:
Lo! God is born!

When sapphires cooled out of molten chaos:
See, God is born! He is blue, he is deep blue, he is forever blue!
When gold lay shining threading the cooled-off rock:
God is born! God is born! bright yellow and ductile He is born.

When the little eggy amoeba emerged out of foam and nowhere
then all the electrons held their breath:
Ach! Ach! Now indeed God is born! He twinkles within.

When from a world of mosses and of ferns
at last the narcissus lifted a tuft of five-pointed stars
and dangled them in the atmosphere,
then every molecule of creation jumped and clapped its hands:
God is born! God is born perfumed and dangling and with a little cup!

Throughout the aeons, as the lizard swirls his tail finer than water,
as the peacock turns to the sun, and could not be more splendid,
as the leopard smites the small calf with a spangled paw, perfect,
the universe trembles: God is born! God is here!

And when at last man stood on two legs and wondered,
then there was a hush of suspense at the core of every electron:
Behold, now very God is born!
God Himself is born!

And so we see, God is not
until he is born.

And also we see
there is no end to the birth of God.

The opening corresponds very closely to Whitman's

Urge and urge and urge,
Always the procreant urge of the world.
Out of the dimness opposite equals advance, always substance and increase,
always sex,
Always a knit of identity, always distinction, always a breed of life.

(*Song of Myself*)

Chaos strains to bring forth identity, distinctiveness. The first
stanza struggles towards the phrase 'light and dark', then con-
vulses with the repeated 'came into existence as' to throw light
and shadow to their polar extremes, between them a cosmos. The
stanza ends, like all the subsequent stanzas, with a direct,

wonderfully naïve, recognition of the miracle. After the 'intangible chaos' we feel the tangible presence of dripping water and spiralling vapour, so liquid and airy is the language. The first sign of organic life, the amoeba which 'twinkles within', is even more miraculous. The lizard, the peacock and the leopard have one line each, but are there, splendid and perfect. Each creature is God, and man who stands and wonders is very God in the sense that God is only visible and has his only identity when he becomes incarnate in the created universe. It is not only the amoeba which 'twinkles within'. There is a quick of being in all substances and creatures which is a little God:

All existence is dual, and surging towards a consummation into being. In the seed of the dandelion, as it floats with its little umbrella of hairs, sits the Holy Ghost in tiny compass. The Holy Ghost is that which holds the light and the dark, the day and the night, the wet and the sunny, united in one little clue (*Reflections on the Death of a Porcupine, Selected Essays*, Penguin, 67).

Lawrence was delighted to find that the Etruscans had, according to his own interpretation, symbolised this divine clue, this quick of being, in their patera or mundum—'the round saucer with the raised knob in the centre, which represents the round germ of heaven and earth':

It stands for the plasm, also, of the living cell, with its nucleus, which is the indivisible God of the beginning, and which remains alive and unbroken to the end, the eternal quick of all things, which yet divides and sub-divides, so that it becomes the sun of the firmament and the lotus of the waters under the earth, and the rose of all existence upon the earth: and the sun maintains its own quick, unbroken for ever; and there is a living quick of the sea, and of all the waters; and every living created thing has its own unfailing quick (*Etruscan Places* 30).

It is this 'undying vivid life electron' which the Rabbi Moses Maimonides cuts from the body of Aristotle the Christian and seals in a jar in the late unfinished story *The Undying Man*. As a guarantee of immortality it links up with all the resurrection stories, and carries over into the poems about death.

God is Born is a microcosm which language serves to people with

bodies and presences, here and now, creatures with a foothold in creation even if it is only a lobster on tip-toe.   (*Demiurge*)

Like Whitman, Lawrence celebrates the 'real poems', the objects in the created universe which the poet can only list or point to. By merely naming in pristine terms, the poem re-enacts creation, as if, here in the poem, the objects were receiving their first incarnation.

Red Geranium and Godly Mignonette is another fine example of this. The opening is colloquial and might almost be prose. But the fourth sentence, organised around the rhythms of the words 'geranium' and 'mignonette' themselves, achieves a poise and liveliness which makes it a poem in itself:

> We know that even God could not imagine the redness of a red geranium
> nor the smell of mignonette
> when geraniums were not, and mignonette neither.

The middle section enacts the comedy of the Most High 'cudgelling his mighty brains' to invent scarlet geranium in the abstract, or rather in a green twilight of moss and mud and mastodons. Nine straining clauses separate the Most High from his eventual utterance. The closing section gives us an alternative, serious, account of the creative process:

> But imagine, among the mud and the mastodons
> god sighing and yearning with tremendous creative yearning, in that dark
> green mess
> oh, for some other beauty, some other beauty
> that blossomed at last, red geranium, and mignonette.

Of this poem A. Alvarez has said:

> It is hard to know whether to emphasize more the ease and originality of the piece, or its tact. There is neither a jot of pretentiousness in the poem, nor of vulgarity, though the opportunity for both certainly offered. Lawrence uses his wit not in the modern fashion, to save his face, but to strengthen the seriousness of what he has to say. There is no disproportion between the colloquial liveliness of the opening and the equally alive tenderness of the close. The wit is not a flourish; it is one of the poetic means; it preserves the seriousness from sentimentality and overstatement, as the seriousness keeps the wit from flippancy (*The Shaping Spirit*).

What I want to emphasise further is the extent to which the whole poem leads up to and achieves a most moving climax in its last four words. Both nouns have occurred often enough in the poem; why should they carry such weight at the end? It is partly that they have never before occurred in quite this simple juxtaposition (not even in the title), and partly the absolute yet spontaneous propriety of the words and rhythms which lead up to them.

In the penultimate poem of *More Pansies*, *Flowers and Men*, Lawrence asks a question which many of the *Last Poems* seek to answer:

> Oh leave off saying I want you to be savages.
> Tell me, is the gentian savage, at the top of its coarse stem?
> Oh what in you can answer to this blueness?

In the Greek and Etruscan heroes there had been a redness to answer:

> Oh, and their faces scarlet, like the dolphin's blood!
> Lo! the loveliest is red all over, rippling vermilion
> as he ripples upwards!
> laughing in his black beard!
>
> They are dancing! they return, as they went, dancing!
> For the thing that is done without the glowing as of god, vermilion,
> were best not done at all.
> How glistening red they are!
>
> *(For the Heroes are Dipped in Scarlet)*

But man is a creature of many colours. What makes him the most miraculous of all creatures is his multiplicity:

> a thing of kisses and strife
> a lit-up shaft of rain
> a calling column of blood
> a rose-tree bronzey with thorns
> a mixture of yea and nay
> a rainbow of love and hate
> a wind that blows back and forth
> a creature of beautiful peace, like a river
> and a creature of conflict, like a cataract
>
> *(Death is not Evil, Evil is Mechanical)*

Modern man has lost this essential manhood, has slipped

> ...through the fingers of the hands of god
> into the abyss of self-knowledge,
> knowledge of the self-apart-from-god.   *(Only Man)*

By abstracting himself from the created universe and from his own body and affective life, he has destroyed his own capacity for real thought or knowledge or belief; has forfeited his birthright—

his kingdom, his power and his glory. Now he must 'suffer a sense-change into something new and strange':

> Become aware as leaves are aware
> and fine as flowers are fine
> and fierce as fire is fierce
> and subtle, silvery, tinkling and rippling
> as rain-water
> and still a man,
> but a man reborn from the rigidity of fixed ideas
> resurrected from the death of mechanical motion and emotion.
>
> (*Climbing Down*)

The poems themselves testify that Lawrence is here describing a process already perfectly realised in himself.

Last Poems has shed the bitterness and bittiness of *Pansies*. Form, as we normally understand it in the analysis of poems, has, in a sense, been dispensed with. The direct confrontation of experience, or total immersion in it, precludes the distancing effect of conscious form. All one can do, deliberately, with free verse, Lawrence claims, is to prune away the clichés, 'of rhythm as well as of phrase':

We can get rid of all the stereotyped movements and the old hackneyed associations of sound and sense. We can break down these artificial conduits and canals through which we do so love to force our utterance. We can break the stiff neck of habit. We can be in ourselves spontaneous and flexible as flame, we can see that utterance rushes out without artificial form or artificial smoothness (*Phoenix* 221).

R. P. Blackmur calls this the fallacy of expressive form: 'The faith that if a thing is only intensely enough felt its mere expression in words will give it satisfactory form' (*Language as Gesture*). That 'mere' is the weak point in Blackmur's formulation. We are not concerned, in the best poems, with a 'mere outburst of personal feeling', but with feelings so fused with and disciplined by intellect, so deeply personal in their response both to experience and to language, that they grow into uniquely fitting, almost impersonally authentic forms: 'The law must come new each time from within' (Preface to *New Poems*). There is nothing lawless or undisciplined about such poetry. Lawrence at this time looked back on his early poems as struggles to say something 'which it takes a man twenty years to be able to say'. And Whitman told Burroughs that he had been searching for twenty-five years for the word to express what the twilight note of the robin meant to him. When Lawrence's imagination is fully engaged, his technique does not fail him. Indeed, it brings him close to what Whitman called 'the Divine Style':

Nothing will do, not one word or sentence, that is not *perfectly clear*—with positive purpose—harmony with the name, nature, drift of the poem. Also *no ornaments*, especially *no ornamental adjectives*, unless they have come molten hot, and imperiously prove themselves. *No ornamental similes at all— not one: perfect transparent clearness* sanity and health are wanted—that is the *Divine Style*—O if it can be attained.

Blackmur's strictures could only come from a critic who brings to the poems strong preconceptions about both art and life. Behind Blackmur's belief in the primacy of imposed form lies the assumption that life itself is chaotic or meaningless until it is transformed by art. Art is asked to provide an ordered reality as against the amorphous flux of life and experience. Such a conception of art goes with the Christian, particularly the Catholic temper: its permanent realities are states of being refined out of temporal experience—mystical, conceptual, sometimes, one suspects, merely verbal. Or it goes with cynicism, for the pose of objectivity often fails to hide disgust or indifference in the face of life. Lawrence takes Flaubert as the classical case:

Physical life is a disordered corruption, against which he can fight with only one weapon, his fine aesthetic sense, his feeling for beauty, for perfection, for a certain fitness which soothes him, and gives him an inner pleasure, however corrupt the stuff of life may be...

And even while he has a rhythm in style, yet his work has none of the rhythm of a living thing, the rise of a poppy, then the after uplift of the bud, the shedding of the calyx and the spreading wide of the petals, the falling of the flower and the pride of the seed-head. There is an unexpectedness in this such as does not come from their carefully plotted and arranged developments (*Phoenix* 312–13).

The opposite kind of art is the product of a sensibility which finds life already meaningful and art a process of discovery, revelation and praise. This is also religious, but in a different sense—more often pagan or pantheistic than Christian (Hopkins being a notable exception). The prototype of the affirmative artist is Whitman, who, by divesting himself of all artificiality transforms himself into a living probe:

His verse springs sheer from the spontaneous sources of his being. Hence its lovely, lovely form and rhythm: at the best. It is sheer, perfect *human* spontaneity, spontaneous as a nightingale throbbing, but still controlled, the highest loveliness of human spontaneity, undecorated, unclothed. The whole being is there, sensually throbbing, spiritually quivering, mentally, ideally speaking...The whole soul speaks at once, and is too pure for mechanical assistance of rhyme and measure. The perfect utterance of a concentrated spontaneous soul (*The Symbolic Meaning* 264).

Every word of this we can apply with equal propriety to *Last Poems*. For all the clarity and coherence, there is no hint of lapidary art. The lustre which the language imparts is far from being a polish or finish. It is the shimmer of something essentially unfinished, transitory, because alive, and therefore not to be grasped or nailed down. These flowers are not, he insists, *immortelles*; they sit confidently on top of their stems. The poems exude a freshness which would be lost if the experience were 'boiled down...cooked in the artistic consciousness' (*Etruscan Places*). Each poem gives us the naïve opening of a soul to life— 'pure jets and bubblings of unthinkable newness'. Lawrence exactly answers Whitman's definition of the prophet as 'one whose mind bubbles up and pours forth as a fountain, from inner divine spontaneities revealing God'.

Form and content are wholly inseparable. The success testifies as much to a skill in living as in writing. Hopkins wrote: 'All things are charged with God, and if we know how to touch them give off sparks and take fire, yield drops and flow, ring and tell of him.' Lawrence knew how to touch them:

The whole tide of all life and all time suddenly heaves, and appears before us as an apparition, a revelation. We look at the very white quick of nascent creation. A water-lily heaves herself from the flood, looks round, gleams, and is gone. We have seen the incarnation, the quick of the ever-swirling flood. We have seen the invisible. We have seen, we have touched, we have partaken of the very substance of creative change, creative mutation. If you tell me about the lotus, tell me of nothing changeless or eternal. Tell me of the mystery of the inexhaustible, forever unfolding creative spark. Tell me of the incarnate disclosure of the flux, mutation in blossom, laughter and decay perfectly open in their transit, nude in their movement before us (*Phoenix* 219).

What we admire, if we admire the poems, is the quality and depth of the vision they spring from, what Coleridge, speaking of Wordsworth, called his sentiments:

No frequency of perusal can deprive them of their freshness. For though they are brought into the full daylight of every reader's comprehension; yet are they drawn up from depths which few in any age are privileged to visit, into which few in any age have courage or inclination to descend (*Biographia Literaria*, ch. 22).

This courage manifests itself supremely in, for example, *Bavarian Gentians*:

Reach me a gentian, give me a torch!
let me guide myself with the blue, forked torch of this flower
down the darker and darker stairs, where blue is darkened on blueness
even where Persephone goes, just now, from the frosted September
to the sightless realm where darkness is awake upon the dark
and Persephone herself is but a voice
or a darkness invisible enfolded in the deeper dark
of the arms Plutonic, and pierced with the passion of dense gloom,
among the splendour of torches of darkness, shedding darkness on the lost
    bride and her groom.

In the earlier versions of this poem, called *Glory of Darkness*, we can trace the emergence of these subtly related images. First comes the perception that the gentians are so deeply blue that they seem to add blueness to blueness until they

        make a dark-blue gloom
        in the sunny room.

The journey of the poet's soul into that darkness is felt, at first, as an experience of joy through penetration into a particularly distinctive kind of beauty, but the idea of a soul journeying into darkness quickly suggests that the fringes of the flower are a doorway and its depths a path to Hades. This, together with the time of year, suggests a parallel between the poet's soul and Persephone returning to her perennial marriage with Pluto in the underworld. In *Bavarian Gentians* itself these elements are subtly reorganised into a miniature myth. Persephone becomes the darkness itself, the darkness, that is, of death, of the return of the soul to oblivion, 'the arms Plutonic', a deeper dark in which she is to be enfolded as in a marriage bed, there to be 'pierced with the passion of dense gloom'—a passion which is at the same time the extremity of dissolution and the first pang of renewed life:

    And if, as autumn deepens and darkens
    I feel the pain of falling leaves, and stems that break in storms
    and trouble and dissolution and distress
    and then the softness of deep shadows folding, folding
    around my soul and spirit, around my lips
    so sweet, like a swoon, or more like the drowse of a low, sad song

singing darker than the nightingale, on, on to the solstice
and the silence of short days, the silence of the year, the shadow,
then I shall know that my life is moving still
with the dark earth, and drenched
with the deep oblivion of earth's lapse and renewal.   (*Shadows*)

The poet's soul has been invited to the nuptials and accepts with joy. The wonderfully tight organisation of the poem is clinched by making the gentian now a blue, forked torch, a black lamp which will guide him down into the living dark and add to the splendour there 'shedding darkness on the lost bride and her groom'.

As the autumn of 1929 advanced and Lawrence felt his last reserves of strength slipping away, he knew that he would not survive the winter, that it was time to be 'dipped again in God and new-created'. The poems about death are poignant, but never waver in their faith that death is only a part of life, the longest journey, perhaps also the greatest adventure:

Now launch the small ship, now as the body dies
and life departs, launch out, the fragile soul
in the fragile ship of courage, the ark of faith.

(*The Ship of Death*)

The little ship is given over to 'the kindness of the cosmos', for the flood of oblivion is also the creative flux. There is always a new dawn and a new birth:

A flush of rose and the whole thing starts again. (*The Ship of Death*)

then I must know that still
I am in the hands of the unknown God,
he is breaking me down to his own oblivion
to send me forth on a new morning, a new man.   (*Shadows*)

245

BIBLIOGRAPHY

I. WORKS BY D. H. LAWRENCE

Details of first publication are given in the chronologies.

(a) Standard editions

The most reliable English edition is the Penguin which includes all the novels; all the short novels; all the collected short stories with the exception of *Mother and Daughter*, *The Blue Moccasins*, *Things* and *The Overtone* (from *The Lovely Lady*), *The Old Adam*, *Her Turn*, *The Witch a la Mode*, *New Eve and Old Adam*, and *Mr Noon* (from *A Modern Lover*); the four travel books; *Selected Essays*; *Selected Letters*; *Selected Poems*; *A Propos of Lady Chatterley's Lover* (which also contains *Pornography and Obscenity* and the *Introduction to These Paintings*).

The Woman Who Rode Away in this edition contains, in addition to the stories originally collected under this title, *A Modern Lover* and *Strike Pay*.

Love Among the Haystacks and Other Stories contains *The Lovely Lady*, *Rawdon's Roof*, *The Rocking Horse Winner*, *The Man Who Loved Islands*, and *The Man Who Died*.

The Heinemann Phoenix Edition abounds in misprints and the texts of *The Rainbow* and *The Lost Girl* are not complete. It contains all the novels except *The Boy in the Bush*; the short novels in two volumes; all the collected short stories except *Mr Noon* in three volumes; the four travel books in two volumes; the Complete Poems in three volumes; *Psychoanalysis and the Unconscious* and *Fantasia of the Unconscious*; and *Studies in Classic American Literature*.

(b) Other works

Movements in European History, O.U.P., 1921.

Reflections on the Death of a Porcupine, Centaur Press, 1925. (The title essay is reprinted in Penguin *Selected Essays; The Novel* and *Love Was Once a Little Boy* are in *Sex, Literature and Censorship; The Crown, Him With His Tail in His Mouth, Blessed Are the Powerful* and *Aristocracy* have not been reprinted.)

The Paintings of D. H. Lawrence, Mandrake Press, 1929.

Assorted Articles, Secker, 1930. (Seven of these twenty-three pieces are in Penguin *Selected Essays*; three of these are also in *Sex, Literature and Censorship*; two others are in *Selected Literary Criticism*.)

Love Among the Haystacks, Nonesuch Press, 1930. (Contains, in addition to the title story, the uncollected story *Once* and two travel sketches from the *Twilight in Italy* period—*A Chapel Among the Mountains* and *A Hay Hut Among the Mountains*.)

A Ropos of Lady Chatterley's Lover, Mandrake Press 1930; Secker, 1931; Penguin 1961 (together with the *Introduction to Pansies*, the *Introduction to*

His Paintings and *Pornography and Obscenity*); also reprinted in *Sex, Literature and Censorship*.

Apocalypse, Orioli, Florence, 1931; Secker, 1932.

The Letters, ed. Huxley, Heinemann, 1932.

The Plays, Secker, 1933; Heinemann, 1938. (Contains *The Widowing of Mrs Holroyd, Touch and Go* and *David*.)

The Tales, Secker, 1934. (Contains all the short novels and all the collected short stories with the exception of those in *A Modern Lover*.)

Foreword to *Women in Love*, Gelber, Lilienthal, San Francisco, 1936. (Reprinted as an introduction to the Random House Modern Library edition of *Women in Love*, 1937.)

Phoenix: The Posthumous Papers of D. H. Lawrence, ed. McDonald, Viking Press, N.Y., 1936; Heinemann, 1936, 1961. (30 of the items in *Phoenix* are reprinted in *Selected Literary Criticism*; 17 in Penguin *Selected Essays*; and 5 in *Sex, Literature and Censorship*.)

The First Lady Chatterley, Dial Press, N.Y., 1944.

Letters to Bertrand Russell, ed. Moore, Gotham Book Mart, 1948.

A Prelude, Merle Press, Thames Ditton, Surrey, 1949. (Lawrence's earliest recorded work.)

Selected Essays, Penguin, 1950.

Sex, Literature and Censorship, ed. Moore, Heinemann, 1953. (This English edition contains reproductions of four paintings: *The Finding of Moses, Resurrection, Fauns and Nymphs* and *Under the Haystack*.)

Selected Literary Criticism, ed. Beal, Heinemann, 1955.

The Symbolic Meaning, ed. Arnold, Centaur Press, 1962. (Original versions of the *Studies in Classic American Literature*.)

The Collected Letters, ed. Moore, Heinemann, 1962.

Paintings of D. H. Lawrence, ed. Mervyn Levy, Cory, Adams and Mackay, 1964. (Contains *Making Pictures* from *Assorted Articles*.)

The Complete Poems, ed. Pinto and Roberts, Heinemann, 1964.

The Complete Plays, Heinemann, 1965. (Contains all eight of Lawrence's completed plays and two fragments.)

(c) Contributions to books and periodicals

The Early Life of D. H. Lawrence, Lawrence and Gelder, Orioli, Florence, 1931. (Contains early essays and many letters.)

Two anonymous reviews of German poetry, *English Review*, January 1912 (373–6), reprinted in *PMLA*, March 1964 (185–8).

A Composite Biography, Nehls, Madison, 1957–9. (Contains *A Burns Novel* and other fragments.)

'The Man Who Was Through with the World', *Essays in Criticism*, IX, 3, 1959.

Prologue to *Women in Love*, *Texas Quarterly*, Spring 1963.

Passages from early drafts of *The White Peacock, Odour of Chrysanthemums*, and *The Rainbow* in Wallace Hildick, *Word for Word*, Faber, 1965.

Uncollected letters can be found in the following books and periodicals:

The New Adelphi, June–August 1930.

The Early Life of D. H. Lawrence, Ada Lawrence, Orioli, 1931.

Lorenzo in Taos, Luhan, Knopf, 1932.
The Savage Pilgrimage, Carswell, Chatto and Windus, 1932.
Reminiscences of D. H. Lawrence, Murry, Cape, 1933.
Reminiscences and Correspondence, Brewster, Secker, 1934.
Not I But the Wind, Frieda Lawrence, Heinemann, 1935.
Amy Lowell, Damon, Houghton Mifflin Co., 1935.
Contacts, Curtis Brown, Cassell, 1935.
T'ien Hsia Monthly, August and September 1935.
A Poet and Two Painters, Merrild, Routledge, 1938.
A Number of People, Edward Marsh, Hamilton, 1939.
The Nineteen Twenties, Douglas Goldring, Nicholson and Watson, 1945.
Encounter, December 1953.
Flowers of the Forest, David Garnett, Chatto and Windus, 1955.
The Intelligent Heart, H. T. Moore, Heinemann, 1955.
Predilections, Marianne Moore, Viking Press, N.Y., 1955.
Twentieth Century, January 1956.
London Magazine, February 1956.
A Composite Biography, Nehls, University of Wisconsin, Madison, 1957.
D. H. Lawrence After Thirty Years, ed. Pinto, Nottingham, 1960.
Memoirs and Correspondence, Frieda Lawrence, Heinemann, 1961.
International Literary Annual 3, Calder, 1961.
The Garnett Family, Heilbrun, Allen and Unwin, 1961.
Review of English Literature, October 1962; July 1965.

2. BIBLIOGRAPHIES

A Bibliography of the Writings of D. H. Lawrence, Edward D. McDonald, Centaur Bookshop, Philadelphia, 1925.
A Bibliographical Supplement, Centaur Bookshop, Philadelphia, 1931.
D. H. Lawrence, His First Editions, Points and Values, Gilbert H. Fabes, Foyle, 1933.
The MSS. of D. H. Lawrence, Lawrence Clark Powell, Public Library, Los Angeles, 1937.
The Frieda Lawrence Collection of D. H. Lawrence MSS., E. W. Tedlock, Jr., University of New Mexico Press, Albuquerque, 1948.
D. H. Lawrence, A Checklist, William White, Wayne University Press, Detroit, 1950.
A Bibliography of D. H. Lawrence, Warren Roberts, Hart-Davis, 1963.

3. BOOKS ON LAWRENCE

A select list (chronologically arranged). A full list will be found in Warren Roberts's Bibliography.

D.H.L., An American Interpretation, Herbert J. Seligmann, Seltzer, 1924.
D.H.L., An Indiscretion, Richard Aldington, Seattle, 1927.
D.H.L., Richard Aldington, Chatto and Windus, 1930.
D.H.L., A First Study, Stephen Potter, Cape, 1930.

BIBLIOGRAPHY

D.H.L., Rebecca West, Secker, 1930.
D.H.L., J. M. Murry, Minority Press, Cambridge, 1930.
D.H.L., F. R. Leavis, Minority Press, Cambridge, 1930.
Son of Woman, J. M. Murry, Cape, 1931.
Young Lorenzo, Early Life of D.H.L., Ada Lawrence and G. Stuart Gelder, Orioli, Florence, 1931.
Lorenzo in Taos, Mabel Luhan, Secker, 1932.
D.H.L., An Unprofessional Study, Anais Nin, Titus, Paris, 1932; Spearman, London, 1961.
The Savage Pilgrimage, Catherine Carswell, Chatto and Windus, 1932.
Footnote to Lawrence, Richard Goodman, White Owl Press, 1932.
D.H.L. and the Body Mystical, Frederick Carter, Archer, 1932.
Reminiscences of D.H.L., J. M. Murry, Cape, 1933.
L. and Brett, Dorothy Brett, Secker, 1933.
L. and Apocalypse, Helen Corke, Heinemann, 1933.
Pilgrim of the Apocalypse, Horace Gregory, Secker, 1934.
D.H.L., Reminiscences and Correspondence, Earl and Achsah Brewster, Secker, 1934.
Not I, But the Wind, Frieda Lawrence, Heinemann, 1935.
D.H.L., A Personal Record, E.T. (Jessie Chambers), Cape, 1935.
A Poet and Two Painters, Knud Merrild, Routledge, 1938.
D.H.L., Hugh Kingsmill, Methuen, 1938.
D.H.L. and Susan His Cow, William York Tindall, Columbia University, N.Y., 1939.
Portrait of a Genius, But..., Richard Aldington, Heinemann, 1950.
D.H.L., Anthony West, Barker, 1950.
The Life and Works of D.H.L., Harry T. Moore, Allen and Unwin, 1951 (revised ed. Twayne, 1964).
D.H.L. and Human Existence, Father William Tiverton (Martin Jarrett-Kerr), Rockliff, 1951.
Fire-Bird, A Study of D.H.L., Dallas Kenmare, Barrie, 1951.
Journey with Genius, Witter Bynner, John Day, N.Y., 1951; Nevill, 1953.
D.H.L., Prophet of the Midlands, V. de S. Pinto, Nottingham, 1951.
D.H.L., Kenneth Young, Longmans Green, 1951.
The Achievement of D.H.L., ed. Frederick J. Hoffman and Harry T. Moore, Oklahoma, 1953.
The Intelligent Heart, Harry T. Moore, Heinemann, 1955.
The Love Ethic of D.H.L., Mark Spilka, Indiana, 1955.
D.H.L., A Basic Study of His Ideas, Mary Freeman, Florida, 1955.
D.H.L: Novelist, F. R. Leavis, Chatto and Windus, 1955.
Poste Restante, A Lawrence Travel Calendar, Harry T. Moore, California, 1956.
The Spiral Flame, David Boadella, Ritter, Nottingham, 1956.
The Dark Sun, Graham Hough, Duckworth, 1956.
D.H.L., A Composite Biography, Edward Nehls, Wisconsin, 1957-9.
Love, Freedom and Society, J. M. Murry, Cape, 1957.
D.H.L. and America, Armin Arnold, Linden Press, 1958.
Brave Men, A Study of D.H.L. and Simone Weil, Richard Rees, Gollancz, 1958.

BIBLIOGRAPHY

A D.H.L. Miscellany, ed. Harry T. Moore, Carbondale, Illinois, 1959.
Tradition and D.H.L., Richard L. Drain, Groningen, 1960.
D.H.L., The Failure and the Triumph of Art, Eliseo Vivas, Northwestern U.P., 1960.
D.H.L. After Thirty Years, ed. V. de S. Pinto, University of Nottingham, 1960.
Frieda Lawrence, The Memoirs and Correspondence, ed. E. W. Tedlock, Heinemann, 1961.
D.H.L., Anthony Beal, Oliver and Boyd, 1961.
The Trial of Lady Chatterley, ed. C. H. Rolph, Penguin, 1961.
The Art of Perversity, Kingsley Widmer, Washington, 1962.
Oedipus in Nottingham, Daniel A. Weiss, Seattle, 1962.
The Utopian Vision of D.H.L., Eugene Goodheart, Chicago, 1963.
D.H.L., ed. Mark Spilka, Prentice-Hall, 1963.
The Deed of Life, Julian Moynahan, Oxford, 1963.
Adventures in Consciousness: The Meaning of D.H.L.'s Religious Quest, G. A. Panichas, The Hague, 1964.
D.H.L., Artist and Rebel, E. W. Tedlock, New Mexico, 1964.
D.H.L., R. P. Draper, Twayne, 1964.
Dark Night of the Body, L. D. Clark, Texas, 1964.
Double Measure, George H. Ford, Holt, 1965.
The Forked Flame, H. M. Daleski, Faber and Faber, 1965.

4. LAWRENCE CRITICISM IN OTHER BOOKS AND IN PERIODICALS

The vast amount of Lawrence criticism has been checklisted up to 1959 by Maurice Beebe and Anthony Tommasi in *Modern Fiction Studies*, vol. 5, no. 1, Spring 1959. I therefore list here only a few interesting items missing from that checklist (A), and some of those which have appeared since 1959 (B).

A

Pound, Ezra, Review of *Love Poems*, in *Poetry*, July 1913. Reprinted in *Selected Literary Criticism*, Faber.
James, Henry, 'The Younger Generation', *T.L.S.* Spring 1914.
Bennett, Arnold, 'D.H.L.'s Delusion', *Evening Standard*, 10 April 1930.
Eliot, T. S., 'Son of Woman', *Criterion*, July 1931.
Chesterton, G. K., 'The End of the Moderns', *London Mercury*, January 1933.
Coombes, H., 'D.H.L. Placed', *Scrutiny*, March 1949.
Danby, John F., 'D.H.L.', *Cambridge Journal*, February 1951.
Stewart, D., 'Immoral Books, *Lady Chatterley* and *The Shropshire Lad*', *The European*, March 1953.
Wilson, Angus, 'At the Heart of L.' *Encounter*, December 1955.
Grant, Douglas, 'England's Phoenix', *Univ. of Toronto Quarterly*, XXVII (1958), 223.
Raleigh, J. H. 'Victorian Morals and the Modern Novel', *Partisan Review*, XXV, 1958.
Traversi, Derek, 'Dr Leavis and the Case of D.H.L.', *Month*, March 1956.
Klingopulos, G. D., 'L.'s Criticism', *Essays in Criticism*, July 1957.

250

B

Adelman, G. 'Beyond the Pleasure Principle: An Analysis of D.H.L.'s *The Prussian Officer*', *Studies in Short Fiction*, I, Fall 1963.

Aldington, Richard. 'A Wreath for L.', *Encounter*, April 1960.

Amis, Kingsley. 'Lone Voices', *Encounter*, XV, I.

—— 'Searcher for Atlantis', *T.L.S.* 12 May 1961.

Armin, Arnold. 'D.H.L. and Thomas Mann', *Comparative Literature*, XIII, i, 33–8.

Auden, W. H. 'D.H.L.' in *The Dyer's Hand*, Faber, 1963.

Baldanza, Frank. 'D.H.L.'s Song of Songs', *Modern Fiction Studies*, 7 (2).

Bartlett, Norman. 'Aldous Huxley and D.H.L.', *Australian Quarterly*, XXXVI, i, 76–84.

Beebe, Maurice. 'L.'s Sacred Fount: The Artist Theme of *Sons and Lovers*', *Texas Studies in Literature and Language*, IV, 539–52.

Benedict, John. 'The *Lady Chatterley's Lover* Case', *American Mercury*, January 1960.

Bramley, J. A. 'The Challenge of D.H.L.', *Hibbert Journal*, April 1960.

—— 'D.H.L.'s Sternest Critic', *Hibbert Journal*, Spring 1965.

Branda, Eldon S. 'Textual Changes in *Women in Love*', *Texas Studies in Literature and Language*, VI, 306–21.

Chamberlain, Robert L. 'Pussum, Minette, and the Afro-Nordic Symbol in L.'s *Women in Love*', *PMLA*, September 1963.

Clements, A. L. 'The Quest for Self: D.H.L.'s *The Rainbow*', *Thoth*, III, Spring 1962.

Corke, Helen. 'Concerning *The White Peacock*', *Texas Quarterly*, Winter 1959.

Cornwell, Ethel F. 'The Sex Mysticism of D.H.L.' in *The Still Point*, Rutgers, 1962.

Cowan, James C. 'The Function of Allusions and Symbols in *The Man Who Died*', *American Image*, XVII, 3.

Craig, G. Armour. 'D.H.L. on Thinghood and Selfhood', *Massachusetts Review*, I, 56–60.

Cross, Barbara. 'L. and the Unbroken Circle', *Perspective*, X, 3.

Dahlberg, Edward and Read, Herbert, on D.H.L. in *Truth is More Sacred*, Routledge and Kegan Paul, 1961.

Daiches, David. *The Novel and the Modern World*, Chicago, 1960.

Dalton, Robert O. '*Snake*: A Moment of Consciousness', *Brigham Young University Studies*, IV (1962), 243–53.

Empson, William. 'Lady Chatterley Again', *Essays in Criticism*, XIII, 101–4.

Engelberg, Edward. '*The Rainbow* as a Modern Bildungsroman', *PMLA*, March 1963.

Englander, Ann. '*The Prussian Officer*: The Self Divided', *Sewanee Review*, LXXI, 605–19.

Enright, D. J. 'A Haste for Wisdom', *New Statesman*, 30 October 1964.

Ford, George H. 'Shelley or Schiller? A Note on D.H.L. at Work', *Texas Studies in Literature and Language*, IV, 154–6.

—— '"The Wedding" Chapter of *Women in Love*', *Texas Studies in Literature and Language*, VI, 134–47.

Foster, D. W. 'L., Sex and Religion', *Theology*, January 1961.

Fraiberg, Louis. 'The Unattainable Self: *Sons and Lovers*', in *Twelve Original Essays on Great English Novels*, ed. Shapiro, Detroit, 1960.

Fraiberg, Selma. 'Two Modern Incest Heroes', *Partisan Review*, XXVIII, 5-6.

Garlington, Jack. 'L. with Misgivings', *South Atlantic Quarterly*, LIX, 3.

Gifford, Henry. 'Anna, L. and the Law', *Critical Quarterly*, Autumn 1959.

—— 'The Defect of L.'s Poetry', *Critical Quarterly*, Summer 1961.

Gillie, Christopher. *Character in English Literature*, Chatto and Windus, 1965.

Goldberg, S. L. '*The Rainbow*: Fiddle Bow and Sand', *Essays in Criticism*, October 1961.

Gomme, Andor. 'Friends and Enemies', *T.L.S.* 27 April 1962.

—— 'L. the Poet, Achievement and Irrelevance'. *T.L.S.*, 26 August 1965.

Goodheart, E. 'L. and Christ', *Partisan Review*, XXXI, i (Winter 1964).

—— 'L. and the Critics', *Chicago Review*, XVI, iii (1963), 127-37.

Gordon, David J. 'D.H.L.'s Quarrel with Tragedy', *Perspective*, Winter 1964.

Grant, Douglas. 'Hands Up, America!', *Review of English Literature*, IV, iv.

Gregor, Ian. '*Lady Chatterley's Lover*', in *The Moral and the Story*, Faber, 1962.

Gurko, Leo. '*The Lost Girl*: D.H.L. as a Dickens of the Midlands', *PMLA*, LXXVIII, 601-5.

—— '*The Trespasser*: D.H.L.'s Neglected Novel', *College English*, XXIV, 29-65.

—— 'Kangaroo: D.H.L. in Transit', *Modern Fiction Studies*, X, 4.

Guttmann, Allen. 'D.H.L.: The Politics of Irrationality', *Wisconsin Studies in Contemporary Literature*, V, 151-63.

Harding, D. W. 'On *Lady Chatterley's Lover*', *Spectator*, 11 November 1960.

—— 'L. and the Unconscious', *New Statesman*, LXII, 1961, 788-90.

Hassall, Christopher. 'D.H.L. and the Etruscans', *Essays by Diverse Hands*, vol. XXXI, ed. Green, O.U.P. 1962.

Heilman, Robert B. 'Nomad, Monads, and the Mystique of the Soma', *Sewanee Review*, LXVIII, 635-59.

Herbert, Sir Alan. 'Thoughts on Lady Chatterley', *The Listener*, 10 November 1960.

Hogan, Robert. 'D.H.L. and His Critics', *Essays in Criticism*, October 1959.

—— 'L.'s Song of a Man Who Came Through', *Explicator*, XVII, Item 51.

Hoggart, Richard. Introduction to *Lady Chatterley's Lover*, Penguin, 1961.

—— 'The Witness and the Law', *Encounter*, March 1961. (Rebecca West, William Emrys Williams, and Martin Jarrett-Kerr also wrote under this title in *Encounter*, March 1961.)

Holbrook, David. *The Quest for Love*, Methuen, 1964.

Idema, J. M. 'The Hawk and the Plover', *University of Houston Forum*, III: VII, 11-14.

Jones, William M. 'Growth of a Symbol: The Sun in L. and Eudora Welty', *University of Kansas City Review*, XXVI, 68-73.

Junkins, Donald. '*The Rocking-Horse Winner*: A Modern Myth', *Studies in Short Fiction*, II, i, 87-8.

Kaufmann, Stanley. 'Lady Chatterley at Last', *New Republic*, 25 May 1959.

Kazin, Alfred. 'Sons, Lovers and Mothers', *Partisan Review*, Summer 1962.

—— 'Lady Chatterley in America', in *Contemporaries*, Secker-Warburg, 1963.

Kendle, Burton S. 'D.H.L. The Man Who Misunderstood Gulliver', *English Language Notes*, September 1964.

Kermode, Frank. 'L. in his Letters', *New Statesman*, 23 March 1962.

Kerr, Fergus. 'Odious Corollaries in D.H.L.', *Blackfriars*, October 1961.

Kessler, Jascha. 'D.H.L.'s Primitivism', *Texas Studies in Literature and Language*, v, 467–88.

Knight, G. Wilson. 'L., Joyce and Powys', *Essays in Criticism*, October 1961.

Knoepflmacher, V. C. 'The Rival Ladies: Mrs Ward's Lady Connie and L.'s *Lady Chatterley's Lover*', *Victorian Studies*, December 1960.

Krieger, Murray, *The Tragic Vision*, 1960.

Krishnamurthy, M. G. 'D.H.L.'s *The Woman Who Rode Away*', *The Literary Criterion*, Summer 1960.

Krook, Dorothea. *Three Traditions of Moral Thought*, C.U.P. 1959.

Kuo, C. H. '*The Rainbow*', *Explicator*, XIX, Item 60.

Leavis, F. R. 'Romantic and Heretic', *Spectator*, 6 February 1959.

—— 'Genius as Critic', *Spectator*, 24 March 1961.

—— 'The New Orthodoxy', *Spectator*, 17 February 1962.

—— 'L. Scholarship and L.', *Sewanee Review*, Winter 1963.

Lerner, Laurence. 'How Beastly the Bourgoisie Is', *Critical Survey*, Spring 1963.

Levy, Mervyn and Wilson, Colin. 'The Paintings of D.H.L.', *Studio*, October 1962.

Lindsay, Jack. 'The Impact of Modernism on L.', in *Paintings of D.H.L.*, ed. Levy, London, 1964.

Longville, Timothy. 'The Longest Journey: D.H.L.'s *Phoenix*', *Critical Quarterly*, Spring 1962.

Lucas, B. 'Apropos of *England, My England*', *Twentieth Century*, March 1961.

MacLeish, Archibald. *Preface to 'Lady Chatterley's Lover'*, Grove Press, 1959.

MacLennan, Hugh. 'The Defence of Lady Chatterley', *Canadian Literature*, no. 6, 1960.

Magalaner, Marvin. 'D.H.L. Today', *Commonweal*, LXX, 1960, 275–6.

Mandel, Oscar. 'Ignorance and Privacy' (on *Lady Chatterley's Lover*), *American Scholar*, XXIX, 509–19.

Martin, W. B. J. 'Significant Modern Writers—D.H.L.', *Expository Times*, March 1960.

Martin, W. R. 'Fancy or Imagination? *The Rocking-Horse Winner*', *College English*, XXIV, 64–5. (Replies by William D. Burroughs and Robert G. Lawrence in the subsequent number, January 1963.)

Maxwell, J. C. '*Lady Chatterley's Lover*: A Correction', *Notes and Queries*, VIII, 110.

Merivale, Patricia. 'D.H.L. and the Modern Pan Myth', *Texas Studies in Literature and Language*, VI, 297–305.

Michot, Paulette. 'D.H.L. A Belated Apology', *Revue des Langues Vivantes*, IV, 1961, 290–305.

Miller, James E. Jr. 'The Dance of Rapture', in *Start with the Sun*, Nebraska, 1960.

Miller, Nolan. 'The "Success" and "Failure" of D.H.L.', *Antioch Review*, XXII, 380–92.

Moore, Everett T. 'D.H.L. and the "Censor-Morons"', *Bulletin of the American Library Assoc.* LIV, 1960, 731–2.

Moore, Harry T. '*The Plumed Serpent*, Vision and Language', in *D.H.L.*, ed. Spilka, Prentice-Hall, 1963.

—— 'L. from All Sides', *Kenyon Review*, XXV, 555–8.

—— 'D.H.L. and his Paintings', in *Paintings of D.H.L.*, London, 1964.

—— 'The Prose Style of D.H.L.', *Langue et Littérature*, Paris, 1961.

Morris, James. 'Reflections on the Chatterley Case', *N.Y. Times Mag.* 4 December 1960.

Moynahan, Julian. 'The Essence of D.H.L.', *University* (Princeton), Summer–Fall 1963.

Myers, Neil. 'L. and the War', *Criticism*, Winter 1962.

Newman, Paul B. 'D.H.L. and *The Golden Bough*', *Kansas Magazine*, 1962, 79–86.

Nott, Kathleen, 'L. by Daylight', *The Observer*, 13 November 1960.

O'Connor, Frank, *The Lonely Voice*, Macmillan, 1964.

Osgerby, J. R. 'D.H.L.'s *The White Peacock*', *Use of English*, Summer 1962.

Pearsall, Robert B. 'The Second Art of D.H.L.' [his painting], *South Atlantic Quarterly*, LXIII, 457–67.

Peter, John. 'The Bottom of the Well' (on *Lady Chatterley's Lover*), *Essays in Criticism*, XII, 226–7, 445–7; XIII, 301–2.

Pinto, Vivian de Sola. 'Poet Without a Mask', *Critical Quarterly*, Spring 1961.

—— 'Mr Gifford and D.H.L.', *Critical Quarterly*, Autumn 1961.

—— 'L. and Frieda', *English*, XIV, Spring 1963.

Porter, Katherine Anne. 'A Wreath for the Gamekeeper', *Encounter*, February 1960.

Potter, Stephen. 'Towards the Great Secret', *Spectator*, 23 October 1964.

Read, Herbert. 'L. as a Painter', in *Paintings of D.H.L.*, ed. Levy, London, 1964.

Requardt, Egon. 'D.H.L.'s *Sons and Lovers*', *Die Neueren Sprachen*, 1961, 230–5.

Rieff, Philip. 'A Modern Mythmaker', in *Myth and Mythmaking*, ed. Murray, Braziller, N.Y., 1960.

—— Introduction to the Viking Press ed. of *Psychoanalysis and the Unconscious*, 1960.

—— 'Two Honest Men, Freud and D.H.L.', *Listener*, 5 May 1960.

Roberts, Walter. 'After the Prophet: the Reputation of D.H.L.', *Month*, April 1962.

Robinson, John. 'The Christian and Lady Chatterley', *Time and Tide*, XII, 45.

Robson, W. W. '*Women in Love*', in *The Modern Age*, Penguin, 1961.

Rosenthal, T. G. 'The Writer as Painter', *The Listener*, 6 September 1962.

Rudikoff, Sonya. 'D.H.L. and Our Life Today: Rereading *Lady Chatterley's Lover*', *Commentary*, XXVIII, 408–13.

Ryals, Clyde de L. 'D.H.L.'s *The Horse Dealer's Daughter*', *Literature and Psychology*, XII, 39–43.

Salgado, Gamini. 'D.H.L. as Literary Critic', *London Magazine*, February 1960.

—— 'Mr Gifford and D.H.L.', *Critical Quarterly*, Autumn 1961.

Sawyer, Paul W. 'The Religious Vision of D.H.L.', *Crane Review*, Spring 1961.

Saxena, H. S. 'The Critical Writings of D.H.L.', *Indian Journal of English Studies*, II (1961), 130–7.

—— 'D.H.L. and the Impressionistic Technique', *Indian Journal of English Studies*, III (1961), 145–52.

Sharpe, Michael C. 'The Genesis of D.H.L.'s *The Trespasser*', *Essays in Criticism*, January 1961.

Shonfield, Andrew. 'L.'s Other Censor', *Encounter*, XVII (September 1961), 63–4.

Slote, Bernice. 'The Leaves of D.H.L.' in *Start with the Sun*.

Smith, L. E. W. '*Snake*', *Critical Survey*, Spring 1963.

Sparrow, John. 'Regina v. Penguin Books', *Encounter*, February 1962.

—— 'Afterthoughts on Regina v. Penguin Books', *Encounter*, June 1962.

—— 'On *Lady Chatterley's Lover*', *Essays in Criticism*, XIII, 202–5, 303. (Colin Macinnes and Stephen Potter replied to Sparrow in *Encounter*, March 1962, and many others replied in the April and May numbers.)

Spilka, Mark. 'Post-Leavis L. Critics', *Modern Language Quarterly*, XXV, 212–17.

Stanley, F. R. 'The Artist as Pornographer', *Literary Half-Yearly*, January 1963.

Stein, Walter. 'Criticism and Theology', *Life of the Spirit*, August–September 1964.

Steiner, George. 'Life of Letters', *Kenyon Review*, XXV (1963), 174–6.

Stewart, J. I. M. 'D.H.L.' in *Eight Modern Writers*, Oxford 1963.

Tanner, Tony. 'The Man Who Lived', *Spectator*, 23 March 1962.

Tedlock, E. W. 'D.H.L.'s Annotation of Ouspensky's *Tertium Organum*', *Texas Studies in Literature and Language*, II, 2.

Tenenbaum, Louis. 'Two Views of the Modern Italian: D.H.L. and Seán O'Faoláin', *Italica*, XXXVII, 1960, 118–25.

Tetsumura, Haruo. 'D.H.L.'s Mysticism: What the Moon Signifies', *Hiroshima Studies in English Language and Literature*, IX (1963), i–ii, 51–65.

Thody, Philip. '*Lady Chatterley's Lover*: A Pyrrhic Victory', *Threshold*, V, ii (Belfast).

Traschen, Isadore. 'Pure and Ironic Idealism. D.H.L.', *South Atlantic Quarterly*, Spring 1960.

Turnell, Martin. *Modern Literature and Christian Faith*, Darton, Longman and Todd, 1961, 30–4.

Vickery, John B. '*The Plumed Serpent* and the Eternal Paradox', *Criticism*, V, 119–34.

Walsh, William. 'Ursula in *The Rainbow*', and 'The Educational Ideas of D.H.L.', in *The Use of Imagination*, Chatto and Windus, 1959.

Waterman, A. E. 'The Plays of D.H.L.', in *D.H.L.* ed. Spilka, Prentice-Hall, 1963.

Way, Brian. 'Sex and Language—Obscene Words in D.H.L. and Henry Miller', *New Left Review*, 27, Autumn 1964.

Welch, Colin. 'Black Magic, White Lies', *Encounter*, February 1961.

Weller, R. H. 'Advocate for Eros', *American Scholar*, XXX, 2.

Werner, Alfred. 'L. and Pascin', *Kenyon Review*, XXIII, 2.

West, Paul. 'D.H.L., Mystical Critic', *Southern Review*, Winter 1965.

Whitaker, T. R. 'L.'s Western Path: *Mornings in Mexico*', *Criticism*, III, 3.

White, William. 'D.H.L. and Marquand', *D.H.L. News and Notes*, II, i, 1962.

Wilde, Alan. 'The Illusion of *St Mawr*: Technique and Vision in D.H.L.'s Novel', *PMLA*, March 1964.

Williams, Raymond. 'L. and Tolstoy', *Critical Quarterly*, Spring 1960.

—— 'The Law and Literary Merit', *Encounter*, XVII, 3.

—— 'Tolstoy, L. and Tragedy', *Kenyon Review*, Autumn 1963.

Wright, Raymond. 'L.'s Non-Human Analogues', *Modern Language Notes*, LXXVI, 426–32.

INDEXES

A: LAWRENCE'S WORKS

Titles of poems are set in italic type. Figures in italic type refer to the chronologies; figures in bold type are main references.

B: GENERAL

INDEXES

Campbell, Gordon, 12
Carlyle, Thomas, 72
Carrasco, Don Ramon (in *The Plumed Serpent*), 145, 159–68
Carrington
  Lou (in *St Mawr*), 151–9, 219
  Rico, 151, 154–6, 196
Carswell, Catherine, 79, 144
Carter, Frederick, 229
Cathcart (in *The Man Who Loved Islands*), 97, 149, 176, 196, 217
Catholicism, 161, 242
Ceylon, 130, 146
Chambers, Jessie, 7, 13, 16, 19–22
Chapala, 145
characterisation, 1, 36, 43–4,
Charon, 164
Chatterley
  Clifford, 179–98
  Connie (in *Lady Chatterley's Lover*), 168, 174, 179–98
childbirth, 49, 54
Christ, 3, 27, 57, 114, 132–3, 153, 158, 162, 173, 205–6, 215–23, 229
Christianity, 65–7, 79, 125, 163, 193, 216–24, 226, 242
Christmas, 51, 56, 150, 167
Cicio (in *The Lost Girl*), 38, 115
Cipriano, Don (in *The Plumed Serpent*), 160–8
civilisation, 65, 67, 76, 83, 84, 93, 96, 123, 140, 149–50, 156, 158–9, 165–6, 174, 179, 182, 189–91, 195, 204, 209–10, 213–15, 227
Clark, L. D., 159, 165
class, 80, 107, 116, 185
Coleridge, S. T., 152–3
  The Ancient Mariner, 125–6
  Biographia Literaria, 243–4
Collings, Ernest, 41–2
Columbus, Christopher, 145
comedy, 122, 134, 154–5, 189
Communism, 74, 135
Conrad, Joseph: *Lord Jim*, 5
Cooley, Ben (in *Kangaroo*), 131–3, 137
Cornwall, 40, 99
Cortés, 145
Corvo, Baron, 169
Crane, Hart, 3
Crich
  Diana, 95
  Gerald (in *Women in Love*), 58, 78–98, 112, 196

Crosby, Harry, 200
Croydon, 8, 16
Croydon English Association, 8
crucifixion, the, 127, 205–6, 217–18

Dahlberg, Edward, 203
  Bottom Dogs, 178
Daleski, H. M.: *The Forked Flame*, 98
dance, 59, 88–9, 148, 164, 173, 191, 198, 210–15, 227, 240
dark gods, 66, 115, 123–4, 136–7, 147, 158, 161–5, 168
Davidson Road School, Croydon, 8
Dawes, Clara (in *Sons and Lovers*), 20, 28–34
Day, Gethin (in *The Flying Fish*), 206–10, 213, 214, 226
death, 33, 46, 59, 78–80, 84, 85, 89–9, 91, 94–5, 111–12, 115–17, 122, 128, 140–1, 148–50, 167, 205, 207–8, 210, 211, 213, 215, 226, 230, 238, 244–5
De Grey, 100
Del Monte, 205
democracy, 77
devil, the, 125, 139, 140, 153, 158, 161, 163, 215–6, 221–3
Dickens, Charles, 5, 36
Diggers (in *Kangaroo*), 131, 133, 135
Dionysus, 78, 90, 229
Dixon, Richard Watson, 120
doggerel, 231
dolphins, *see* porpoises
Dostoevsky, Fiodor, 229
Douglas, Norman, 204
dragons, 161–3, 221–2
Dukes, Tommy (in *Lady Chatterley's Lover*), 182, 195
Dunlop, Sir T. D., 39

eagles, 146–7, 150, 162
Eastwood, 7
Easu (in *The Boy in the Bush*), 138–9
Eden, 157, 163, 166, 171, 176, 187, 193–4, 210
egg, the, 127, 187, 216, 224
ego, 57, 89, 124, 196
Elan Vital, 161
Eliot, George, 5, 10, 66
Eliot, T. S., 2, 5, 233
Elliott, John R. Jr., 176
England, 38, 39, 73, 77, 100, 125, 137, 145–6, 178, 202, 206, 227

263

INDEXES

English Review, 7, 8, 14, 16, 39, 40, 73, 99
Etna, 123
Etruscans, 128–9, 170, 198, 199 210–19, 238, 240
Eve, 194

Fall, the, 182, 193, 196, 198, 240
fascism, 109
Fiedler, H. G., 16
Field, John (in *Sons and Lovers*), 22
Flaubert, Gustave, 2, 70, 103, 242
flowers, 13, 25, 30, 31, 53, 83–4, 92, 104, 120, 185–9, 205, 220, 221, 231, 236–45
Fontana Vecchia, 129
Forster, E. M., 74, 77
France, Anatole, 70
Franklin, Benjamin, 124
Franks, Sir William (in *Aaron's Rod*), 108
Frankstone, Dr (in *The Rainbow*), 62
free verse, 119–20, 232, 241–4
Freud, Sigmund, 20, 124

Galsworthy, John, 36–7, 69–71, 171
    The Man of Property, 37
Gardiner, Rolf, 173, 178
gargoyles (in *The Rainbow*), 53, 211
Garnett, Edward, 8, 18, 20, 41, 43, 70, 72
Garsington, 74–6
Genesis, 66, 78
Germany, 16, 17, 136, 143, 170, 180
Gertler, Mark, 91
Ghiselin, Brewster, 203, 235
Gill, Eric, 230
Glen, Isa, 170
God, 42, 57–8, 65, 66, 79, 112–13, 125–6, 133, 136–40, 153, 158, 162–3, 191–2, 217, 218, 220, 222, 224, 236–9, 240, 243, 245
grace, 67, 164, 188, 196
Graham, R. B. Cunningham, 171
Grannie (in *The Virgin and the Gypsy*), 116
Gray, Cecil, 40
Greeks, the, 151, 210, 240

Hades, 244
Halliday (in *Women in Love*), 81, 89
Harby, Mr (in *The Rainbow*), 62
Hardy, Thomas, 5, 10, 35, 40, 66, 70
    Tess of the D'Urbervilles, 36
Hemingway, Ernest, 171

Herbertson, Captain (in *Aaron's Rod*), 111
hermits, 176–7, 183–4
Heseltine, Philip, 40
Hesperides, 213
Hinduism, 176, 221, 233
Hoggart, Richard, 231
Holy Ghost, the, 111, 114, 137, 222, 238
homosexuality, 112–13
Hopkins, Gerard Manley, 120, 153, 187, 224, 234, 242–3
horses, 27, 64, 65–7, 80–1, 117, 151–9
Hough, Graham: *The Dark Sun*, 21
Hueffer, Ford Maddox, 8, 9, 14, 19
Huitzilopochtli (in *The Plumed Serpent*), 165, 167
Huxley, Aldous, 2
    Wordsworth in the Tropics, 65

Ibsen, Henrik: *Peer Gynt*, 148
Incas, 145
Indians (American), 142–50, 168, 213
industrialism, 15, 60, 79, 83, 86, 96, 189–91
Inger, Winifred (in *The Rainbow*), 59–60, 62
insouciance, 192, 214, 224–8
Isaiah, 66, 78
Isis (in *The Man Who Died*), 219–20
Italy, 39, 99, 100, 107, 128–9, 135, 202

James, Henry, 5
Jeremiah, 78
Jesus, *see* Christ
John Bull, 76–7
Juta, Jan, 118

Kangaroo (Ben Cooley in *Kangaroo*), 131–3, 137
Kessler, Jascha, 159
Kew Gardens, 19
Kierkegaard, Soren, 67
Kiowa, 147
Kotelianski, S. S., 74, 100, 101, 103, 104
Krout, J. A., 169

Lasca, Il, 31, 202
Lawrence
    Arthur, 42
    Frieda, 1, 17, 20, 35, 38, 39, 40, 43, 63, 79, 99, 131, 159, 205–6, 224; *Not I But the Wind*, 163
    Lydia, 16, 21–2, 42

INDEXES

Pantheism, 65–7, 242
paradise, *see* Eden
Paradise Lost, 226
Parkin (in *The First Lady Chatterley*), 195, 197
Passos, John Dos, 171
patera, 238
Persephone, 183, 244
phallus, 105, 125–6, 133, 166, 174–5, 182, 191–8, 211, 213, 220–1, 235
Phoenix (in *St Mawr*), 152, 155
phoenix, 162, 191, 215
Picasso, 211–12
Pickthall, Marmaduke, 169
Pini, Piero, 200
Pinker, J. B., 69, 73
Plato, 244
plot, 10
politics, 107, 109, 112, 134–5, 185
Polynesia, 166
porpoises, 208–10, 213, 226, 240
Pound, Ezra, 2
power, 112, 148–9, 192
propaganda, 134, 159
prose, Lawrence's, 13, 15, 71, 77, 151, 181, 224–5, 233
prostitution, 150, 223
puritanism, 137

Quetzalcoatl, 137, 142, 145, 160–8, 178, 192, 215

rainbows, 50, 55, 65–8, 72, 78, 87, 96, 135, 162, 175, 191, 213, 240
Ramon, Don (in *The Plumed Serpent*), 145, 159–68
Rananim, 74–6, 213
realism, 5–6, 71, 197, 234
religion, 23, 41, 43, 53–4, 63, 65, 67, 147–9, 156, 212, 224, 242
resurrection, 128, 148, 161, 172, 175, 182–3, 188, 194, 205–10, 215–25, 238, 244–5
revolution, 75
rhyme, 120, 243
rhythm, 44, 45, 50, 52, 59, 64, 119–21, 224, 231, 240–2
Robinson, John: *Honest to God*, 67, 163
Rocky Mountains, 157–9
Roddice, Hermione, (in *Women in Love*), 28, 81, 83, 85, 88, 97
Romans, 129, 211, 219, 222–3
Rozanov, V. V., 199, 229

Ruskin, John, 161
Russell, Bertrand, 74–6, 132

St Mawr, 151–9, 183
salvation, 177, 215, 217–18
Sargent, J. S., 212
Satan, *see* devil
satire, 37, 231–2
Sayula, Lake of (in *The Plumed Serpent*), 162, 164
Schofield, Anthony (in *The Rainbow*), 56
Schorer, Mark, 197
Scott, Sir Walter, 5
Shakespeare, 5, 70, 226
Shaw, George Bernard: *Heartbreak House*, 57, 77, 108
Shestov, Leo, 100
Shortlands (in *Women in Love*), 86
Sicily, 118, 123, 136
Siebenhaar, W., 170
Signature, The, 40
Skinner, Mollie
 The House of Ellis, 130, 139–40
 Black Swans, 144
Skrebensky, Anton (in *The Rainbow*), 51, 58–9, 62–4
snakes, 54, 84, 119–26, 150–5, 161–5, 174, 207, 215–16, 221–2
socialism, 75
Sodom, 81, 103
Soho, 81
Somers, Richard Lovat (in *Kangaroo*), 112, 131–7
song, 173, 191, 213, 223, 227
Sophocles, 5, 70
South Sea Islands, 142, 146
sun, the, 123–4, 147–50, 162, 165, 173–5, 177, 206, 208, 219, 220–1, 224, 238
Sydney, 134
symbolism
 in *The White Peacock*, 12
 in *Sons and Lovers*, 30–2
 in *The Rainbow*, 45, 50, 53, 64–5, 72
 in *Women in Love*, 78, 83–4, 88–90, 94, 97
 in *Aaron's Rod*, 105–6
 in *Snake*, 124–6
 in *St Mawr*, 152–3
 in *The Plumed Serpent*, 161–3
 in *Lady Chatterley's Lover*, 188–9, 191–5, 197–8
 in *The Man Who Died*, 216, 219

266